GIGANTIC GLOBAL HOPE

Our First *Woman Pope*

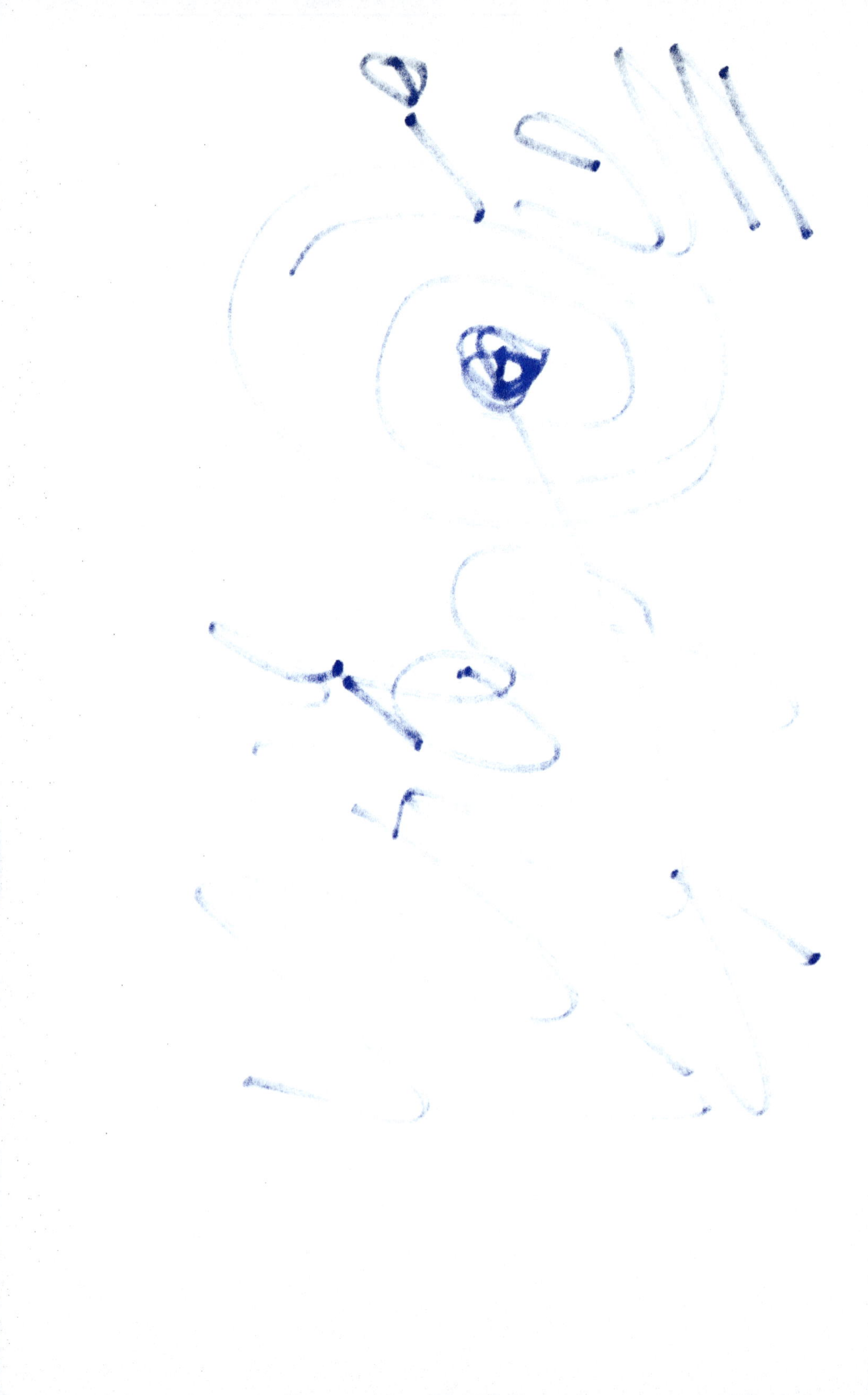

GIGANTIC GLOBAL HOPE

Our First *Woman Pope*

VICTOR VILLASEÑOR

Waterside Press

Cardiff, California

Cover and interior design by Teri Rider

Printed in the United States of America

ISBN-13: 978-1-958848-45-6 (hardcover)
ISBN-13: 978-1-958848-46-3 (paperback)
ISBN-13: 978-1-958848-47-0 (ebook)

Our First Woman Pope is co-published by:

Waterside Press
2055 Oxford Ave.
Cardiff, CA 92007
www.waterside.com

Burro Genius Productions
1302 Stewart St.
Oceanside, CA 92054
www.victorvillasenor.com

Dedicated to
Our First Woman Pope
and to
Women of Vision
Women of Power
Women of Substance
and to
Men of Empathy
Men of Compassion
Men of HeartCorazón
and to
Children of Joy
Children of Laughter
Children of Mischief
Who United Together are the Key for All of Humanity
helping Us Heal Our Beloved Mother Earth,
and thusly taking Us off the Most Endangered Species List.

Burro Genius Productions

Oceanside, California

QUOTES

"I know God will not give me anything I can't handle. I just wish that He didn't have so much Trust in me."

Mother Teresa of Calcutta

"Before civilization you, me, we, all of us were like weeds, because a civilized plant like a rose you've got to feed and water and spray for bugs or it will die. But a wild uncivilized plant like a weed, you give it nothing and it lives. You poison it and it comes back the following year with the rains. You pour cement over it and it will break that concrete reaching for the sunlight. And this is how we, humans, all used to be all over the earth. Uncivilized and Wild of Heart, Alive of Soul, and Indestructible in Faith as we reached for the Light of God!"

Doña Margarita

"It took me a long time not to judge myself through someone else's eyes."

Sally Field

"A successful person is one who can lay a firm foundation with the bricks that others throw at him or her."

David Brinkley

"It's not who you are that holds you back, it's who you think you're not."

Painted on a dumpster in Ocean Beach,
by a homeless woman known as the
Dumpster Poet of California.

"Thousands of geniuses live and die undiscovered—either by themselves or by others."

Mark Twain

"Whatever you can do or dream you can do, begin it. Boldness has genius, power and magic."

Johann Wolfgang von Goethe

"Our deepest fear is not that we are inadequate. Our deepest fear is that we are powerful beyond measure. It is our light, not our darkness, that most frightens us. We ask ourselves, who am I to be brilliant, gorgeous, talented, fabulous? Actually, who are you not to be? You are a child of God. Your playing small does not serve the world. There is nothing enlightened about shrinking so that other people won't feel insecure around you. We are all meant to shine, as children do. We were born to make manifest the glory of God that is within us. It is not just in some of us; it is in everyone. And as we let our own light shine, we unconsciously give other people permission to do the same. As we are liberated from our own fear, our presence automatically liberates others."

Marianne Williamson, A Return to Love: Reflections on the Principles of "A Course in Miracles," *1992 (commonly attributed to Nelson Mandela, 1994 inauguration speech)*

"What lies behind us and what lies before us are tiny matters compared to what lies within us. And when we bring what is within out into the world, miracles happen."

Ralph Waldo Emerson

"The Kingdom of God is within you."

Jesus Christ

CONTENTS

Bonus Stories

PS—Three Miracles

DEFINITIONS

Daniel Webster's New World Dictionary of American Language pre1990

Genius: guardian deity, or spirit of a person; spirit, natural ability. According to ancient Roman belief, a guardian spirit is assigned to a person at birth.

Catholic: universal, all-inclusive; of general interest or value; hence, having broad sympathies or understanding; liberal.

Balance: an instrument for weighing, especially one that opposes equal weights, as in two matched scales hanging from either end of a lever supported exactly in the middle. The imaginary scales of fortune or fate, as an emblem of justice or the power to decide; hence, the power to decide human fate, value, etc. A state of bodily equilibrium: as he kept his balance on the tightrope. Equilibrium in design, painting, music composition, harmonious proportions. The constellation Libra, or the seventh sign of the zodiac.

God: any of various beings as conceived as supernatural, immortal, and having special powers over the lives and affairs of people, and of course nature. An image that is worshipped. In monotheistic religions, the creator and ruler of the universal, regarded as eternal, infinite, all-powerful, and all-knowing; Supreme Being; Almighty.

Miracle: an event or action that apparently contradicts known scientific laws, and is hence thought to be due to supernatural causes, especially to an act of God. A remarkable event or thing. A marvel.

Angel: a messenger from God. A supernatural being, either good or bad, to whom is attributed more than human power, intelligence. A guiding spirit or influence.

Author's Own Dictionary

Godvolution: the understanding that there is no contradiction between God and evolution or between God and science; they do, in fact, work together.

Follow Infront: the understanding that for over 20 million years, the big male snow geese, who fly in front of the V-formations of geese migrating north and south don't lead, but 'Follow Infront.' It's the female and young geese who set the pace and lead from behind with their joyful sounds of laughter and cackling. And the big brave male snow geese are the ones who drop out of the sky making themselves vulnerable to hunters and other predators. In other words, heroically risking their lives to make sure it is safe before the rest of the flock comes in for landing.

DreamVoyage: A dream which is so real and full of detail that you just know deep inside yourself that it really did occur, and hence was not just a dream, but a reality within your own on-going DreamVoyaging Consciousness that has occurred, or is going to occur.

MoonFlow: Originally women were revered by men and our whole of society, because everyone knew that women's menstrual cycle was connected to the cycle of the moon and happened every 28 days. This is also why Indigenous People referred to the moon as Mother Moon, and why the yearly calendar had 13 months of 28 days each and is still considered the most accurate of all calendars.

Hollow Bone, Buffalo Bone: This is who we Human Beings really are. We are Our Almighty Creator's Sacred Instruments for receiving and giving and keeping nada, nada, nothing for when it's all said and done, we want to be "empty vessels" ready to return to Our Almighty's Loving Arms for Eternity.

SoulSpinning: This usually starts with our ArmWings stretched straight out and us, at first, spinning counter-clock-wise towards Our HeartCorazon side, opening up Our Heart and activating Our Soul. And in doing this, we joyfully slipslide out of our restrictive Five-Sensory Perception and into Our Multi-Sensory Perception of Limitless Dimensions.

GodBreathing: In many Indigenous languages the word for God and Breath are the same word. And so when we take in a deep Breath and hold it, then blow out real fast, we are filling up our whole Being with Supreme Being. This is why you will find throughout the book that I take in many deep Breaths.

Please, I invite you to take in these deep GodBreaths along with me and hold them for a count of 1, 2, 3, 4, 5, then blow out fast, and you'll find that your thinking-busy-brain will dissolve and you'll automatically slipslide into your own Center of Being, which Ralph Waldo Emerson refers to in his wonderful quote.

Capitalization: This is done throughout the book, giving a special Emotional and Spiritual emphasis to a word or a group of words. This is how I was raised with my family and especially by my dad giving a lively importance to certain words and phrases with his eyes lighting up and a strong tone of voice and great flying hand movements.

Then secondly, I took note that this was done in comic books with a flare of capitalizations and huge WOWS and BANGS! And I later saw that even my all-time favorite comic strip Peanuts did it, too, and this is when I came to realize that what was being done was taking the written word out of its up-tight proper world and actually energizing language and the written page itself.

Truly, it's no accident the yearly convention of the American Book Association has drastically lost so much of its membership, and on the other hand, the Comic Book Convention has exploded into the millions

How This Book Came to Be

Okay, ready? Here we go! So to start with, I'd like you to Know how this book came to be, because you see this book wasn't my idea.

The year was 2010, and I was on my way to give a talk in Riverside, about 70 miles northeast from my home in Oceanside, California when my cell phone rang. My good friend Gary was driving, so I picked up. To my great joy it was Marc Jaffe, my long-time editor. In fact, I'd met Marc back in the early 1970s when I'd sold my first book *A La Brava* to Bantam Books, and they'd convinced me to change the title to *Macho!*

"Hello, Marc! Great to hear from you!"

"Thank you, good to hear your voice, too. Is this a good time? I have something that could, well, be quite important I'd like to discuss with you."

"Sure, it's a great time. I'm on my way to give a talk."

"Oh, you're driving. I'll call you back later."

"No, I'm not driving. My friend Gary is driving."

"Oh, the school teacher, principal, school superintendent?"

"Exactly."

"Well, then, this might be something you'd both like to hear."

"Okay, I'll put you on speaker. Shoot."

"Hello, Gary."

"Hello, Marc."

"Well, you know this manuscript we've just wrapped up?"

"Sure," I said. "*Beyond Rain of Gold* that I think we'd been working on for nearly ten years."

"Well, Vic, in the manuscript you have a piece about being invited to speak to a group of retired nuns and priests and you didn't want to go."

"That's true, Marc. I didn't want to go."

"But you went."

"Yes, on my mother's insistence."

"Exactly, and so I've been thinking, as your editor, that you could take that little piece from *Beyond* and make it into an entire book."

I was taken aback. I had no idea how to respond.

"Are you still there?" asked Marc.

"Yes, I'm still here. But, Marc, I don't see how a whole book is possible. I only spent three or four days with those old nuns and priests."

Marc started laughing. "After working with you all these years, I bet you could do three volumes on what happened in those few days."

"Really? You think so?"

"Sure, you had a mountain of resentment towards nuns and priests and the very institution itself, but your mother kept insisting, and so you finally went."

"That's true, Marc, and those old nuns and priests had only read *Rain of Gold* and I hadn't written that well of the Church in *Rain*, so I had no idea why they'd invite me to go and speak to them."

"That's the point, you had no idea why they wanted to see you, and yet you went because of your mother's insistence and explaining to you that some of the very things she and your father didn't want to do were the exact experiences that caused them to learn and grow the most so they'd be able to fit into our American mainstream society."

"You're right, Marc, and my visit with those old nuns and priests did cause me to learn and grow so much that by the end of my visit I no longer saw them as nuns and priests, but as regular human beings trying to make sense of their lives and prepare themselves for their Passing."

"And that's a book, my friend!" said Marc with energy.

"WOW! I think you really got something going here, and I never thought of it. My God, my Heart*Corazon* is already pumping with all these flashes of anger and frustration, and yeah, a few good things, too."

"Exactly," he said. "So go for it, Vic, and call me any time. I have a hunch this is going to be a big important book! I can hardly wait to see a thick bunch of pages you'll be sending me!"

"That might be quite a while."

He laughed. "I doubt it."

I laughed, too. "Thank you, Marc."

"The pleasure is all mine," he said.

Then I'd no more than hung up when Gary, who was Irish and had almost become a priest before becoming an educator, shouted:

"And I know the title for the book, *Revenge of a Catholic School Boy*!"

I burst out laughing, and we continued laughing all the way to our destination.

"You know," I said, as we pulled in the Riverside University parking lot, "I've been with Marc for over 40 years. He must be close to 90 and he's still as full of the energy as when he was in his 50s and top dog in the New York publishing world."

"Of course, the man is really excited about this new book you two will be working on together."

"Yeah, he is," I said, smiling, "And wow, do I look forward to working with him. He doesn't try to control and put his own stamp on my writing like most of all the other editors I've had. He inspires, giving me rein so I can keep my eyes focused on the twisting, leaping path of writing."

"In other words," said Gary, "he has a lot of faith in you."

"Yeah, I guess you're right. It really does all come down to faith, doesn't it?"

AND SO FOR A COUPLE OF YEARS I WROTE WITH THE TITLE Revenge in mind and Gary was very helpful with all his knowledge and experiences he'd had with the Church, and especially why he'd ultimately decided to not become a priest.

But something wasn't quite right, because I could also see that Gary and I, like most ex-Catholics, had just experienced too many negative and horrible things with the Church, so it was difficult for us to be objective.

Then my youngest son Joseph came home from Humboldt State University in northern California, so I asked him to read the manuscript. He hadn't gone to Catholic school, so he had no axe to grind. In fact, his mother Barbara and I had deliberately raised him in the Jewish Culture for her side of our family, and in the Mexican Indian Catholic Culture for my side of the family, and on top of that, he was totally All-American.

"Okay, Dad, I've read it," he said, "and some parts are very good, but the title is misleading. I didn't find any revenge anywhere. All I found were complaints about the Church, but that's not revenge."

He had me. I didn't know what to say. Marc had come up with this, too.

"And Dad, you've always told me that if a writer can't verbalize in a couple of words what he's writing about, then the book will be sure to fail, because readers need to immediately know where they are going, or they'll quickly lose interest."

I gripped my forehead. He was totally right, and yet I had such a mountain of crap rushing inside of me having been raised Catholic that I just couldn't put a finger on what my revenge really was in just a couple of words. Hell, the whole of Catholicism was no more than an extension of the Roman Empire, raping and conquering globally, destroying all other forms of beliefs. But then, amidst all my agonizing memories came a LIGHTNING BOLT STRAIGHT INTO ME FROM HEAVEN!

"A LADY POPE!" I shouted. "This would be REAL REVENGE for me and all of the world, and especially for Our Indigenous Native Mexican American *Mamagrandes* who loved the Church, and yet were slaughtered and double-crossed at every turn by this arrogant all-male institution that has DOMINATED WITHOUT MERCY THE WORLD FOR 2,000 YEARS!"

Joseph started clapping. "You got it, Dad! A lady pope with women cardinals and bishops and priests would be a thorough revenge!" His whole face lit up with a beautiful smile. "Now Dad, I'm really interested in this book, even though it's about old nuns and priests. Who of my generation doesn't want to see one of our most powerful self-righteous social pillars transform into modern mentality of respect and inclusion for all humanity."

"Thanks," I said, "thank you for pushing me, *mijito*."

And I meant this with all my Heart and Soul. For in Native Indigenous Sacred Knowledge my son had just become my Spiritual Father, and this was the highest Honor any son could attain

— for it ensured each generation to further Our Ongoing Tribal Path Of Wisdom.

We hugged and touched foreheads, then I called Marc. He loved it, saying this new direction would certainly appeal to a much wider audience.

So now with the title *Our First Lady Pope*, Marc and I surged with a revitalized new energy, mining for the gold nuggets of those few days I'd spent with the old retired nuns and priests.

More years passed and they were exciting and wonderful, and Marc was now in his 90s when a whole new perspective presented itself to us. But in fact, it wasn't really new, and was something my mother had initially mentioned when I'd received the invitation to go speak to the nuns and priests. She'd used the Indigenous Term "Sacred Elders," saying that maybe these servants of the Church had seen in *Rain of Gold* how older Native People didn't fear death, but looked forward to become Sacred Elders as they prepared for their Own Passing Over to the Other Side Of Living.

So with Marc and I both getting older, this new title *Sacred Elders* felt really good and our energy changed. In fact, we both became more confident that we were working on a global impacting book. Also, more people liked this title, because they weren't Catholic or ex-Catholic or even very religious, and so this title spoke to them.

More years passed and the manuscript improved in many ways, and yet something was amiss. The title of *Revenge of a Catholic School Boy* had more energy, and the title *Our First Lady Pope* gripped the imagination. But we didn't want to go back to those two titles, so we were stumped, and also I was tired and very sure that Marc was even more tired than I was.

Then the Covid Virus had come in and dominated the world and people became angry if I spoke about religion and God, and especially if I spoke with enthusiasm, saying that my new book was about a Wonderful Collective Global Hope FOR ALL OF US!

I quit calling Marc. I felt too beaten down. And also, I was half afraid if I called, I'd be told that he'd died. Hell, a bunch of my relatives and friends had died in the last few years, and four of them that had passed had nothing to do with the virus, but more about just getting old.

It felt stupid to keep writing with such enthusiasm for Global Hope. Who was I kidding? Marc and I were old farts. We didn't have it within us anymore to pull off a big important book. That took the power of young energy. And it was one thing for me to have gone up and spoken to a group of old retired nuns and priests, and a whole other ballpark for me to write about it and think that Marc and I and Gary could help change the course of the world's largest and most powerful institution.

Oh, I was stumped, and so I did what I usually do when I'm stumped. I let go, quit all of my man-made-word-thinking, and turned everything over to Our Lord God Almighty. Instantly, with this load off my back, I felt better and decided to go down to the beach just north of Buccaneer Beach and visit with my big black rock that some young surfers, who were geologists, told me that the rock was part of an asteroid that had come to earth tens of millions of years ago.

I got on my old fat tire bike that I'd purchased for $39.00 brand new and rode down to the beach and sat on the bluff looking out over the great expanse of the sea.

"I need help God," I said, taking in a great big deep Breath and holding it for a count of 1, 2, 3, 4, 5, then blowing out fast. "I really, really do. And remember when I made my deal with You to become a great writer, I said that You'd have to stick with me, because I couldn't do it without You." Tears came to my eyes. "And that was in May of 1960 and in all these years I haven't chickened out on You, and so don't You dare chicken out on me now, dear God."

The tears were streaming down my face, so I took in a couple more deep GodBreaths, got to feeling a little light-headed, then BOOM, here I was surrounded by HEAVEN! The crashing music of the breaking waves. The high-pitched calling of the happy seagulls. The silent mystic grace of the gliding pelicans. And of course, my big black rock facing south and laying in the surf like a magnificent large-maned male African lion.

I smiled.

I laughed.

Oh, I was so happy now! BIG BIG HAPPY! So I closed my eyes and took in a few more great big deep GodBreaths. This big rock and I had become SoulMates when I was eight years old and my brother Joseph 16 years old had Passed Over. He'd been my best friend. He'd taught me how to play marbles.

Tears of joy continued pouring down my face as I was remembering my kind wonderful big brother, and yet my sneaky-thinking-head still kept trying to tell me that maybe, just maybe, Marc and I had wasted 10 years of our lives.

I laughed, shaking my head to this Doubting Thomas crap, and then I heard something else. It was like the sound of a faraway happy singing and barking. And it was getting closer and closer.

I opened my eyes, and there below me was a robust older woman dressed in a colorful dress and blouse, and she was skipping and dancing along in the shallow surf with her beautiful large Golden Labrador Retriever and singing "I am Woman!"

I leaped to my feet ROARING WITH *CARCAJADAS*! Big belly-shaking laughter that keep at bay all sickness, according to Indigenous Healers. Oh, she was a sight to see! A ROBUST ANGEL sent to me by GOD ALMIGHTY with her arms and legs

FLYING and her big dog RACING and LEAPING in the surf with SUCH JOY!

And their BARKING and SINGING Harmonized with the Music of the CRASHING waves and the CALLING of the seagulls and the SQUEALING of the tiny quick-legged shore birds that rushed all about them!

Oh, my Heart*Corazon* and *Alma*Soul were suddenly FILLED TO THE BRIM with this Angel woman's GREAT FEELING ENERGY! And I Knew in my BONES that this was it! "I AM WOMAN" echoing out of over the sea and land was the Theme Song of our new title, *OUR FIRST WOMAN POPE*!

I called Marc. He loved it, saying that this title had all the earthiness that was prevalent throughout the manuscript, whereas "Lady Pope" had suggested that old class distinction that was the bread and butter of Catholicism throughout the ages!

So now with this title *Our First Woman Pope* a BIG BIG EXCITING ENERGY came EXPLODING into us! Once more I'd AWAKE before daylight. Not slowly. But leaping out of bed like a kid on Christmas Day! And the Stars would speak to me, Gifting me Insights I hadn't seen before, and I'd go into a Trance, working 10-12 hours a day just as I'd done when I'd been in my 20s and 30s and 40s!

Oh, Marc and I were now FLYING and feeling younger and younger and full of BIG BIG HAPPY ENERGY!

Then last November 5, 2021 when Marc had his 100th BirthDay, he said, "Yes, 100 and going on 75, just as when I was 90 going on 65, and when I was 80 going on 55 just like you, my good young *amigo*, are presently doing! SERVICE IS OUR FOUNTAIN OF YOUTH!"

And Marc was EXACTLY RIGHT! For this coming May 11, 2022 I'm turning 82 years old and yet I feel 50 years old, and 50 years just happens to be how long Marc and I have been reaching together for the STARS FOR THE GREATER GLORY OF ALMIGHTY GOD!

And now with this book *OUR FIRST WOMAN POPE* finally finished after umpteen years and approximately 40 rewrites, I ask you, dear people, could Marc and I have pulled off this Totally Inspired Gift from the Other Side of Being at a younger age? I think not. For Marc and I both had to become of that same age as those old nuns and priests for us to truly understand what really happens when we, Human People, strive to become Sacred Elders as my mother had initially suggested.

You see, Sacred Elders don't strive to go into retirement, thinking they're done and want to rest. OH, NO! THEY LEAP INTO INSPIREMENT with BURNING FIRE in their bellies, realizing what Emerson said in his wonderful quote! And in this act, a LIGHTING BOLT OF GENIUS AND MAGIC comes into them just as Goethe said and this is exactly what happened to Marc and me, giving us PURPOSE AND MEANING ALL THESE YEARS!

So ARISE all of you Well-Seasoned People! ARISE AROUND THE WHOLE WORLD, no longer worshiping Youth, but instead stepping up to the PLATE OF ANCIENT HOLY INSPIREMENT, realizing that it is up to us at this WONDROUS AGE to hit HOME RUNS with all of our well-earned WISDOM, giving Our Future Generations GIGANTIC GLOBAL HOPE!

And we can do it! You, Me, We, for All of Us United Together in SPIRIT ARE HONEST TO GOODNESS REAL SUPER-WOMEN and SUPERMEN!

NO JOKE!

Just take in a GREAT BIG DEEP GODBREATH, and you'll

instantly feel your own NATURAL PURE GOLDEN SPIRIT ENERGY COME BURSTING into you just as Marc and I have been feeling throughout all of our ups and downs with this writing and within our own preparation for OUR WONDROUS PASSING OVER to the Other Side of BEING WITH SUPREME BEING!

Oh, yes, I AM WOMAN is Our Holy Song for Our Transformation of realizing that as Human People, Our Earth Mission has always been to become Sacred Elders and Inspire Our Tribe Youth to hear their OWN DRUM BEAT in their own planting of Heaven on Earth. For there's only One Race, Our Human Race, and Ann Frank said it best that even as they were exterminating her people, she still thought people were basically good of Heart-*Corazon*.

AMEN!
AWOMEN!
ACHILDREN!

Book One

Chapter One

I WAS SHOCKED.

A group of retired nuns and priests were inviting me to go and speak to them up by the Great Lakes near the Canadian border. But I didn't want to go. I mean, as a kid, I'd been beaten by the nuns and threatened with damnation and the fires of hell by the priests. So, of course, I hadn't written that well about the Catholic Church in my book *Rain of Gold*, and yet it was this very book that had caused these old nuns and priests to write to me.

I decided to sleep on the matter as my dad had always done whenever he'd had an important decision to make, and in the morning, much to my surprise, I awoke with the realization that I still had a lot of love and even some good memories of the Church.

In fact, looking back I could now see that it had been the sounds and smells that had first caused me to fall in love with the Holy Roman Catholic Church. I'd just been a little kid, and the smell of the smoking incense, and the quiet sounds of the people praying, and the old deaf priest's large booming voice full of warm sing-song sounding language, and then the altar boys singing back to the priest with beautiful high-sounding voices, pretending to also be speaking in Latin, but in actuality they'd be singing to the old priest in Spanish, telling him that they agreed with him and it was best to cook the wild turkey in Mexican green sauce. Oh, it had all been so much fun. The old priest dressed up in an elaborate dress like a queen and chanting with such seriousness, and the altar boys, also dressed in elaborate dresses, chanting back to him with so much *gusto*.

"Gua-jo-lote! Co-cido en sal-saaa verrr-de!" would chant the altar boys, and most parents would get mad, hearing that the boys were tricking the half-deaf old priest, but my dad would join us kids and sing along with the laughing, giggling altar boys.

Oh, it was the best show in town and these first wonderful memories began for me at Saint Patrick's Holy Catholic Church in the Mexican *barrio de Carlosmalo* of Carlsbad, California with the smell of burning incense being whirled about in a little silver bell, and the quiet rolling whispers of my mother and grandmother saying the rosary.

Then, when I got a little older, it was the bells of Saint Mary's Star of the Sea in Oceanside, a few miles north from the *barrio de Carlosmalo*, with which I fell in love. The loud-clanging bells, and the smell of the sea mixed with cutting flowers and incense, slightly different smells than the ones in Carlsbad, but the sounds of the people praying were exactly the same and wonderful.

Then came the San Luis Rey Mission, king of all the missions of California, with its great towering bell that could be heard across the whole valley full of luscious green fields and best of all the hundreds of beautiful goldfish in the water fountain right across from the entrance of the huge magnificent great-smelling mission where, on some lucky Sundays, we got to see wild pigeons flying about inside of the church as the old priest and the altar boys chanting back and forth to each other about the best way to cook wild turkey in Mexican green sauce.

And also, looking back, I could now see that it had felt very *especial* to get all dressed up every Sunday and listen to the sounds of the Holy Roman Catholic Church, and then get to go out for breakfast as one big happy hungry *familia* who'd confessed our sins, received Holy Communion, and now that we were all at peace with God Almighty, the Holy Creator of the whole Universe, we'd get to eat whatever we wanted. And I, of course, always got waffles with plenty of whipped cream and syrup and a side-order of bacon. *Huevos rancheros con chorizo* was what we usually ate for breakfast at home, and so this was a real treat.

But for days I procrastinated, because I still just couldn't see myself going to see a bunch of old retired nuns and priests. Hell, I could also still remember all the abuses that I'd received at Catholic school.

WHAT HAPPENED WAS THAT I'D BEEN GOING TO PUBLIC school in South Oceanside just a few blocks from our home and everything had been going . . . well, not too bad, until I got to the third grade, then I just couldn't seem to be able to learn how to read.

I mean, reading in second grade had been difficult enough for me, but reading in third grade had just been beyond my comprehension. School became a nightmare. The kids began making fun of me. I became a bed wetter. And I flunked the third grade. I was told not to worry, that by taking the third grade over, I'd surely learn how to read. But I didn't, and this was when even my best friends began to call me a stupid Mexican and wait for me after school so they could throw rocks at me and beat me up. Oh, I'd felt so double-crossed that I'd start to cry and get so mad I'd grab and bite my tormentors.

But then to my surprise, my parents were called in and my teacher told them that I was a trouble-maker and constantly getting into fights. I started to cry again. My teacher knew this wasn't true, but my dad winked at me and took my hand as my mom told my teacher to pass me on to the fourth grade, and they'd then take me out of public school and put me in Catholic school out at the San Luis Rey Mission.

At first the teacher said she couldn't do that, but this was when my dad leaned in so close to her with his big smoking cigar and a lug of avocados with an envelope full of money, that my teacher's eyes got full of fear. She quickly agreed to pass me on, and driving home my mother explained to me that the nuns and priests weren't Protestants, they were Catholics and so they'd be kinder and more patient with me and surely I'd now learn how to read.

And my mom and dad were almost right, because Sister Theresa, the little nun who was assigned to teach me how to read after school, was wonderful and kind and never got mad at me when I didn't get it. Within a week I was in love with her and so one afternoon I asked her if she would marry me when I grew up.

She smiled, I'll never forget, and took my hand and explained to me that she was already married to Jesus.

"He's dead, you know," I said.

"Yes, but I'm married to Our Lord Jesus in spirit," she said, still smiling.

"Oh, that's okay," I said, "we can then get married in body and have babies."

But she was never able to give me her answer, because just then the big, old mother superior came crashing through the door, screaming at me that I was the devil and slapped me so hard that she knocked me out of my chair, and then she went after my little nun, slapping her and slapping her. And this was when Sister Theresa's habit was knocked off of her head, and I saw that her long, beautiful dark red hair was the same color as my horse's mane and tail. And she was so young and beautiful and yet she wouldn't fight back or even defend herself, and the big, old mother superior just kept hitting her.

This incident I would never forget. I'd only been eight years old, but still I'd been so full of Love*Amor* for my little nun that I'd leaped up off the floor and attacked the smelly old mother superior, getting under her long robe and biting her leg and gouging my nails into her soft flesh.

She screamed bloody murder and quit hitting my little nun and began hitting me on the head. But still I continued biting her until a priest came rushing in and grabbed me by my hair and dragged me down the hallway, then locked me in a broom closet. After that, I was never allowed to see my little nun again, and months later when I did see her, her face instantly filled with terror and she took off running.

My heart died. What had they done to her? And also after that incident, it was like the old mother superior and the priest now thought that they had an open license to beat me every day, and after each beating explain to me that I'd been born with Original Sin, and so it was their sworn duty and for the good of my soul for them to beat me and keep me away from all the other kids.

And so no, no, no, now as an adult I couldn't see myself going to see any old retired nuns and priests. After all, what I'd written about in *Rain of Gold* was that God was full of Love*Amor*. Not wrath. And that every day was *otro milagro de Dios,* every day was another miracle gifted to us by God, and that our job here on Mother Earth was for us, five-pointed Walking Stars, to help Our Holy Creator plant His ongoing Sacred Garden of Heaven on Earth.

But then finally, after a few days of still not being able to make up my mind, I decided to just go across the grass past the chicken coops and see my mother who lived in our new, smaller house. My dad had passed over more than ten years ago in March of 1988, and so I now spoke to my mother, who was almost 90 old, but she'd never been much of a talker like my dad. To go to church and pray her rosary had always been more of my mother's style of how to deal with difficult situations. Getting to her house, her front door was open, which was okay. At our little *ranchito* in South Oceanside we hardly ever locked our doors at night, and during the day we didn't close them half of the time.

"*Mama*," I called out as I went inside, "I'd like to speak with you."

"Okay," she called back, "I'm in the kitchen. I'm making myself a *quesadilla*. Would you like one?"

I'd already had breakfast about two hours ago, but still the thought of having one of my mother's delicious *quesadillas*, meaning a handmade *tortilla* folded in half with cheese and homemade salsa in the middle, sounded pretty good.

"Yeah, sure," I said, licking my lips. "Do you also have avocado? I can go and pick a couple if you'd like."

"No, I already picked a few this morning," she said. "You slice one while I do the *quesadillas* on the *comal*."

"Okay," I said, and so I washed my hands, dried them, then began feeling the avocados to see which one was the ripest.

Sitting down with my mother, we ate our *quesadillas* with fresh slices of avocado and homemade *salsa*, then I came right to the point.

"*Mama*," I said, "I've been invited to go to Wisconsin up by the Great Lakes to give a talk to a bunch of old retired nuns and priests, but I don't know if I can go."

"Oh, you don't think you have warm enough clothes?" she said. "Well, that's no problem, *mijito*. Just do as your father always said he learned to do up in Montana and wear many layers. You'll be okay, *mijito*. Don't worry."

"*Mama*, I got the clothes. That's not the *problema*," I said. "The problem is that I was, well, you know, abused by the nuns and priests out at the San Luis Rey Mission so much that part of me just doesn't want to go."

"But didn't you bite a nun? Isn't that what started the whole problem?"

"Oh, *Mama*," I said, "I've told you a thousand times that that's not how it happened!"

"Well, the priest, he told your father and me that you bit a nun so hard that they'd had to take her to the hospital."

"*Mama*, please stop it! You just don't know what happened, and every time I've tried to explain, you twist things all around."

"Well, okay, maybe I do," she said, "but let's be practical and realize that all those things happened to you a long time ago, *mijito*, and you're now a grown man with a wife and kids. Do you think your father and I could have succeeded in this country if we'd held onto all the bad things that happened to us? Oh, no, *mijito*, we all got to let go and keep going. That's our only hope," she said, making the sign of the cross over herself and adding the words, "*con el favor de Dios*." Meaning, with the blessing of God.

"Yes, *Mama*, I can see that that," I said, taking in a deep breath, and I almost said 'but if this was really true, then why have you held onto so many bad things all these years?' But I didn't need to say this. It was my mother who now, looking at me said it best.

"And I also know, *mijito*, that I haven't always been a very good example of doing this," she said. "After all, it was your father, not me," she added, "who went to see Doctor Hoskins when he was sick and dying of cancer. I couldn't do that. In fact, it enraged me that your father would do such a thing, because it had been that no good drunken doctor's fault that your brother Joseph died! Oh, he was the only doctor in town back then, and he caused so many deaths because of his stupid, drunken ways!"

She stopped and tears came to her eyes, and I took in another deep breath. I, too, remembered my brother's death very well. Joseph had been sixteen years old and I'd been eight years old and he'd been like a second father to me.

Oh, I loved him so much. If he had lived I don't think that I would have flunked the third grade for a second time, because he'd always had a way of teaching me how to do things with such patience and good natural horse sense. In fact, he was the one who'd taught me how to play marbles and, with his teachings, I became the marble champion of my whole school.

"And yet looking back," continued my mother, "I'm beginning to now see how your father was able to do that, because, well, I'm approaching the end of my life, *mijito*, so I . . . I can now see that if we don't show forgiveness, then how can we expect God to show us forgiveness when we pass over?" And it was now my mother who took in a big, deep GodBreath. "*Mijito*, you've got to go and see those nuns and priests," she added. "Truly, it will help you, yourself, deep inside of your own Heart and Soul."

"Oh, *Mama*," I said, shaking my head.

"You say that they are old retired nuns and priests, right?"

"Yes," I said.

"Well, then, remember what happened to your little sister Teresita when the old dying nun asked to see her?"

"Remind me," I said.

"Well, they called me from Saint Mary's Star of the Sea and said that one of the nun's old helpers was in the hospital dying and she wanted to see your little sister. I took Teresita, and the sick old woman called your sister to her bedside, but she refused to go near the old lady."

"How old was Sita at the time?" I asked. Most of us never called our youngest sister Teresita. We called her Sita for short and she liked it.

"She was about, well, I guess, maybe ten. And the woman begged her to come close, but you know how your sister is when she sets her mind to something."

My mother was absolutely right. Our little sister could be strong as iron.

"Well, finally, the sick old woman said, 'Child, in the name of God, could you please forgive me for how I treated you all these years?'"

"I remember now," I said. "Sita shook her head, telling her no, that she would not forgive her, and she walked out of the room."

"Yes, exactly," said my mother, taking in another deep breath, "and I saw that old sick woman's face fill with fear, and all the nuns around her tried to console her, telling her that she'd been a very good person, but none of this helped. It was like, well, I guess, she was seeing hell itself deep inside of herself."

I nodded. "Yes, she probably was, *Mama.*" And this was going to be tough, but I wasn't going to chicken out. "And do you remember who Sita was even more mad at than . . . than at that old nun's helper?" I asked.

"No, tell me."

"You, *Mama,*" I said with tears bursting from my eyes. "You! Because during all those years of abuse you never once believed Sita! You always believed the nuns and that nun's old helper!"

"That's true," said my mother with tears also bursting from her eyes.

"Yeah, you'd thought that Sita had made it all up, just like you'd thought Linda and I had made up all our stuff about the nuns and priests."

"That's true, that's true," said my mother. "But how could I think differently? Those nuns would talk to your father and me with such respect and kindness, and . . . and they'd dedicated their whole lives for the love of God and the good of humanity, so how could we believe that those same nuns and their helpers could be so abusive? It just didn't make sense, *mijito*."

"OH, *MAMA*," I shouted with my Heart*Corazon* pounding! "AND THIS IS EXACTLY why I don't want to go to speak to those old nuns and priests! Am I just going to pretend that everything is Jim Dandy okay? Or am I going to be blunt and ask these old nuns and priests how many of them slapped kids, pulled their hair, and sneaked into the boys' bathroom, trying to see if they were touching themselves, so they could then scream at them that they were GOING TO GO TO HELL AND BURN FOR ETERNITY!

"Can't you understand, *Mama*, that it was no accident that these nuns and priests knew how to handle you guys? We, your kids, came into this world with Original Sin and all that crap, so we couldn't be trusted, and you, the adults, had your own daily ongoing sins, and so you couldn't be trusted either, and so these nuns and priests had us all by the balls, trained to divide and conquer our *familia* just like armies divide and conquer nations. This is what Cortez did to *México*. His little group of soldiers could have never won if they hadn't been experts at manipulation and deception!

"Truly, I'm now beginning to realize that a lot of nuns and priests don't even believe in Jesus or in God. What they really believe in is . . . is the survival and expansion of their institution, and in keeping all the power in their own hands, so they can, then, accumulate huge amounts of wealth for their diocese and THE VATICAN AND THE POPE HIMSELF!"

"Oh, *mijito,* do you really believe this?"

"Absolutely! Look at all the gold they stole from the New World, and you, more than most people, should know this, because you were raised in a gold mining town in *México*!"

"But those were Americans who were taking the gold."

"Yes, but before the Americans it was Spain and the Church who raped all of the Americas! Let's not kid ourselves, *Mama,* it's been the Church who's been backing up the rich for centuries, so they can get their share of the spoils.

"Can't you see that, *Mama?* You and *Papa* were adults and you were rich on top of that and . . . and . . . extremely generous with your donations, so of course, they spoke to you with respect and kindness. Truly, *Mama,* I just don't know how I can possibly go to see these old nuns and priests without WANTING TO RIP THEIR HEARTS OUT! And bluntly tell them what I really think of their manipulating, abusive ways!"

I stopped and took in a great big deep Breath and held, trying to calm down. "Oh, *Mama,*" I now said after blowing out fast, "I'll never forget how I climbed over that wall to go looking for my little nun and when I saw her sitting in the rose garden reading her Bible and I went up to her, she smiled at first, but then her whole face twisted into terror and she ran away from me in fear." The tears were streaming down my face. "What did they do to my beautiful, kind little nun? *S*he must've been no more than eighteen years old, and she . . . she was the first teacher I ever had who was kind to me and didn't look down her nose at me when I didn't get it. Truly, I wish I'd bitten that smelly old mother superior's leg COMPLETELY OFF!"

"*Mijito,* how can you talk like this?"

"Easy, *Mama,* easy," I said, wiping the tears off my face with the back of my hand, "it used to enrage me the way they'd always talk to you and *Papa.* They're all great actors. All the nuns and priests. And the best actors among them become the bishops and cardinals and mother superiors. I swear, they really got their pious little mannerisms down to a science. Remember how that old head nun out at the mission so quickly changed her whole position that first day of theirs being primarily a girls school when you slipped her that envelope full of money across the desk? Suddenly she became all smiles and told you that yes, of course, they'd be most happy to accept me and assign a nun to help teach me how to read after school.

"And then when that little young nun was so kind and nice to me that I fell in love with her and asked her if she would marry me when I got big, what did that old smelly nun do? She, who, I guess, had been outside of our door listening the whole time, came bursting into our room, slapped me across the face so hard that she knocked me out of my chair, called me the devil, and then she began slapping my little nun. And, *Mama,* Sister Theresa wouldn't fight back or even try to protect herself," I said with tears pouring down my face. "So this was when I leaped up off the floor and began biting the big old nun so she WOULDN'T KILL MY LOVING, KIND LITTLE NUN!" I added with a scream.

My mother was stunned. "But why didn't you tell us all this years ago? All we knew was that you'd bit a nun and they'd had to take her to the hospital."

"I tried, *Mama,*" I said. "I really tried to tell you, but I just couldn't find the words because I was a child, and they'd convinced me that I was evil and Mexican and sub-human. Truly, they were even worse to me than they'd been in public school when the teachers allowed the kids to keep calling me a stupid Mexican, because I couldn't learn to read."

My mother reached into her pocket and brought out her handkerchief with the little pink flowers and green leaves, which she had embroidered while she and my dad watched T.V. together, and she handed it to me. I took the pretty little handkerchief and dried my eyes.

"Oh, *mijito*," she said, taking in a couple of great big, deep GodBreaths, "it just seems to me that your father and I were so busy trying to be successful in this country that we failed as parents for you kids. Your older sister Tencha, just a young innocent girl and getting pregnant, or maybe even raped and having a child out of wedlock, and us being so ashamed and trying to keep up appearances that we quickly got her out of town and put her in a home down in San Diego where no one would know her.

"And then your brother, not liking football because he was so gentle, but still he played with all his heart so he, too, could fit in at school, and the coaches kept egging him on to keep playing until he injured himself. And then when we took him to see Dr. Hoskins, what did that no good drunk say, 'He only has growing pains, so keep him playing.'"

Tears came to my mother's eyes. "And your father and I could see that there was something very wrong with your brother, but we believed Dr. Hoskins because he was an American doctor, and we were too busy doing business to pay much attention. And it wasn't until the new young doctor named Pace came to town, who'd just gotten out of the Navy, that he took just one look at your brother and rushed him to Scripps Hospital in La Jolla. But it was too late. His football injuries had turned to yellow jaundice, injuries that could have been so easily taken care of at an earlier stage. Oh, we failed, *mijito!*" said my mother, with tears pouring down her face. "Your father and I, we failed all of you children!"

"Oh, *Mama*," I said, handing her back her embroidered handkerchief, "it's not you and *Papa* who failed. It's this whole system in which we live that has failed all of us."

"What do you mean?" she said, drying her eyes.

"Look, Dr. Hoskin's license should have been revoked years ago, *Mama,* and nuns and priests should never have been allowed and even encouraged to be abusive. You see, it's the very structure of these old out-of-date, male-based institutions that are failing us, the people, because they're full of secrecy, control, and have no real love and respect for ordinary people.

"Think about it, *Mama,* the very foundation of the Catholic Church is based on the . . . the concept of an all-male angry god who's full of wrath, and then we're told that we humans come into this world with Original Sin, so this then tells the Church to treat all of us as basically evil, and hence gives them the right to be abusive. Can you see that?

"It's an all-male-based set up so that then a few old impotent men can . . . can manipulate all of us with ease. So, then, your failure wasn't your failure. You and *Papa* were always very good wise people, because both of you were raised by your Indigenous American Indian mothers who were towers of faith and strength and believed in a kind, loving God who was both male and female."

"Well," she said, looking at me in a new way, "if this is what you really think, then maybe this is exactly what you should go and tell these retired nuns and priests."

"Are you kidding? This is what got me slapped until I was bloody out at the mission, *Mama*! Priests and nuns don't want to hear about any of this!"

"Yes, I'm sure that was true," she said. "But these nuns and priests have read your book, and so maybe their Heart*Corazones* have opened up."

"That would be a Miracle," I said.

"Yes," she said, "and did we not raise you kids to understand that every day is, in fact, *otro milagro* gifted to us by God?"

I nodded. "Yes, that is how you raised us, *Mama*," I said. "And this is also what I have been writing about all these years."

I stopped and my mother and I kept looking at each other. My dad had done this, too, and it was called *Ojo*Eye Gazing, which, according to Native People, was a Sacred Form of Heart to Heart and Soul to Soul Touching.

I pushed back in my chair and got to my feet. I'd never expected to get into such a deep conversation with my mother. It was almost as if the Spirit of my dad had come into her now that he was on Our Other Side of Living and she, too, had become a great talker.

"You're right, *Mama*," I said, "they have read *Rain of Gold.* That's why they've contacted me, so maybe they will be open for me to tell them what I really think and feel.

"But, oh, no, *Mama*," I added, shaking my head, "I don't know if I can do this! Not when I can't get it out of my head all the horrors that the Church has done! Hell, the Catholic Church alone, mostly through Spain and Portugal, slaughtered well over sixty to eighty million Native Americans in the name of God! And not just the men, but the women and children, too, like they slaughtered your mother's own Yaqui people! And damn it, nobody knows anything about this! Hell, what the Germans did to the Jews is small potatoes compared to what the Church has done worldwide! *Papa* KNEW THIS, and he wasn't afraid to admit it!"

"Yes," she said, with tears once more coming to her eyes, "and your father is also the one who found it in his Heart*Corazon* to go and . . . and Forgive the man who was responsible for your brother's untimely death. He was only sixteen years old," she added, "only sixteen, and still your father was able to Forgive."

Hearing this, I now stopped all my talking and took my mother into my arms. I, too, remembered what my dad had done very well. I'd been about seventeen years old and going to the Army Navy

Academy in Carlsbad where my brother Joseph had also gone, and that day I'd just gotten home from school when I found out that my dad had driven up California Street to see Dr. Hoskins.

My mother had been screaming with rage and she'd demanded for me to get in our ranch truck and drive after my dad and stop him from seeing the doctor. But I hadn't wanted to get involved. Yet seeing my mother so angry, and she was normally such a calm person, I'd finally agreed to do what she asked and I'd gotten into our old ranch truck and drove after my dad.

And I'd gotten there just as my dad was walking past the corrals to where Dr. Hoskins was in his riding ring with one of his Tennessee Walkers. I'll never forget watching my dad in his big western hat walking up to the doctor in his English gear. Both of them were old, distinguished-looking grey-haired men. I watched the doctor dismount and take off his right-hand glove to shake my dad's hand.

Then I couldn't believe it. My dad was actually accepting the hand of the man who was responsible for my brother Joseph's death. I quickly turned to leave, but this was when my dad spotted me and waved me to come over so he could introduce me to this man that I'd avoided all of my life. I didn't know what to do, but my dad insisted and so I finally walked over, feeling like a traitor to my brother and mother.

"This is our other son, Edmundo," said my dad. My parents always called me by my middle name Edmundo at home.

My eyes flashed with rage and the doctor saw it, but still he reached out to take my hand. And what did I do? I couldn't believe it, I, too, reached out and took his hand, but if he had so much as squeezed my hand just a little bit, I would've jerked him to me and side stepped him, slamming him to the ground as we did at our wrestling workouts every afternoon at the Academy. But he didn't squeeze my hand like a lot of old men do trying to show that they still have power. No, he shook my hand with such gentleness that in his own way he was saying he . . . he was sorry. So I didn't slam him, but still I quickly took my hand back and just stood there listening.

And my dad and the old doctor continued speaking about horses and the price of hay and not one single word was ever mentioned about my brother. And yet before my dad and I left, I could see in both of these old men's eyes that a Peace had been made between them, and that the doctor, who was now himself dying of cancer, was truly grateful that my dad had come to see him. I took in several deep GodBreaths, remembering all this.

"Okay, *Mama,*" I finally said, "maybe you're right, and I should go and see these old retired nuns and priests. But truly, I don't know what I'll do when I get there."

"You will pray, *mijito,* you will pray and ask God for guidance, and then you will Know what to do, and who knows, this . . . this might end up Being the most important talk of your life."

"What? Why would you say this, *Mama*?"

"Because, *mijito,* over and over again your father and I found in business here in the United States, that that which we really didn't want to do was often the very thing that caused us to learn the most and grow the most."

"Well, yes, but this isn't business."

"Oh, isn't the business of religion the biggest business in all the world? You, yourself, spoke of this only moments ago."

I nodded. "Yes, I guess you're right."

"Look, *mijito,* your father never wanted to stop bootlegging, but then when he was forced to stop because prohibition was over and we got that pool hall from Archie in Carlsbad and we went legal, our whole life changed in a way that we'd never dreamed possible. Doors that had been previously closed to us suddenly opened up.

It was like now that we were business people, the *Americanos* no longer saw us as *Mexicanos,* but instead as other business people.

"It was like a Miracle, I tell you, so you now go and see these nuns and priests and do not be surprised that—with the help of Our Sacred Blessed Mother and Her Son Jesus—that this might end up . . . not just being the most important talk of your life, but also a whole New Miraculous Change of life for you here in your Heart*Corazon, con el favor de Dios,*" she added, making the sign of the cross and then kissing the back of her right thumb which she'd placed over her index finger, making a cross.

"Oh, *Mama,*" I said.

"Eh, don't you 'oh, *Mama*' me," she said. "You pray tonight, *mijito,* you pray and ask Our Lord Jesus to teach you how to find it in your Heart to Forgive just as He did on the cross and how your father was also able to do with Hoskins. And I'm not saying that this is easy, *mijito,* because only now that I'm approaching my last few years am I finally beginning to understand what Forgiveness is really all about."

"And what's that, *Mama*?"

"Forgiveness, *mijito,*" she said, "I'm now beginning to see is . . . is the only way we mortals can find Peace in *nuestra* Heart*Corazones.*" She stopped and took in a big deep GodBreath. "So I can now see that your father was absolutely right that day he went to see that no good doctor, but I just couldn't see it back then, and . . . and, well, sometimes I still have trouble seeing it even today."

It was me who now took in a big, deep GodBreath, held, then blew out fast. This was a big one for my mother. Maybe even the biggest. Yes, my mother was showing a lot of guts to admit this.

"Me, too, *Mama,*" I now said, "me, too. Oh, that little nun! Do you realize that every woman I've ever been attracted to since then has had some kind of likeness to my little nun? AND THEY

DESTROYED HER, *MAMA!*" I yelled. "THEY REALLY DID!"

But my mother didn't panic or get flustered by my outburst and simply said, "Well, then, *mijito,* maybe this is exactly what you're supposed to speak about to these old nuns and priests. Remember, they, too, were young once and . . . and maybe they, too, were destroyed, and this is why they got mean."

I nodded, and nodded again. Maybe what my mother was saying was right. All through my writing I always wrote—like Anne Frank had so wisely written in her diary—that no matter what, she still believed that people were basically good of heart.

"Okay, *Mama,*" I said. "I'll pray, I really will, and I'll ask for guidance, and I'll go see them. Thank you. You've really been a big help. Thank you very much."

"I'm glad I was able to help you, *mijito,* because . . . as you well know I've never been a very good talker like your father and his mother. Oh, how that little skinny Indian woman could talk. I swear, the birds would come out of the sky to hear her speak," she added with laughter.

And so we hugged in a big *abrazo,* and then I went back across the grass and the chicken coops to the big old house that was so rundown with roof leaks and broken toilets that my parents had been very smart to want to move into the nice new smaller house that Barbara and I had built.

I could hear the goats and the horses in the distance and, of course, the chickens. I was feeling pretty good now. I was no longer all-divided and confused inside. No, I was now Centered, and the teaching of my Native American *Mamagrandes*—through *mi mama*—had done it once again. After all, when it was all said and done, we, Human People, really were like the weeds, as my dad's mother *Doña Margarita* always said, "indestructible as we reached for the Light of God!"

Chapter Two

OH, I'D ALWAYS LOVED FLYING!

In high school my best friend, John Folting, got his pilot's license when he was sixteen years old and he immediately took me up in a little propeller powered plane that had no doors and flew so slowly that the cars below us would go past us. We flew just a few hundred feet above the earth, and the land below us became alive with jackrabbits in the valleys, quail in the canyons, and deer on the *mesas*. Oh, seeing the world from a bird's point of view was spectacular and totally all new to me. Then I'll never forget, up ahead I saw that we were approaching some green meadows and little ponds and this was when I saw a waterfall that I'd never known even existed in San Diego County, but John then banked the little plane and we headed back.

"NO!" I shouted over the noise of the propeller. "Let's keep going! I want to see that waterfall and those meadows and little ponds!"

"WE CAN'T!" he yelled back at me. "That's *México*! We can't cross international borders without advance notice and approval!"

"What border?" I shouted. "I don't see any border! That's the same kind of brush and oak trees and rocky hills as we've got here all around us!"

I'll never forget, John started laughing and laughing. "What did you expect to see, a concrete wall like they have in China?"

"Well, no," I said, feeling all embarrassed, "but I guess I did expect to at least see something."

That day I was totally shocked to find out that . . . that in reality the world was borderless, and so incredibly beautiful and full of natural abundance, and now here I was aboard a huge commercial jet and once again looking out my window as we flew across the western United States.

And once more I could see that our whole Mother Earth was so fantastic and beautiful and full of abundance as I flew northeast from San Diego, California to the city of Minneapolis at the border of Minnesota and Wisconsin. And I still couldn't see any visual borders.

No, everything just worked together in unity and color. First came the rocky thick-brush hills of Southern California that looked like they were covered with fur and a few trees in the canyons, then came the huge valleys of agriculture with those great big green circles—so easy to irrigate because it only took one huge turning sprinkler on monstrous wheels per circle—and then there were also long straight rows of orchards stretching out for miles, and then all of this was surrounded by vast deserts painted in colors of orange and red and white with veins of blue.

Then when I thought I couldn't take in another ounce of beauty, here came the sculptured Grand Canyon with all its wonder and majesty, then, of course, next came the great tall snowcapped Rocky Mountains.

Oh, I was once more in Love*Amor*, taking in Beauty with a capital 'B' as my *mamagrande* had always taught me how to do. In fact, I'd forgotten that I was going to see old retired nuns and priests until we landed, and then it all came rushing back into me. And even though I'd prayed and asked for guidance as my mother had suggested, I still had no real idea why I'd accepted this speaking engagement.

At the airport a man dressed in a dark suit had a sign with my name on it. I hadn't expected this. Usually when I spoke at high schools and universities, I was picked up by the teachers or professors. This was really pretty extravagant. These old nuns and priests were really putting on a show for me. The man immediately took my luggage and took me out to a long black limousine, put my bag in the trunk, and then quickly opened the back door for me. I almost laughed. This really wasn't my style.

"And in a little cooler you'll find water and beer and wine and some snacks that were prepared for you," he said. "You see, we'll be taking a two-hour drive from the city of Minneapolis out into the country."

"Thank you," I said, and I slipped off my small day backpack and got into the back of the big luxurious car.

Normally I liked to sit up front with the driver and visit when I came to a new place, but this time I didn't want to talk to anyone. No, I had to gather myself. My mother's words had truly gotten deep inside of me. If she was right and this was going to maybe end up being the most important talk of my life, then I still had a lot of heavy *Alma*Soul searching to do.

I took in a great big deep GodBreath and held. Ever since I'd had my talk with my mother, it also seemed like I just couldn't get Sister Theresa out of my mind. Yes, I'd only been an eight year old, and yet I'd never quit loving that kind, soft-spoken little nun. How could I? Something deep inside of me had known, within the first moment I met her, that she'd been meant to be the Love*Amor* of my life.

And now Breathing easy, real easy, I looked out the window of the big dark car. There was a little snow on the ground and most of the trees had lost their leaves. Then we were out of the city and traveling across farmland with large barns, then we were travelling alongside a huge lake, and I could see that all this terrain was mostly flat and wooded, a very different type of terrain than the dry, rugged, wide-open western United States that I was used to. But still, I also found it to be just as breathtakingly beautiful as the land that we'd flown over.

Oh, looking out at the huge lake with its tiny splashing waves, I wished that I'd really come to go fishing so I could get to know the local people and we could talk about what kind of fish they caught and what did they do to keep their lake so clean and beautiful. A large part of me still wished that I really hadn't come to see these old retired nuns and priests.

I mean, yeah, sure, my mother had explained to me that Forgiveness was our only Hope, and I agreed with her, but also I had to admit that Forgiveness had never been my style. After all, I wasn't my brother Joseph who'd always been so kind and gentle. I was Cain. Not Abel. In fact, at my first public talk back in 1973 when my first book *Macho!* had come out, and the keynote speaker, a famous author, was too drunk to do the keynote, it ended up that I spoke to the 500 English teachers in Long Beach, California, and believe-you-me, I'd shown no Forgiveness.

Sure, I'd had notes, and I'd been prepared to give a nice little friendly talk about all the research and interviewing that I'd had to do to write *Macho!* But then when I'd looked out at that sea of white teachers' faces and I hadn't seen one Black, Asian, or Mexican face, my Heart*Corazon* EXPLODED and I'd tossed my notes away, pulled down my Stetson, and gone for the jugular!

"I understand you're all English teachers," I'd said with a huge booming voice.

They'd laughed, thinking that this was a compliment.

"Well," I'd continued, "I'd like you all to know that I once had an English teacher, and I hope that English teacher dies a painful death that lasts at least a week! BECAUSE!" I'd screamed, "I can forgive bad parents because maybe it was an accident, and they didn't even want to be parents, BUT ENGLISH TEACHERS ARE NO ACCIDENT!" I'd yelled. "You guys study to become teachers! You study for years, and so no, I will not forgive you English teachers who are abusive and torture kids with commas and periods and misspelling, making them feel like less than human, because they can't seem to be able to GET IT RIGHT!"

My publisher's representative, a woman from back east who was standing to the right of me behind the stage curtains, went bonkers and came rushing towards me to get me off the stage. But I'd turned and yelled at her, too.

"GET BACK AWAY FROM ME! I will not be silenced! These teachers came to hear a writer speak, AND THEY WILL NOW HEAR A WRITER SPEAK!"

And with that conviction, I continued with my foot to the pedal, and told the 500 English teachers that, on the other hand, I prayed to God with all my Heart and Soul for teachers who were patient, attentive, considerate, and kind, that these would go to Heaven when they Passed and they'd be rewarded with apple pie and vanilla ice cream for all of Eternity.

Tears started pouring down my face and my publisher's representative was shitting square bricks, but then her shock and mine, when at the end of my talk I received a standing ovation that lasted for several minutes, she quickly changed her position, acting like the whole thing had been her idea. And my book *Macho!* became a west coast bestseller, and it was reviewed by the *L.A. Times* and compared to the best of John Steinbeck.

So, well, then, maybe my mother was wrong and it wasn't about Forgiveness and I should just go straight for the jugular with these nuns and priests, too. I mean, that time back in 1973, I'd just gone for it with all my Heart and Soul, and so maybe I should do the same thing again.

Hell, this was also how I'd become a writer.

I'd just gone for it with all my Heart and Soul come hell or high water! The year was 1960. I was nineteen years old and I'd just come back from *México* to the U.S. three days before, and all those old horrible racist feelings that I'd had growing up with since kindergarten had come EXPLODING back up inside of me, but, well, that was also another story, so I won't go into that right now.

Anyway, these were the kind of memories that were going through my head until I got hungry and reached for the little cooler that was by my feet alongside my backpack, and I saw that there was a pretty pink little bag attached to the cooler. I took the pretty little bag in hand and opened it and there was a red rose inside with a note.

Instantly, a smile came to my face. Who would have ever thought? I took the rose in hand and smelled of it and it smelled of Heaven, and then I read the note. It was handwritten in wonderful penmanship and simply said, "Please enjoy your drive alongside our beautiful lake, and you'll find that your pastrami sandwich has extra hot mustard just like you like it." And there was no signature. Just a little hand-drawn heart with the word "love" below it.

I was stunned.

What was all this about? And how had they found out that I liked pastrami with extra hot mustard? Then when I got a beer out of the cooler. It was a Stella, my favorite, along with Modelo and Pacifico. Had these old nuns and priests spoken with my mother or with my wife Barbara? I couldn't stop smiling as I ate my thick, delicious pastrami and drank down both beers. I was sound asleep when we drove up to the huge retirement home.

Waking up, I took in several deep GodBreaths, centering myself, and glanced around. This retirement home was a great big old beautiful mansion built on a knoll over-looking the large expanse of water that we'd been following. There were Canadian honkers on the grass and the well-maintained lawn rolled all the way down to the water's edge.

I took in another great big deep GodBreath, held for a count of five, then blew out real fast. Yes, I could now see that my mother had been absolutely right. There were no accidents, and I was no longer a kid. I was now an adult. A published author. And so if I couldn't get past my own crap, then how could I ever expect for others to get past theirs? The buck stopped here. My God, a rose, and then a pastrami with lots of hot mustard and a Stella, my favorite next to Modelo.

Yeah, sure, no doubt about it, it was me who had to change my way of thinking, because the change we wanted for the world had to start within each of us, here deep inside us. Not over there with abusive nuns and priests and teachers, but right here within me, you, we, all of us.

I got out of the car. I didn't want the driver to open the door for me. I really didn't like all that subservient crap, especially when I was dressed in old worn out Levis, cowboy boots, western hat, and a beat-up sheepskin jacket. An elderly man came out to greet me. He was smiling and in regular street clothes, but I guessed he was a priest.

"Hello," he said, with a voice full of joy. "We're so happy you accepted our invitation." He laughed. "A few of us were getting a little worried that you might not come, because of the interviews you've done and you mentioned all those abusive things that happened to you in Catholic school. Father James," he added, sticking out his hand with a big smile.

I took his hand. "Well, you guys were right," I said. "I almost didn't come. It was my mother who talked me into coming."

"Well, then, we need to thank your mother. Lupe, correct?"

I nodded. "Yes, Lupe."

"A beautiful woman," continued Father James. "Here, let me help you with your backpack. You've had a long trip."

"No, thank you," I said. "I always like to keep my pack in my own hands at all times."

"Oh," he said, as the three of us went up the stairs. And it was one of the most deliberate "oh's" I'd ever heard.

"My God, this place is beautiful," I said once we were inside.

And I meant it. The whole backside was made up of tall magnificent windows that looked out on the rolling hill of green grass and the large expanse of water. I walked up to the windows. There were two nice big fat whitetail deer just beyond the Canadian honkers by the water's edge.

"WOW! What a gorgeous place! The deer, the honkers, the natural grass, and this huge body of water that looks like a whole entire sea! Truly, a land of plenty! Is this Lake Michigan?"

"No, it's Lake Superior."

"Really? I thought Lake Michigan was the big one."

He smiled. "All five Great Lakes are very large," he said.

"Oh, and this structure, who built it?" I asked. "The fine woodwork, the window panes, the arches, the marble floors. What great expansive architecture."

"I'm glad you appreciate it," he said with a big smile. "You see, at the turn of last century this was built as a hunting lodge by a few very rich powerful men, who liked to get together now and then, so they could make some of the major decisions for our country."

"Really? For our entire nation, eh?"

"Yes, and they had barges of material brought in from Europe and floated across the lake to this remote location so they could meet in total privacy."

I started laughing.

"What is it?" he asked.

"So those tough, greedy, old conniving so-and-so's finally began to fear death, and decided to give the whole place to you guys for insurance for their Souls, eh?" I said, cracking up with *carcajadas*, meaning big belly-shaking laughter.

"Well," he said, "I hadn't quite thought of it like that, but you might be right. Come this way," he added. "You have time to go to your room and rest before dinner, which will be very simple, then you can get a good night's rest for tomorrow's events. I hope you don't mind, but we've invited some outside teachers and administrators to join our activities."

"No, of course not," I said. "The more, the merrier!"

"Good," he said. "After reading your books, I told them that you wouldn't be intimidated."

"Which of my books have you read?"

"*Macho!*, *Jury*, and of course, your most fabulous book, *Rain of Gold*. But I must say, I do believe that in some ways *Jury* might just be my favorite. Did Naomi really change her vote to guilty because of cat food?"

Jury was the true story of the minute-by-minute deliberations of the Juan Corona murder trial, the largest mass murder ever committed in the United States at that time.

I laughed. "Yes, she really did, and it shocked people when Juan Corona was convicted because Hawk, the defense attorney, had torn the prosecution case apart."

"So I read," he said, "but the foreman, Ernie Phillips, guided the jurors with such, well, honesty and simplicity that they all finally voted for guilty except for Naomi."

"Exactly," I said.

"But then Naomi's sister called her and told her she was leaving, that she was going back to her own home, and her cats were out of food. I couldn't put the book down, because this then told me that the whole course of history can be changed by the most trivial and meaningless of reasons."

"Yes, but also the right decision was made by the jurors," I said, taking in a deep breath, "because after the trial . . . well, Juan Corona's priest came to me and he talked, but, of course, I can never write about what he told me."

"Really?"

"Yes."

"Oh, if I'm guessing correctly it must've been haunting his Soul," said Father James, also taking in a deep breath.

"Amen," I said. "Truly, I learned a lot by doing *Macho!* and *Jury*. In fact, I'm sure I could have never done *Rain* if I hadn't done those two books first."

"I can now understand that very well," he said. "*Rain of Gold* is a monumental work," he added.

"Really, you think so?" I said.

"Absolutely," he said. "I've read it three times already, and I've never done that with any other book, except, of course, for the Bible."

Hearing this, I took in a deep GodBreath. Maybe these nuns and priests had really opened up, and so maybe, just maybe, they weren't going to panic if I told them what I really thought about the Roman Catholic Church.

"Well, I'm very glad to hear this," I said to Father James, "because, you see, I quit on *Rain of Gold* many times. I'd just get all full of doubt, and the years would pass, but then I'd re-interview my parents and give it another try. I swear, the truth is that I didn't have the talent or brains with which to pull *Rain* off, and yet, each time I'd go back to it, it was like I now had, well, new insights and . . . and a deeper understanding what it was that my parents were really telling me." I laughed. "Both my dad and mom got so frustrated with me a few times that they told me I'd just become so *gringo*-ized that I was constipated in the brain, and so I could never understand the world that my two Native American *Mamagrandes* had come from, and so I just kept trying and trying."

"Well, we're all very glad you did," he said, "because the book shows that it was Inspired by God."

"Really? You think the book shows that? I mean, it took me sixteen years to write *Rain* and by the time I turned it in to my New York publisher, Marc Jaffe, and all the other people I'd known at Bantam-Random House were no longer there, or had died."

"Well, I can tell you that we've all read *Rain of Gold* and we're very happy you didn't quit and completed the book," he said. "But I also believe that we should save the rest of this conversation for the others. So now please let me just take you to your room."

"Sure, of course," I said.

And as we walked further into the grand great-looking old place, I didn't see any people anywhere. The whole place seemed deserted.

"Where is everyone?" I asked.

"At chapel, or in their rooms."

"Oh," I said, and it was now my turn to give a very deliberate 'oh.' I'd been so caught up in the grandeur of the place and talking about *Rain* that I'd almost forgotten to whom it was that I'd be speaking.

My room was on the second story and was large and beautiful with a balcony overlooking the lake. There were now four deer on the grassy area by the water's edge and another big bunch of honkers had flown in. There were now about 200 birds. I'd never been in a natural setting of such beauty and abundance. It reminded me a lot of Yosemite, California, and the famous world class Ahwanee Lodge.

I unpacked, then decided to lie down to rest for a few minutes. It was a good comfortable bed. Firm but not too firm. And I guess that, well, I fell into a deep sleep, because the next thing I knew, I awoke and it was dark and yet there was some light coming from the far end of my room. I got up on my elbows and saw that a man was standing across the room from me and a bright and yet soft golden light surrounded him.

I rubbed my eyes, thinking that I was still asleep and dreaming all this, but then I realized I was awake and breathing fast, and the man was now gone. And for the life of me, I couldn't remember where I was. So I lay back down and, little by little, I began to remember that I was at a retirement home of old nuns and priests by Lake Superior and not Lake Michigan. And that the last time I'd had a man come to me surrounded by a bright and yet soft golden light had been in Madrid, Spain and . . . and that man had been Our Lord Jesus Christ.

I sat up, took in a big deep Breath, and blew out fast. And back then in Spain, when Jesus had come to me, made total sense, because my *familia* and I and a group of Native Americans had gone to Spain in the name of worldwide Harmony and Peace and Abundance for all, and I'd been totally Open of Heart*Corazon* to complete Our Mission. So what was I now being told by Jesus? Was I now being told that I was on another worldwide Mission, and that Forgiveness wasn't enough, but that I also had to have a Completely Open Heart*Corazón* with these nuns and priests?

OH, MY LORD GOD! I got up and went to the restroom, took a long pee, then washed my hands and face. At times like this I sometimes felt like I was crazy*loco*. Who did I think I was to really believe that Jesus had come to me in Spain and then once again here in Wisconsin?

But then, as I continued washing my face with cold water and my *Mamagrandes'* teaching began coming back to me, I once more realized that there really was no separation between us and the Spirit World once we let go and we started seeing with our HeartEyes and not just our HeadEyes. So then yes, of course, Jesus had just come to me Right Now as He'd come to me in Spain and . . . and as He'd come to me that first time just north of Buccaneer Beach in South Oceanside when I'd been eight years old.

I smiled, remembering that my brother Joseph, my best friend, had just Passed over a few days before. I'd suddenly awakened with a start just before daybreak and was told in no uncertain terms that I was supposed to go to the corrals and saddle up my brother's big horse Midnight Duke.

I got up, slipped on my Levis and boots, and quickly went out to the corrals and Midnight Duke came walking up to me out of the dark as if he, too, had been told that we were supposed to do something very important.

After saddling up the big all-black horse, I pushed him against a fence so I could mount up, and I turned inland, figuring that we were supposed to go up our valley towards the new cemetery where my brother Joseph was buried. But no, Midnight Duke refused to go that way and he turned going down our valley towards Buccaneer Beach at the west end of our ranch.

The Father Sun, the Right Eye of God, had just begun illuminating the world with beautiful colors of yellow and orange and dazzling streaks of silver when we got to the beach. Suddenly Midnight Duke began calling out to sea with great big belly-expanding screeches that spread my little short legs apart.

Then with a couple more great big powerful screeches, he leaped into the huge rolling waves. I was terror-stricken. I didn't know how to swim, so I yanked on the reins with all my might, but then Midnight did something I didn't know horses could do. He just turned his big long horse head to the right, and gripped the side of his bit with his huge horse teeth, and yanked the reins completely out of my hands.

Desperately, I grabbed hold of the saddle with all my might as he kept screeching and the waves came in crashing over us. Then I saw these fins coming toward us and I'd thought they were sharks and they were going to tear us apart. But to my surprise, Midnight Duke didn't get frightened. In fact, he calmed down as the fins came in all around us, and he now began talking to them with little cute bird-like chirping sounds that I also didn't know horses could make.

And . . . and these large sea creatures now also began making little chirping bird-like sounds back to Midnight Duke, and this was when I realized they weren't sharks. No, they were Dolphins.

I smiled, getting warm all over. Oh, this was a Whole Wondrous Miracle. Why Midnight Duke and these Dolphins were talking together like best old friends. But then Midnight Duke stopped talking to his dolphin friends and lifted his head, looking to the left and let out the LOUDEST BIGGEST HORSE SCREECH I'd ever heard. I turned, too, and saw that there was my brother Joseph walking on water alongside Our Lord Jesus just beyond the big black rock and the breakers.

I gulped. I rubbed my eyes. I looked again, and sure enough Midnight Duke was still screeching with such joy at seeing my brother whom he'd loved so much, and I was now also seeing my brother Joseph who was, indeed, walking alongside Jesus.

Tears came to my eyes, I felt so Blessed and I made the sign of the cross over myself for I now Knew without a shadow of a doubt that when One Of Our Loved Ones Passed Over, we weren't losing them. Oh, no, what was really happening was that we were gaining an even closer relationship with Our Lord God Jesus.

And now remembering all this so vividly, I smelled WILDFLOWERS! Wonderful WILDFLOWERS, and looking in the mirror above the sink, there was Jesus.

"Hi," I said to Jesus.

"Hello," He said back to me.

"Thanks for coming with me," I said.

And saying this, I began laughing with *carcajadas!* What a ridiculous thing to say. There were no boundaries for Jesus once we accepted Him. He was, then, always with us. It wasn't like He would have stayed behind in California and I'd come to Wisconsin by myself. Oh, He was now laughing with *carcajadas*, too, and this felt wonderful. Yeah, sure, of course, and it wasn't like I was crazy*loco* that I was seeing and talking with Jesus. After all, Life, *la Vida,* was a DreamVoyage, and Confucius said it best:

Row, row, row your boat,
Gently down the stream,
Merrily, merrily, merrily,
Life is but a dream!

Oh, the fragrance of Wildflowers, and the sight of Jesus always felt SO VERY! VERY GOOD! I slipped on my Levis, and went across the room to the balcony to look up at Our *Familia* of Stars. But opening the balcony door, the freezing cold hit me like a wall of ice. I quickly closed the door.

Shivering, I went across the room and got back in bed under the big warm comforter. And as I lay in bed, I began to realize that Jesus was always really, really, really with me, with you, with all of us when we were Open of Heart*Corazon* and Alive of *Alma*Soul as

I'd been in Spain and Jesus had come to endorse our movement of Snow Goose Global Thanksgiving, meaning that we were taking Our Greatest U.S. Celebration when Native Americans and Europeans ate in Harmony and Peace together, AND GOING GLOBAL WITH IT! And now Jesus had come to me again, because I guess, He was also endorsing this Talk I was going to have with these old retired nuns and priests.

Tears came to my eyes. Yes, of course, THIS WAS IT! My mother had been ABSOLUTELY RIGHT ONCE AGAIN! And I just hadn't seen it, because it was so easy for me to be a Doubting Thomas!

I took in a GodBreath, held, blew out fast, then took in Another and Another and went back to sleep. Only in our DreamVoyaging did we bypass our forever examining busy-thinking head and accept our Natural Human Beingness which was, of course, Forever Connected To Supreme Being.

The next thing I knew, I awoke, and there was sunlight coming in my window. Why, I'd slept the whole night through. The whole eastern sky was now painted in gorgeous colors of red and orange and pink with spectacular streaks of dazzling silver and blue and soft purple. I took in several deep GodBreaths, blew out fast, got up, found I was still wearing my Levis, and crossed the room to step out on the balcony, and to my surprise, the cold didn't hit me like a wall of ice this time. No, it was like the cold now embraced me with a crisp, good feeling of ENERGIZING LOVE*AMOR*!

I smiled.

I laughed. Oh, it felt so invigorating that I put both of my hands over my Heart*Corazon*, and gave greetings to Our Father Sun as I'd done with my Yaqui Indian *Mamagrande* as a child.

"GOOD MORNING! GOOD MORNING! GOOD

MORNING, FATHER SUN!" I shouted, pounding my Heart*Corazon* with both of my open hands and looking out at Our Sun, Our Right Eye of God.

"FROM MY HEART*CORAZON*!" I now shouted still pounding the left side of my chest. "Good morning, Father Sun! Goodnight, Mother Moon," who was, of course, Our Left Eye of God. "*Con Todo Mi Corazón y Alma,* good morning, good morning, Father Sky, Mother Earth, and All Our Holy Stars, *nuestra familia!* Our great great grandparents and aunts and uncles! All of Our Ancestry, who've already come here to *Tierra Santa* and completed their Holy Work of planting Our Almighty's Sacred Garden of Heaven on Mother Earth!

"GOOD MORNING, *FAMILIA*! GOOD MORNING!" I shouted even louder, giving Love*Amor* to Our whole entire *Familia's* Universe! "Good morning! Good morning! Good morning! GOOD MORNING!"

And now feeling so good deep inside, I laughed with *CARCAJADAS!* Oh, it felt so good to do this SACRED HOLY RITUAL of Giving Thanks that *mi Mamagrande* had taught me to do when I'd been a child.

Glancing around, I saw that the honkers were already up and munching, like an army of great big birds, bobbing their heads up and down in a quick singing rhythm as they ate the tips off the grass. And the lake waters were shimmering and the trees were singing in the breeze. Oh, Life, *la Vida,* was truly a Symphony of Sound and Color. Then suddenly, two white tail deer came prancing into the midst of honkers with their tails up and their ears pointing forward in high alert.

Something must've startled them, and then I saw them, Five Native Americans, dressed in buckskin and fur, and they were walking about three feet above the ground just like Jesus had hovered about two feet above the floor when He'd come to me this morning and when He'd come to me in Spain.

I called out, waving to my Five Native Brothers, and they turned and waved back to me. Then they, too, ShapeShifted out of this Dimension and into another just as Jesus always also did so easily.

Chapter Three

So I went back inside, did my floor exercises, showered, dressed, and went down for breakfast. I was starving. In the lobby, I saw people going to a room to the right just off of the huge, beautiful main dining room. I followed them, thinking they might lead me to food. There were about thirty people in the smaller room. They were all elderly and dressed in street clothes and most of them were women. The men, who were very few, were all over by the food which was set out on two long white linen-covered tables by the large expanse of windows overlooking the grass and the lake.

I could now see that it had been a good thing that I'd slept through the whole night and I hadn't met any of these people for dinner last night, because, well, I'm sure that if I'd met them last night, I would have probably just been looking at them and trying to figure out which nun had been the meanest and which priest had been the child molester. But now that I'd slept the whole night through and Jesus had come to me as He'd done in Madrid, Spain, I was seeing things very differently. Simply, I was seeing these nuns and priests as just happy-looking old people.

Father James was the first one to come up to me. "Good morning," he said with a great big smile. "How did you sleep?"

"Very well, thank you," I said. "How about you? How did you sleep?"

"Not so good. It's hard to sleep at my age."

"Oh, how old are you?"

"I'm going on eighty-two," he said.

"My dad was older than you and every night he slept like a baby," I said.

"Well, I wish I knew his secret," he said, laughing. "In fact, I bet many of us would like to know."

And I almost said, "Well, maybe my dad slept like a baby because he had a clear conscience and a lot of you guys don't." But I didn't say this, and instead just kept quiet. After all, I had to keep an Open Heart*Corazon* as Jesus had let me know, especially if I hoped to accomplish anything worthwhile with all these old nuns and priests.

"I'll be introducing you," he continued. "Is there anything special that you'd like me to say?"

"No, not really. Just go for it, but please keep it short, okay?"

"Of course," he said.

Then he walked me over to the two tables where the food was laid out.

"As you can see," he said, "we mostly have rolls and coffee and fruit, but there are also eggs and bacon available. You never came down for dinner last night, did you?" he added.

"No, I didn't," I said, "and I'm starving, so yes, I'd really like to have a big full breakfast." I laughed. "I had such vivid wonderful dreams, I awoke laughing!"

"Really? You awoke laughing?"

"Yes, and it was wonderful!"

"I'll be," he said. "Maybe it's hereditary. Your grandmother, *Doña Margarita*—I hope I pronounced it right—if I'm not mistaken, awoke laughing many times, too."

"Yes, you pronounced very well, and you're right. My

grandmother would explain to us that when we sleep, our Guardian Angel takes us back up to Heaven to sleep in the Holy Arms of *Papito Dios*, so how can we not awake laughing, eh?"

"Well, maybe this is something you can tell us all about, too," he said. "You see, this is what many of us found so fascinating about your book. It was almost like your grandmothers didn't worship God, but instead—how can I say this—they lived with God."

"Exactly, because in many native languagings, breathing and God are the exact same word."

"Really? Oh, you will definitely need to tell us about this!"

"I'll be glad to," I said.

Wow, I was really beginning to see that it was a Godsend that I'd come. What a waste it had been for me to carry around inside of me all this hate and rage for nuns and priests all these years. But, well, on the other hand, maybe it hadn't been a waste, because my rage and hate had also been part of my main driving force for getting through all those years of writing and rejection.

Father James had them prepare two eggs and four crisp pieces of bacon for me and also a mountain of country potatoes, and a couple of slices of rye toast with butter and strawberry jam on the side. I ate everything and drank down two full cups of my own Yogi herbal tea that I always carried with me in my backpack, and now I was ready.

Most people had taken their seats, and I could see that almost everyone had a copy of *Rain of Gold,* and a few also had *Macho!* and *Jury.* My next two books, *Thirteen Senses* and *Wild Steps of Heaven,* that would complete the trilogy of *Rain of Gold,* wouldn't be out for another year.

Father James and a very handsome young-looking man were making a final check of the microphone. I took in a deep Breath and walked across the room in my western boots over to the podium that was by the large expanse of windows.

Glancing out, I saw that the whitetail deer were gone, but most of the Canadian honkers were still grazing on the grass outside the huge windows. Other honkers were lying down and resting. I smiled. Oh, I just loved this beautiful natural land of plenty.

Then Father James called people to order and did my introduction, but he didn't keep it short like he'd agreed to do. Instead he did like a lot of teachers and professors did and he praised my work, my talent, and especially my tenacity of having endured over 265 rejections from New York publishers.

Then he still didn't stop and he went on to say how my first book *Macho!* was immediately compared to the best of John Steinbeck by the *Los Angeles Times*. This always embarrassed me to no end, because, in my opinion, John Steinbeck—and not Hemingway or Fitzgerald—along with William Faulkner had to be the best writer of our country, truly giving voice to real people. Then to further embarrass me, he added it was an honor that I'd come to be with them.

"In fact, he almost didn't accept our invitation until his mother Lupe convinced him to come," he added with laughter.

After receiving some applause and cheering, I walked over to Father James and gave him a great big hug, which at first he resisted, but then relaxed and hugged me back. I thanked him and stepped up to the podium as he walked over and took a seat along with the priests who were all in the back.

"Thank you," I said. "Thank you very much, and the honor is really mine to be here. And I loved that red rose and the note and that thick wonderful pastrami with lots of extra hot mustard that you guys put in the little cooler for me in the limo."

The faces of the nuns directly in front of me lit up with joy. I smiled and nodded to them, and they all smiled and nodded back, except for one cute little short nun with grey curly hair who turned all red with embarrassment, and quickly glanced away. Oh, then this probably meant that the other nuns didn't know about the flower and the note.

I laughed and glanced around. All the nuns were in the first three rows, and the priests were all behind them, and some of these hadn't even taken their seats yet. I closed my eyes. I wasn't going to let this bother me, so I just took in a big GodBreath, and held it as I gathered myself deep inside, then . . . then I realized that I had absolutely no idea where to begin. I'd never spoken to a roomful of nuns and priests before. I usually spoke to teachers, professors, students, law enforcement groups, and/or other community organizations.

I kept my eyes closed, asking for guidance, and it came to me to start out with a story, and maybe even the story of my nephew Erik and how I'd taken him to the beach one day. Yes, yes, especially if I concluded about the incoming and outgoing waves being like our Mother Earth's 26,000 year cycle of Male and Female Global Energy coming in and going out.

Then after I accomplished this, I would ask them to please join me in a Native American Prayer that I'd learned a few years back from Lydia Whirlwind Soldier of the South Dakota Rosebud Reservation, and by doing these two things, then I'd have a better feel of where I could go with these nuns and priests without losing them.

"GOOD MORNING!" I said in a loud happy voice. "Good morning! Good morning! Good morning! How did you all sleep? Good, I hope. Myself, I slept like a baby and awoke smiling and laughing, then I went out on my balcony and I saw the Father Sun, the Right Eye of God, coming up with all His splendor and wonder, which, according to my two Indian *Mamagrandes,* makes every day *otro milagro de Dios*, another Miracle straight from God, as you already know since . . . since you've read *Rain of Gold.*"

I stopped. My whole Heart*Corazon* was pounding! Something huge was happening to me deep inside. I just couldn't start out with a little story. No, first I'd have to bluntly tell them why it was that I almost hadn't accepted this speaking engagement.

"But now," I said, "before I can begin my talk with the little story of taking my nephew Erik to the beach one day or . . . or even ask you to share with me why you invited me to come to see you, I first need to let all of you know that Father James was right, and I almost didn't accept this speaking engagement, because . . . because of all the abuse I received at the hands of nuns and priests as a young boy."

Tears came to my eyes and I could well see that I'd definitely surprised them, and a few even looked like they were ready to bolt.

"But please bear with me," I said, closing my eyes, "because, you see, it's going to, well, turn out for the good." I opened my eyes and blew out fast. "After days of procrastination, I went to see my mother and we had a *quesadilla* with homemade *salsa* and avocado, and she, who you all know as Lupe in the book and is now almost ninety years old, told me in no uncertain terms that I had to find Forgiveness in my Heart just as Our Lord Jesus had done on the cross, and come and see all of you, because this could very well end up being the most important talk of my life."

The tears were now streaming down my face. "Look, I was eight years old when I fell in love with the little young nun who was teaching me how to read after school in the fourth grade." I wiped the tears off my face. "She was so kind to me. In fact, she was my first teacher who didn't make me feel stupid because I didn't get it. You see, I'm dyslexic and didn't learn to read until I was twenty, and it's a miracle that I was ever able to become a writer."

"Would you like some water?" asked the little short nun with the curly grey hair.

"Yes," I said. "Please."

She quickly got up and went to the two tables where the food had been laid out, poured me a glass of water from a large pitcher, then brought the water and a handful of napkins for me.

"Thank you," I said, taking the water and napkins, "And you are?"

"Mary, Sister Mary, but just call me Mary," she said.

"Thank you, Mary," I said, drinking down the whole glass and then wiping my tears with the napkins. "Are you the one who wrote me the note and put the rose in the little bag?"

"Yes," she said, getting embarrassed, "but please just go on. We really do want to know this man who wrote *Rain of Gold.* Most of us girls just knew that it had to be a woman."

I laughed. "Well, in a way it really was a woman," I said, "because it was my mother and my aunts and my godmother whom I interviewed, and *mi papa* had also been raised in the old Indian way as a woman by his old Indian mother for the first seven years of his life, meaning that he learned to cook and sew and do the work around the house and helped in the birthing process of the goats and dogs and cats, and then even of his older cousins and sisters, and such a man," I now added, "doesn't grow up thinking that women are the weaker sex, but instead are in complete awe of women, and . . . and this is one of the Eight Indigenous Concepts that will help us all over the world reverse the destructive course of modern civilization."

I could see that what I'd said had rattled a lot of cages, but I wasn't going to stop. "So anyway," I continued, "getting back to the story of my little nun, my dad had always told me that the most important decision any man can make in his life is choosing the right woman to marry, because the woman a man married isn't just a man's wife, but the first teacher of his children. And so after a couple of weeks of being with my little nun every day after school, I could see that she was by far the kindest, smartest, most wonderful woman I'd ever met, and so naturally I asked her if she would marry me when I grew up. But she told me that she was already married to Jesus.

"'He's dead, you know,' I'd said.

"'Yes, but I'm married to Our Lord Jesus in Spirit,' she'd said.

"'Oh, then that's okay,' I'd said, 'we can get married in body and have babies.'

"And she then smiled, and looking back, I can guess that she was now going to explain to me what she meant by being married in Spirit, but she never got to say this to me, because at that very moment the big mother superior came bursting in through the door and she slapped me so hard she knocked me out of my chair, called me the devil, then started hitting my kind, wonderful, little nun who wouldn't fight back or even try to defend herself. This was when I attacked the old nun, biting her leg so hard that she quit hitting my little nun."

I stopped. I could see that I'd startled half of the nuns and priests, and a few of the priests looked like they wanted to do me in.

"BUT NOW LET'S NOT STOP HERE!" I said in a loud booming voice. "Because I'd like to bring that incident that happened forty-some years ago to the present, and ask how many of you had experiences with a little kid like this? And please you don't have to raise your hands. No, what I really want for you to do is . . . is to just go within yourself to your own Kingdom of God, and see if you ever behaved like this mother superior or the little nun, because this wasn't the end of that situation.

"Oh, no, after that the young priest, who was attached to the school, and the old mother superior thought it was their duty to keep beating me on a regular schedule and explain to me that I'd been born with Original Sin, and so it was their duty to punish me for my own good, so I wouldn't go to hell and burn for eternity!"

I wiped my eyes. "What a bunch of crap! But also now looking back, what I think was really going on was that both the young priest and the old mother superior were in love with my beautiful little nun and they were jealous that they'd never proposed to her."

I glanced around. "And I'm not joking," I added. "Recently, I've had the good fortune to become friends with some ex-nuns and ex-sisters of different religious organizations, and they've told me that part of the reason they left their organizations was because of the sexual advances that had been made on them by their superiors, both male and female.

"And I'm not blaming or finger pointing. I'm just saying that there are no accidents in life. You see, we are a very emotional and sexually driven planet, and so we need to understand this and admit it, so that then every day can, indeed, become *otro milagro de Dios,* instead of a living hell, because of all of our hypocrisy and hidden agendas and lies!

"So are you glad I came, eh? Myself, I'm now glad that I came to see you guys, because the buck stops here! Right now! So that, then, together we can do some serious healing, and . . . and not just of the body and mind, but also of our Hearts and Souls. For you and I now have a great opportunity to —" Two priests had gotten to their feet. "No, please, don't leave! This is good! This is wonderful!"

"Yes, he's right, you know," said a tall elegant nun who was sitting beside little Sister Mary. "Mother Teresa always says, 'I know that God will not give me anything I can't handle, but I only wish that He didn't have so much trust in me.'"

Several nuns laughed and nodded in agreement, but not the priests. In fact, it now looked like quite a few of the priests were ready to bolt, and not just these two who'd stood up. I closed my eyes, Praying for Guidance, and instantly I Knew what to do. I'd simply take the bull by the horns.

"Look," I said to the two priests, "leave if you must, but also realize that this will only cause people to think the worst of you." I opened my eyes. "And so I suggest that you two stay and we all see this through together. Because, like my mother so well said to me before I left, '*Mijito,* all my life I've found that Miracles often come to us when we least expected it, and when we're doing exactly what it is that we've been avoiding and not wanting to do.' And then my mother told me to open up my Heart*Corazon* and pray, realizing that there are no accidents, only situations that can cause us to Spiritually grow beyond OUR WILDEST DREAMS! So please, stay and let us DreamVoyage together!"

"Yes," spoke the tall, elegant-looking nun again, "and this was exactly what Teresa was talking about and what is now causing me to consider if I ever behaved like that mother superior when I was in that position."

"Thank you," I said to this ex-mother superior, "this is truly wonderful, and so now what I'm proposing is that we all fasten our seatbelts because we're now going into the Kingdom of God that's within each of us, and hence into a reality beyond our five-sensory perception and into OUR NATURAL MULTI-SENSORY PERCEPTION OF INFINITE POSSIBILITIES!

"And this is NO JOKE! But the very foundation of *Rain of Gold,* which means a Golden Rain of Miracles coming down to us from Our Holy Creator on a daily basis! You see, most people miss the point and simply read *Rain* as a history book about two families and the Mexican Revolution, and then coming to the United States. But this isn't what *Rain of Gold* is really all about. It's about—"

"FAITH IN GOD!" shouted Sister Mary. "And learning how to see nature in a way I'd never read about in any other book! And about your mother Lupe, a seven-year-old child, waking up every day to the first three miracles of the day."

"It's about a family, who in their innocence, still believe they live in the Garden of Eden," said another nun. "And they understand that every woman needs her own Crying Tree, meaning her very own Special, Quiet Sacred Place."

"It's about butterflies coming into their box canyon in a dancing cloud of dazzling golden color and landing among all the beautiful wild orchids and other gorgeous flowers!" said another nun.

"It's about the Love of a seven-year-old girl for her knight in shining armor, and how she has to make tough decisions that would intimidate even grown women," said yet another nun.

"It's about Forgiveness and Gratitude and going on, no matter what."

"It's about seeing every day as another Miracle given to us by God."

"It's about life and a kind loving God, and never getting bitter, even after witnessing your own beloved children being raped and killed before your very eyes."

"Yes," said Sister Mary, turning to the nun who'd spoken last, "but it doesn't stop there. Even after *Doña Margarita,* my favorite character, loses eleven of her fourteen children, she still goes to her outhouse, smokes her little *cigarillo,* drinks her coffee laced with *whiskito,* and she says her rosary. Oh, to have such relaxed, Natural Faith no matter what, this is what *Rain of Gold* IS REALLY ALL ABOUT!"

I pulled up a chair and sat down. My eyes flooded with tears of joy. These nuns had really read *Rain of Gold* and they'd really, really gotten it, and the priests, as a group, hadn't said anything yet.

"Oh, thank you! Thank you! Thank you!" I said, getting up. "And I almost didn't come. Oh, what a Doubting Thomas I am! But truly, I can now see that we're going to have a fine time, because a lot of you here are ready to receive beyond your WILDEST DREAMS! You see, myself, that's what I do. I've been receiving beyond my Wildest Dreams ever since I took an oath before God up in the wilds of Wyoming to become not just a writer, but a writer as great as Homer or greater with the help of Our Lord God!"

"How old were you?" asked a priest.

"Nineteen, or maybe a week into twenty. You see, I'd just gotten back from *México* where I'd found my roots just as Alex Haley had found his in Africa."

"You were only nineteen when you took such an oath?" asked this same priest.

"Well, yes, of course. Didn't most of you here take a similar oath at eighteen, nineteen, or twenty to dedicate your lives to the Service of God? So that's what I did, but I can tell you that it wasn't until my dad Passed Over and I was in my late forties that my Spiritual Education EXPLODED INTO MIRACLES! And the full realization came to me that I'd been receiving from the University of the Heavens ever since I'd taken my oath. And you guys have also been receiving from this same Divine University whether you realize it or not.

"And this evening after dinner," I continued, "I'll be able to show you how to receive in your sleep, just as my dad showed me on the night he Passed Over."

I stopped and glanced around. The nuns as a group all seemed to be open to what I was saying, and some of the priests, too. And yet a few now looked even more ready to bolt than ever.

I smiled.

I laughed, sending good-feeling Love*Amor* Energy to everyone.

"Then tomorrow," I said in an easy happy tone of voice, "I'll ask you to please share your Dreams, and you'll see how as a group, as a Collective Consciousness of DreamVoyaging, you people will now be on the cutting edge of LEADING ALL OF HUMANITY, back to Our Garden of Heaven, because as Sacred Elders, you automatically Follow Infront!"

"Follow Infront?" asked a priest.

"Yes, that's what the big male goose does when he's at the head of a migrating V-formation of geese, cutting the wind so that all the rest of the geese can then use 30% less energy to keep up. But no more about this right now. Right now I need for all of you to fasten your seatbelts, because . . . because we first need to gain the understanding of the Eight Western Civilization Concepts that are holding us back from worldwide Harmony and Peace and Abundance for All.

"For once we grasp these eight concepts," I said with a great big smile, "we will then be able to slipslide back into Our Indigenous Concepts that will Free Us All! Then BOOM! We'll EXPLODE into Our Natural All-Knowing Cellular Memory, and each of you will then start remembering that we come from the Stars! That's Our True Home! And you'll also KNOW deep inside of yourself all about Our Six Sister Planets and realize that Our Beloved Mother is ALIVE and has a Pulsating Spiritual Heart*Corazon* which over Timeless Time has been moving from Sacred Location to Sacred Location."

I stopped and took in a great big deep GodBreath and I could see that many of them were now doing this GodBreathing along with me. I smiled. Our Energies were finally Harmonizing together.

Sister Mary raised her hand.

"Yes," I said.

"Is India the Sacred Location of Our Mother Earth?" she asked.

"Interesting that you'd ask that. Why, yes, you're right. India has been the Sacred Heart and Soul Location for the last few thousand years, but now it's moving, and these moves will now not be done in increments of thousands of years, but in increments of hundreds. And Our Holy Catholic Church now has the chance to jump abroad and move every 100 years, too. First Ireland, then Mexico, then the Philippines, and keep moving and Being of Service for the Sacred Heart*Corazon* Energy of Our Almighty.

"And all of you Here already Feel and Know this deep inside of Our Collective Cellular Memory, and this is why Jesus so well said that what He did, we will do more. And in doing more, we will automatically Harmonize into World Wide Peace and Abundance for All, because this is a Natural Part of Our DNA, and all of Our Six Sister Planets have already realized this Eons of Timeless Time Ago."

I stopped.

I could smell Wildflowers again, and I now saw that Jesus, along with my brother Joseph and a bunch of my Ancestry, were over there towards the rear of the room and they were SoulSpinning and sending us all their BLESSED SACRED ENERGY.

In fact, many of the nuns and priests were now smiling and looking so happy. BIG BIG HAPPY! And yet the same two priests were on their feet again and ready to bolt.

"Oh, please," I said, closing my eyes, "just sit back down! Didn't Jesus say that we all have the Kingdom of God within us? Well, then, the Kingdom of God must include everything there is, and so I'm not really saying anything new. Come on, guys, just sit back down, and I promise you that all this will start making good common horse sense in just a little bit.

"You see," I said, opening my eyes, "*Rain of Gold* is just the first book of a trilogy, so what you people have read is only the tip of the iceberg. Remember, Hemingway said that the dignity of the movement of an iceberg is that 7/8 is under water, and so we're just getting started, guys."

Hearing this, reluctantly, both old priests sat back down.

"Thank you," I said, "thank you very much. You see, I didn't come here with loaded guns. I really did as my mother told me to do and I asked for guidance, and when I went to bed that night I understood that yes, I was supposed to come out here and see you, and then last night, right here, in my room upstairs, *mi papa,* who'd passed over ten years ago, came to me in my sleep and he assured me that my mother was right, and that it was pre-ordained that all of us come together. So come on, let's just go for it! Okay?" One priest nodded. "Good. Thank you. And so now I'm going to first start with a little story, and then I'm going to ask you all to join me in a Native American Sacred Prayer that will help set up what this whole talk will really be all about. Okay, ready?"

Once again all the nuns nodded, but many priests still looked pretty guarded.

"Okay, not long ago I read an article about two young *Latino* astronomers," I said, "and the article explained how these two young guys had come to the conclusion that all the telescopes around the world had grey-green lenses, and that grey-green wasn't part of the natural colors of a rainbow. So these two guys then speculated that if the rainbow color of rose was put on the huge telescope in Baja, California, where the sky is still relatively clean and there are no city lights for 100s of miles, then these new stars that had recently been found would turn out not to be stars, but entire new galaxies and galaxies, because of the higher frequency of their natural rose-colored lens.

"Well, these two young Chicano astronomers were finally able to get the funding to do it, and they found out that these new stars were, indeed, new galaxies. Then when they turned their rose-colored lenses to other well-established parts of the heavens, they discovered other new galaxies, too, and our comprehension of the heavens quadrupled exponentially, and they almost hadn't been allowed to do their work by the old, well-established astronomers. Pretty good, eh? And so this is what I'm now proposing that we do. That we put on rose-colored glasses like in that old Frank Sinatra song, and that you please join me in this Native American prayer that I learned from my good friend Lydia Whirlwind Soldier of the Lakota Nation.

"Eh, would you please do me the honor and join me? You see, this is also what my two Indigenous *Mamagrandes* always did. They'd wouldn't look at the world through the low frequency of the grey-green glasses of Western Civilization, but instead, they'd keep their vibrant rose-colored glasses on, and they'd mix their Indian Spirituality with their Catholic Christianity, and, in doing this, they'd come up with a wonderful new way of giving Daily Thanks to Our Holy Creator. All right, now everyone please stand up!" All the nuns immediately stood up. The priests were a little slower to follow, but they all finally got to their feet, too.

"Okay, good," I said. "Thank you. And now, put your left hand, palm open, and facing up, and put your right hand, palm open, and facing down. Good. Good. Perfect."

All the nuns were participating, but even though all of the priests had stood up, only about half of them were doing what I asked. I closed my eyes. I was not going to let this bother me. I sent them all Love*Amor*, and then when I opened my eyes, a few more of the priests began participating. And I also noticed that the young, very handsome priest, who was sitting next to Father James, looked totally open and very happy.

"Okay, now, please, everyone close your eyes," I said, "and realize that in many Native Indigenous Languages around the world, the word for God and for Breath is the same word, and so when we take in a great big deep Breath we are taking in a great big part of God. And in doing this, what we're actually doing is that we are activating Our Kingdom of God that's within each of us as Our Lord Jesus so wisely told us about.

"Good," I said, smiling. "Good. Good. I can feel that most of you are participating. Great! Wonderful! Fabulous! And now imagine yourself to be a Hollow Bone. A Buffalo Bone. And with your open left hand facing up, you are receiving, receiving, receiving Good-Feeling Harmonious Energy from our Whole Entire Universe! Just like Albert Einstein did when he received his great theory!" I said with a loud clear voice and with my eyes still closed. "And with your right hand open and facing down you are flooding the Mother Earth with all this good, wonderful, healthy, Pure Love*Amor* Energy you are receiving even from the FURTHEST REACHES OF OUR UNIVERSE!

"Breathe! Breathe! You're a Human Being filling yourself up with Supreme Being, and realize that the faster you give, the faster you receive, so you keep giving and giving and giving as you keep receiving and receiving and keep *nada, nada,* nothing for you are a Hollow Bone! a Buffalo Bone! And you are so huge, so great that your head and hands and feet stretch out to the ends of Creation! And Our Sacred Mother Earth is no larger than a grain of sand on the Seashore of Creation, and we, Human Beings, now full to the brim of Supreme Being are Our Creator's Holy Instruments of Receiving and Giving!

"And understand that old Albert Knew this to HIS BONES! That we are all Hollow Bones! Buffalo Bones once we've Activated Our Kingdom of God that's within each of us! For at this point we, all of us, become Our Almighty's HOLY INSTRUMENTS of planting His/Her LOVE*AMOR* throughout the UNIVERSE! Because this is who we, Human Beings, really are, Holy Sacred Instruments of Receiving and Giving and this is why, when I was eight years old, I was able to receive the vision of seeing my brother Joseph, a few days after he'd Passed Over, walking on the ocean just out beyond the breakers alongside Jesus."

"You saw Jesus?"

I opened my eyes. "Yes, I saw Jesus," I said.

"In full three-dimensional form?"

"Well, yes, of course, but please, just let me go on, because, you see, the time has come in Our Godvolution for all of us to start walking alongside Jesus right now, right here on Mother Earth."

"Godvolution?" mumbled another priest, opening his eyes, too.

"Yes," I said, "Godvolution is also one of the Eight Indigenous Concepts that we need in order for us to slipslide and dissolve ourselves back into the Holy Garden. Evolution and God do not have to oppose each other."

"Makes perfect sense!" shouted a nun, who was keeping her eyes closed.

"Not to me," said a priest, opening his eyes.

And I could now see that almost everyone had their eyes open.

"Okay," I said to the priest, "I can understand why you'd say that, but now tell me, have you ever walked into a room and you instantly knew something was wrong? Come on, how many of you have had this experience?"

Almost everyone raised their hands, especially the nuns who still had their eyes closed.

"Good. Excellent. And you didn't think this," I said, "you knew this, because thinking is done with manmade words which are very recent in our development as Human Beings, and, on the other hand, feelings are ancient. Maybe 100s of 1,000s of years old, if not millions of years, and we feel not just with our hands, but with our whole body twenty-six arm-lengths in all directions.

"And old cops immediately know what I'm talking about, because when they come to a potentially violent situation, they automatically quit their thinking and start trusting their gut-feelings, their instinct, which is the voice of our genius which processes information 10,000 times faster than thinking."

I stopped and glanced around. Only a few still had their eyes closed. "And so what I'm saying," I continued, "is that we all now need to quit our thinking, so we can get out of our Head Computer and move into our Heart Computer. Only then can we access our Soul Computer, and enter into the Kingdom of God that's within each of us.

"Truly understand that our five senses we got from the Greeks, from Aristotle, I believe, is one of the Eight Western Concepts that is holding us back, and Our Full Natural Thirteen Multi-Sensory Perception, that came to me from my *Mamagrande* from *Oaxaca, México,* will free us, because we do, in fact, have three computers for processing information.

"The Head Computer with four senses, the Heart Computer with three senses, and the Soul Computer with six senses, and 'thinking' is to the Head Center as 'intuition' is to the Heart Center and 'psychic powers' are to the Soul Center. This is why a few years back I was able to tell a skinny young Black guy with big ears in South Chicago that he is going to be President of the United States for two terms, and yet his greatest work will happen six months after he leaves the oval office on a Thursday, and why I also Knew—like Bishop Malachy of Ireland Knew back in the 12th Century—that our next Pope, number 112, will be Our Last Pope.

"But what Bishop Malachy didn't know, because Columbus hadn't sailed to the Americas yet, was that this last Pope himself will be from the New World, and with his Intuitive Heart*Corazon* Instincts, he'll set up Our Global Foundation for Our Vatican to move to Ireland for 100 years where we will have Our First Woman Pope. Then Our Vatican will move to *Oaxaca, México* for 100 years and will keep moving every 100 years for the next 50,000 years, so our presently stagnant Church can then keep Growing, Expanding, and Changing just like all the rest of CREATION CREATING!"

Hands were going up all over the place. I closed my eyes. "Please, no, no, questions yet. Right now, just Breathe. GodBreathe. And understand that the longest journey any of us will ever make are these eighteen inches from Our Head Center to Our Heart Center."

I stopped and Breathed. "Good, good," I said. "I can see that most of you are now participating with me and GodBreathing deeply. Only a few of you are shaking your heads and your eyes are wide open with very mixed feelings. EXCELLENT! You're now out of your comfort zone, and so now I'd like you to Know that this Native American Prayer we just did is one if Our Keys for moving us those eighteen inches. Eh, it feels pretty good deep inside to start seeing ourselves as Hollow Bones! Buffalo Bones! And as Our Almighty's Sacred Instruments for planting Eternal Love*Amor* throughout OUR WHOLE UNIVERSE!"

A lot of people were now nodding and saying yes.

"Good. I'm glad to hear this, because I'll tell you," I said, sitting down, "The first time I heard this prayer, it touched me to the depths of my Being! My God, for us to be Holy Sacred Instruments of planting Love*Amor* for Our Creator was SO BEAUTIFUL! SO FANTASTIC! And . . . and it made so much good horse sense!

"Then we, Human Beings, really can walk on water alongside Jesus because we, too, are part of God's Creating Light, and this, in a nutshell, is what Albert Einstein did to receive his theory and what I'll be talking about for the next few days. Okay, now all of you open your eyes," I said. "And please turn and look at each other. Do you now see yourselves differently?" I asked. "Eh, do you see a Glowing?"

Several nuns nodded, saying they did.

"Good," I said, "so will one of you tell us about this Glowing Light you see?"

Mary, the curly grey-haired little nun, spoke first. "When I first opened my eyes I thought I saw a Glowing Light surrounding Sister Margret, but now I'm not quite sure."

"Exactly," I said. "When I first began to see a bright and yet soft Golden Light around people, I thought it was just my imagination. But then I also began to see a crescent shaped little Moon just off to my right when I'd get up to write or go to the bathroom. Then it soon began happening to me so regularly that I just Knew it was really real and not just my imagination.

"So what I'm saying is that this Glowing Light that some of you saw, especially you people who kept your eyes closed the whole time so you were able to keep your focus, will now start happening to you more and more regularly, and then BOOM! You, too, will then one day see your own Crescent Moon, and soon that Moon will be so bright and steady that you won't have to turn on the bathroom light when you get up in the middle of the night to go to the bathroom. And . . . and most important, you'll be feeling, oh, so happy! BIG BIG HAPPY!"

"That's true," said Mary. "When I saw this Holy Light surrounding Margret, it was like I was receiving all this understanding, all these feelings that we're all Holy, and that I still have a lot of life to live," she said, with tears of joy coming to her eyes. "Like I now understand that my life of service is far from over, and this makes me so happy!"

"BIG, BIG HAPPY, eh?" I shouted.

"Yes! BIG, BIG HAPPY!"

I laughed. She laughed.

"And all of you, who were able to keep your eyes closed the whole time, you are now going to start understanding that there's a whole world that hasn't been Touched yet, and will now come ALIVE within Our Living Breathing Almighty."

"Is this why you continually close your eyes," asked a nun who had not spoken before, "and take in such deep breaths?"

"Yes, exactly," I said. "And I'd like all of you to notice that when Mary spoke she never used the word 'thinking' in reference to the Glowing Light she saw. She used the words 'understanding' and then 'feelings', and this is because thinking, which processes information through manmade words, is so superficial and limiting that we can never come to Know God with thinking. Albert Einstein wasn't thinking when he came up with his theory. No, he was flashing with Light of Divine Understanding, and this is called receiving through your Guardian Angel and/or Genuising."

"Yes," said a nun in the second row, "it was a wonderful experience for you to have us close our eyes, because with my eyes closed I wasn't distracted even with what was being said, and I actually got to feeling so strongly connected to God that, of course, I just wanted to keep giving and giving forever!"

"Exactly," I said. "You see, greed is not part of human nature. What is part of human nature is Birthing God."

"Birthing God?!" said several priests and one nun.

"Yes, this is another Indigenous Concept that we all used to understand when we Know Our Original Instructions. Why do you think that religions are so strong all over the world? We're all trying to Birth God, to give Life to God from deep inside of us. Truly, greed only happens when we lose Our Holy Contact with God that's here within us.

"Do you all remember reading in *Rain* how my grandmother *Doña Margarita* gave away all the money that the rich man gave her in Arandas, Jalisco when she was on her way to save her son, Jose, the Great, from execution?"

"That's only a little bit in *Rain of Gold,"* said a nun.

"That's right," I said, laughing. "I didn't get into at all that in *Rain.* It's in *Wild Steps of Heaven* that I told the Miraculous Whole Story. You see, originally *Rain* was 1,500 pages, so I ended up breaking it down into three books. Anyway, my dad explained to me that when people think money will solve all of their *problemas,* then it is very difficult if not impossible for them to see or ever receive any Miracles from the Almighty.

"Truly, Collectively, understand that we all need to once more start becoming Hollow Bones, Buffalo Bones, Instruments of receiving God's Holy Light, just as Albert Einstein did when he saw himself riding on that beam of light and he came up with his Theory of Relativity. You see, this is exactly who we, Human Beings, really are once we activate Our Kingdom of God that's within each of us; we become . . . Beams of the Almighty's Holy Light, giving and giving and giving in ABUNDANCE!

"Remember, Supreme Being is one of the original terms we used for God, and we are Human Beings, and so old Einstein was right when he saw himself riding on a beam of light. No, actually saw himself become a beam of Holy Golden Light, and this is who we all really, really are.

"And I, myself, I could never really grasp this until I first learned to see myself as a Hollow Bone, a Buffalo Bone, a Holy

Instrument of receiving and giving and keeping nothing. Then the words Supreme Being and Human Being made sense to me, and I could also then see that when Einstein ShapeShifted and became a Beam of Light, he was then of Total Service for the Greater Glory of God, and this kind of ShapeShifting is another one of the Eight Natural Indigenous Concepts that we need to activate in order for us to slipslide back into our Natural Flow of Godvolution."

Three hands shot up. "Yes?" I said.

"Isn't ShapeShifting a term used by Native Americans?"

"Yes, and it can also be called SongShifting. You see, when God created the Universe, He/She created One Song, One United Verse, and so it is really all about Energy Frequencies, meaning that each of us comes to Mother Earth with our very own Song, our own unique Vibrational Frequency.

"Okay, no more, please. I need a little break," I said, "then when we come back we can . . . well, understand why it is time in our Godvolution for all of us to stop worshipping Jesus and start doing Jesus, because remember Jesus told us that what He did, we would do more?"

"JUST WAIT!" shouted a tall thin priest who was in the back row. "Are you now insinuating you've walked on water?"

"What? Why do you ask this?" I said. I had no idea where he was coming from.

"You just said 'do' Jesus, and Jesus walked on water, and so for us to do Jesus, then we, too, would need to walk on water."

I gripped my forehead. I could feel his frustration from clear across the room and I almost said, "What are you so afraid of?" But I didn't and I closed my eyes, asked for guidance, and I immediately knew deep within me that this guy had been a very abusive priest, and only now, that he was old and fearing death, was he beginning to be haunted by what he'd done. I opened my eyes and said,

"Father, it's not too late for you to ask God for forgiveness."

Rage exploded across his face. "How dare you speak to me like this!"

I closed my eyes once again, taking in several deep breaths.

"Please, Father, understand that it's going to be okay," I said, opening my eyes. "Truly, God is all about Love, and nothing but Love*Amor*. It's our own fears that caused us to come up with all this business of an angry God who's full of wrath, and . . . and we'll get into all this after our little break. Okay, take ten," I said.

I quickly walked out of the room. I could feel his eyes glaring at me with hate. I needed to get to my room as fast as I could. I wanted no part of his destructive vibrational frequencies.

Chapter Four

TAKING TWO AND THREE STAIRS AT A TIME, I RAN UP TO the second story and rushed down the hallway to my room. Going inside and closing the door, I rushed into the bathroom, closed that door, and I took the biggest dump I'd ever taken in my life. It smelled awful! I had to open the window. My God, what was coming out of me? I guess it was all these years of holding resentment and anger that had fermented into a terrible shit inside of me.

I went to the sink and washed my hands and my face with cold water. I guess my mother had been right once again. It really was helping me deep inside to have come to see these old nuns and priests. I turned off the water and turned to get a towel and this is when I saw that my dad was standing behind me.

"Hello," I said, reaching for a towel.

"*Buenos dias,*" he said with a big smile.

"*Papa,*" I said, drying my hands and face, "I'm glad you're here. I can't do this alone."

"You're not alone," said another voice.

I lowered the towel from my face and I saw that my brother Joseph was standing alongside our dad.

"Joseph?" I said. "OH, WOW!"

I hadn't seen my brother in full form since I'd been eight

years old and he'd come walking across the water just beyond the breakers and the big black rock alongside Jesus.

"We're all here with you," he said. "You have nothing to worry about."

"Really?" I said.

"Yes, just lie down for a few minutes so we can transmit into you," he added.

"Transmit? You mean like a radio receives transmissions from different stations?"

"Yes, through Our Lord God Jesus we will feed you Heart to Heart and Soul to Soul."

I did as told. I went out of the bathroom, into the bedroom, and fell across my bed. Instantly I was out like a light, and when I awoke I felt totally refreshed and ready to go. And looking at the clock by the bed, I could see that I'd only lain down for about eight minutes. It was totally amazing. In just eight minutes it felt as if I'd gained as much rest as a whole night's sleep. But then I remembered that our Eighth Sense was Music and Music activated Our Soul Computer, and once we moved into this computer, then our Ninth Sense, Time, and our Tenth Sense, Space, were both relative, and/or disappeared.

I got up. My dad and brother Joseph were both gone, but I knew that they hadn't left me. No, I could still feel them totally here with me. Oh, I was now ready! No more doubt! No more confusion! Now all was smooth sailing inside of me once again. I went whistling down the hallway stairs. I was now a Hollow Bone, a Buffalo Bone. Oh, I'd never felt better in all my life. Seeing me come into the room, all the nuns and priests took their seats. Their energy was very different.

"Good, I can see that you all came back," I said. "Thank you very much. And I want to apologize for my behavior. I had no right to suggest that one of you needed to ask for Forgiveness. What I should have done was addressed the question that I'd been asked and that was . . . was I insinuating that I've walked on water. And, well, now the Truth is that I didn't know how to answer the question, because—" I blushed. "I had to take a dump, and I barely made it to my room in time."

People laughed.

"And I'll tell you," I continued, "it turned out being one of the biggest and most foul smelling dumps I've ever taken, and I think it had a lot to do with the fact that I've been holding on to so much crap inside of me for all these years that it had fermented," I added, laughing. "Did anyone else ever have a similar experience?"

Two nuns burst out laughing and nodded their heads, and then the tall, thin priest who'd spoken up, laughed, too.

"I had a big one, too," he said, "and I'm sure that if I hadn't had a big one, I wouldn't have returned."

"Well, I'm very glad that you did," I said, "so we can now address that question of yours. You see, after my dump, my dad and my brother Joseph came to me."

"In spirit?" asked the priest.

"No, yes, I mean, yes, in Spirit, because they've both passed over but they also came to me in full three-dimensional form, and they told me to address your question with a specific question." I Breathed. "Tell me, where would we be today if . . . if Peter had not looked down and he had walked side by side with Jesus on water? Eh, where would we all be today?"

I glanced around. My God, the question had really worked. You could hear a pin drop.

"Well, one thing would be for sure," said a nun in the back row who had not spoken, "if Peter hadn't looked down and he'd walked on water alongside Our Lord Jesus, then we wouldn't be as fearful today, because we'd know that if Peter could do this, then maybe we can do it, too."

"We'd all feel closer to Our Lord Jesus," another nun said with tears of joy streaming down her face.

"Everything would be different for us, because we would have been raised to think that walking on water and other such miracles were a normal part of life," said Margret, the tall, elegant nun.

I smiled and they continued and I could now see why I'd been told to address this question with this specific question. A Miracle was taking place before my very eyes. These nuns were now stepping forward and taking the lead.

"My parents would have felt safe to just love me, and not be so critical," said another nun.

So I continued listening and it was beautiful, then I finally said, "Amen! Awomen! Achildren! And now I'd like you to know that this was how I was raised by my Yaqui Indian *mamagrande,* that Miracles are a Normal Part of Life, and so yes, straight out, I can now tell you that no, I haven't walked on water, but I've done much more.

"You see, back at one time when we were All, All, All Indigenous People the world over, we Knew that ordinary people walked on water and they started doing this when they reached our most perfect human age of 78, because between 78 and 104 is our normal age for Passing."

"What in the world are you now talking about?" asked another priest. "I was just beginning to follow you, and now you throw a whole new wrench INTO THIS MESS!"

I closed my eyes and took in a great big deep GodBreath. "Please, just let me explain," I said, opening my OjoEyes. "You see, within our Multi-Sensory World of Thirteen Senses our natural aging process also happens in stages of thirteen years. And our first thirteen is, of course, puberty, give or take a couple of years. Our second is twenty-six which is our full male and/or female powers. Our next is at thirty-nine, and this is when women stop caring what men think or do and they start coming into their own male powers, and in our society at thirty-nine men start looking at young girls, because they start feeling the lessening of their male powers and so they feel the need to prove themselves.

"And then fifty-two is the big one for both sexes, because women stop their moonflow, give or take two years, and they go through men-o-pause, meaning that they pause before they come into their full male powers.

"Women actually get a little hair on their upper lip and a few around their nipples, and they become Women of Substance. And at this age you met my two grandmothers and you witnessed them being cunning and tough and strong. And men at this point, go through women-o-pause and get unsure and kinder and/or mean.

"Then at sixty-five, both women and men start to Balance Out their male and female powers, and then at seventy-eight BINGO! People start living with one foot in This World and the other foot in the Other World, and like I earlier said, to the degree that they accept their Spirituality, to that degree there is no aging between 78 to 104."

"How do you know all this?" asked a priest.

I looked at him and I could see his question was sincere. "Because," I said to him, "I was educated in our Original Instructions by my Yaqui Indian *mamagrande* before I started school and my parents followed up that education, because they, too, had been home schooled by their mothers and grandmothers. Then, also on the night my dad Passed, he told me that he'd be coming back to educate from the University of the Divine once he checked in with his mother, the rest of our *Familia*, and the Grand Masters."

"And we, too, can receive this Divine Education?" asked the same priest.

"Absolutely," I said. "Look, about three years back, I was the keynote speaker in Seattle, and after I'd spoken I went to one of the workshops and this big burly guy with a huge grey beard sprinkled with a lot of red was leading a workshop. His audience was mostly teachers and administrators, and he asked them if they'd ever had the experience of driving in a mall parking lot and had a group of young teenage boys about fourteen and fifteen walking real slow in front of them. Most of the people raised their hands.

"He laughed and gave a slow strutting gait to demonstrate his point, then said, 'And if you're dumb enough to honk at them, what do they do? They don't get out of your way. Oh, no, they turn and look at you as if you're the one with a problem, and now they walk even slower. So who's had this experience?'

"With laughter, almost everyone raised their hands. 'And now I want you to know that those boys were doing exactly what they are supposed to be doing,' he said, 'because Socialization is 100s of 1,000s of years old, if not millions of years, and Civilization is only 20 to 40,000 years old at best, and we're trying to get boys to conform to Civilization instead of Socialization.'

"Then he explained to us that when young male bear cubs reach this age of about 200 pounds and they start behaving this way, their mothers take them to a spot where they know the bear cub can make it on his own and they leave them and never return. 'At first the male cub gets angry,' he said to us, 'but then as night falls he gets scared because he's never been alone, but by daybreak he's so hungry that he just starts fending for himself.

"And it used to be that when boys got to be fourteen and fifteen years old, we'd push them out of the nest like the Falcons do, but now in modern times we don't just throw them out of our homes.

Instead we program our kids for school and college, and not for life, and so they're tough where they should be kind, and wild when they should be cautious. And we parents do this, because we've lost our Original Instructions, and don't have a clue how to live a sustainable life or how to pass on information to our children.'

"This was the first time I'd ever heard the term Original Instructions and that there used to be a way to live in Harmony with Nature instead of conquering the wild and raping our planet. And then this big guy told us that little female bear were kept for about a year longer, so the mother could give her the advanced knowledge of how to be a mother bear, then he explained to us that he'd learned all this from the Native Americans of the Northwestern United States.

"Oh, I tell you I could've listened to that big burly guy all day long. He was WONDERFUL! And he was validating how I'd been raised, telling us things just like my *mamagrande* used to tell me, and he said to us that the ducks and geese Knew when to migrate, and salmon Knew when to go down river and out to sea, and then with their last dying breath they Knew how to fight back upstream and spawn."

"And so now after sharing all this background, I can answer your question of how come I Know all this. Simply, I came to Know all of this because I was raised with the understanding that every day is *otro milagro de Dios,* and so, of course, if Peter had Known his Original Instructions, he could have walked on water, because when people reached this most perfect age of 78, with one foot on This Side of Living and another on the Other Side of Living, it was then Our Normal to walk on water and to perform Daily Miracles.

"And all of you here in this room are at this age and/or approaching this perfect age of 78, and so it's now time for all of you to go for it! As I said earlier, not into retirement, but to go into INSPIREMENT! Because Miracles are Our Norm!

"Look, my whole family and I have done more than just walk on water! We've walked on fire that was measured at 1,200 Fahrenheit, and we've had L.A. rush hour traffic part for us like the Red Sea so we could travel at 60, 70, 90 miles an hour while all the rest of the traffic crept along at five and ten miles an hour, and personally, I've walked off a thirty foot rock cliff into thin air, and . . . and God assisted my every step by providing a rock staircase that allowed me to get down from the cliff."

I stopped.

I Breathed. I held, then blew out fast. "And I'm not special," I added with a calm easy tone of voice. "Remember in *Rain* when my mother Lupe turned into a fern so those renegade soldiers wouldn't rape her and kill her? And do you remember when my dad turned into stone along with the two Yaqui Indians so the prison guards and their pack of dogs didn't tear them to pieces? Both of these Miracles are forms of ShapeShifting, SongShifting, and/or Ghosting, and my parents were able to do them, because my parents had been educated in Our Sacred Ancient Indigenous Way how to GodBreathe with their every Breath, and then with the Sacred Holy Breath of God you are now Goding," I added with a smile.

"JUST WAIT!" shouted a priest. "Are you then saying that you didn't write all of these things as metaphors? And your mother Lupe actually turned into a fern?"

"Yes," I said, taking in a deep breath. "This is exactly what I'm saying, and why I got 265 rejections before I got published and . . . and why my New York publisher wanted to bring out *Rain* as fiction, and why my mother—God Bless Her Soul—was willing to mortgage her home, her last possession in the world, so we could buy the rights back from Putnam." Tears came to my eyes. "My mom was in her 80s!" I yelled.

"My dad had passed! And still she had the guts to mortgage her home and . . . and . . . oh, my God!" I said, "Can you see it? Can you see it? All of Life, *la Vida,* is an ONGOING MIRACLE ONCE WE OPEN UP OUR HEART AND SOUL EYES, and begin to see that we live within Seven Dimensions here on OUR SACRED HOLY MOTHER EARTH!"

I stopped, wiping the tears out of my eyes. "And you guys just glimpsed that," I added, "when you saw how different our world would be if Peter had walked on water. So let's not lose that Vision that we all just had together, because what I'm saying is that we all need to get beyond Peter and take Jesus off all the crosses in the world and stop worshipping Him and start Being like Him. This was His message. Not that negative story of Him needing to save us from our sins, but instead a positive story of Him coming to Mother Earth to INSPIRE US TO GREATNESS!

"Just imagine what a world we would have if all Christians were into Forgiving, as Our Lord Jesus did on the cross, instead of being so judgmental and into finger pointing, and thinking their way was the only way.

"And I'd like you to Know that this is exactly why He came to me when I was eight, so I could learn that when one of Our Loved Ones Passes Over, we don't lose them," I said with more tears coming to my eyes, "but instead we gain an even closer relationship with Jesus. And this is also why He came to me in Spain and why He even came to me last night, here in your place, because JESUS HAS ALWAYS BEEN ALL ABOUT LOVE*AMOR* AND INCLUSIVE ENERGY!

"You see, it's simply out of date for us to be living in fear of God, and it's out of date to—here, let me tell you a story that will show you that people have really, really, really been walking on water all over the world for eons of timeless time. Okay, ready?" I said, walking away from the podium and getting an empty chair out of the front row and turning it around so I could face them.

"Oh, yeah, this feels so much closer and so much more better," I said, laughing, then I closed my eyes. "In the hallway to my writing room, I have an old black and white picture of Einstein riding a bicycle. He's my hero, because he's happy. Big Big Happy! And this is where we are all now going! Ready? Good. Good. And now just close your eyes, so you don't get distracted and you can slipslide into our Collective Happy Consciousness of the Kingdom of God."

People closed their eyes and a hush came over the room. And I could also feel that all of the nuns were with me, but the priests, for the most part, were still either ready to bolt and/or were shitting square bricks. And sure, I understood that I'd taken them out of their comfort zone, but I wasn't going to slow down. No, I had to keep going if we were ever going to get anywhere.

"All right," I now said, opening my eyes and looking at the tall, old priest, "to now address your question about walking on water, or parting the Red Sea, or any of those other old Miracles of the Bible, let me share with you this story about my Great Great Great Great Great Aunt, Mother Of No Specific Child, who, like so many of our Sacred Elders, became a Miracle Maker and a Water Walker at Our Blessed Age of 78.

"And so *mi Papa* told me that one afternoon our aunt was walking on water from peninsula to peninsula doing her Sacred Holy Healing Work down in the lower part of *México* when some young Spanish soldiers saw her walking across the water. Instantly, they dropped to their knees and started praying, thinking she was of Jesus Christ. But when the old priest found out about this, he screamed blasphemy, and he had her arrested and raped and burned at the stake, so he could prove to these young soldiers that she was a woman of the devil and not of Jesus Christ.

"But it backfired on the old priest." I said, getting out of my chair, "for a young priest named Jose-Maria saw her dignity and purity of Love*Amor* even as she burned, and so he Knew Soul to Soul that she was, indeed, of Our Lord Jesus Christ. Jose-Maria ripped off his collar and a bunch of the young soldiers joined him and together they united with the local Indians and they revolted against the Church and Spain with SUCH CONVICTION that they almost turned the tide of the European invasion!

"And this, all this, you will, of course, never find in any history book, but this is what my dad told me that his mother *Doña Margarita* told him, and her father Don Pio told her, and Don Pio's mother told him. And now the big one, that I'd like all of you to know, is that from the Other Side, my dad also told me that our Great Great Great Great Great Aunt, Mother Of No Specific Child, was 165 years old when she was arrested, tortured, and then burned at the stake, and so she was Totally of Jesus!" I added, with tears streaming down my face. "And she could have lived 200, 300 years, or 900 years just like Moses."

"And you say your dad told you all of this from the Other Side?" asked a nun.

I nodded. "Yes, I don't think he ever even mentioned her when he was on This Side of Living," I said.

"Why do you think he never did?" asked the same nun.

I laughed. "Look, I had enough trouble believing in the big snake my dad told me about and the dancing clouds of butterflies that my mother spoke to me about, so I'm sure my dad Knew that only after he Passed Over and came to me in my sleep, educating me from the University of the Divine, would I be able to hear him and accept what he told me.

"And this is what we'll do today after dinner. I'll give you the Tools of Genius that my dad gave me on the night he Passed in order for you to receive in your sleep as I've been receiving ever since *mi Papa* Passed. And much of this is being written about in a book called *Beyond Rain of Gold*, but this book will not come out until after I finished the *Rain Trilogy*," I added.

"Then you truly believe that your father comes to you in your sleep and it's not just wishful thinking?" asked a priest, with that well-practiced little smile of superiority.

Seeing this smile, all the abuses of my childhood came EXPLODING up inside of me and I almost rushed across the room to grab this arrogant old priest by the throat and yank him out of his chair, but I didn't. No, instead I Breathed deeply, closed my eyes, and asked for help, and I was immediately told to address his question with a specific question. I opened my eyes.

"Tell me," I said, "do you believe in the Bible?"

"Well, yes, of course, but the Bible is the word of God," he added.

"Okay, I understand that that's what you've been taught, and . . . and particularly because of the word 'the' which is only European based, but we'll get into that later. And right now," I said, "what I'd like to Know is did you read *Rain of Gold*?"

His face caved in. Oh, yes, I'd been given the right question. "Well, not all of it," he said.

"How much is not all of it?" I asked.

"I read the first part of it, and glanced through the rest," he said.

I closed my eyes. "Look," I said, "I didn't become a writer because I wanted to get rich or famous. Hell, I didn't even like books. I became a writer because I made a deal with God." I opened my eyes. "I was nineteen years old and I'd just gotten back from *México* a few days before, and I'd been happy in *México*. My stomach didn't hurt. But my dad had explained to me that the United States was now our home, that my older uncles and cousins had paid in blood for this country in World War II and Korea and that my two grandmothers were buried here.

"So I returned to the U.S. with my dad and I'd only been here a few days and my stomach was hurting once again with all the racism I saw against Mexicans and Blacks. A HATE AND RAGE CAME EXPLODING up inside of me, especially now that I was no longer ashamed of being Mexican, but actually proud of my Indigenous Ancestry!"

I took in a great big deep GodBreath and blew out fast. "Oh, I was so full of rage that I wanted to kill all of the abusive teachers I've had in public school and also in Catholic school, but then it came to me to pack my rifle and handguns and a few thousand rounds of ammo and get out of town.

"Loading this arsenal in our old ranch truck, I took off. I drove east to the rising Father Sun through the back country of Southern California, then through Las Vegas, Nevada and St. George, Utah, then I drove north through Salt Lake and to the southern tip of Idaho, and here I turned east and was going across Wyoming when a herd of antelope ran across the road in front of me. I slammed on my brake, got my Winchester .06 model 70, my .357 Smith and Wesson revolver, and my always-with-me backpack, and took off after the antelope to kill them.

"But then I saw that they had yearlings and these little ones looked so innocent. They weren't even afraid of me. In fact, two of them came towards me to see what I was. I guess they'd never seen a human before. And this was when I saw the beautiful snowcapped Teton Mountains, and I remembered that my *Mamagrande* had always told me that it was Our Job, Our Mission to help *Papito Dios* plant His/Her ongoing Garden of Heaven on Mother Earth.

I began to cry, then I screamed, demanding God to tell me how I could plant any Stardust Seeds with all this rage and hate I had inside of me!

"All this I'm writing in a book called *CrazyLoco Love* which is the second book of my *Burro Genius Trilogy* and this is when God spoke to me, not in words, but in Flashes of Understanding and I learned that God never chose the Jews. No, it was the Jews who chose God when they took their oral story and put it into written form.

"And in that moment of utter clarity, I understood that there were 1,000s and 1,000s of Bibles that needed to be written from all over Africa, Asia, and the Americas before we could have Peace on Earth, and that I, myself, had to write my own people's Holy Book, so we, too, could then become the Chosen People of God like the Jews.

"So, please," I now said to this priest, "no more questions, and especially not from you guys who haven't read *Rain of Gold* in its entirety, because . . . BECAUSE I DIDN'T WRITE IT!" I screamed. "It came through me just as Einstein's theory came through him and Edison's stuff all came through him and . . . understand that I'm not accusing you of being a bad person or anything like that. Hell, I mean, Heaven, I, too, was totally a Doubting Thomas until my dad Passed Over in March of 1988, and then he came to me a few months later in New York City in my hotel room, and ever since, he's the one who's been giving me an education straight from Heaven."

I stopped.

I had to sit down. I was shaking, I was so upset. That old priest had no idea how close I'd came to rushing across the room and slapping that little grin off his face.

"And he's right," said Sister Mary. "You wouldn't even be asking these questions if you'd read the book as we asked you to!"

Oh, she was pissed!

"I suggest that we listen to Victor. May I call you Victor?" asked Margret.

"Of course," I said.

"And I suggest we listen to him as if he's teaching us how to fly an airplane," she said, "or as if he's guiding us through this new world of computers."

"Thank you," I said, calming down and wiping the tears out of my eyes. "Thank you very much, and to learn how to fly and/or use a computer there is an entire new language of concepts that we need to learn. Thank you, Sister. Your suggestion will be a big help."

"Call me *Margarita*, if you don't mind. *Margarita* like your grandmother."

I smiled. "Of course, *Margarita*," I said to her.

Six hands shot up.

"No, please, no more questions," I said, laughing. "In fact, no more words, no more talking. Let's all just take a little break, so we can digest all this within our own Kingdom of God, then BOOM! We'll come back and go for it ALL THE WAY BACK TO THE FUTURE!"

"It's almost lunch time," announced Father James, standing up, "so why don't we just call it quits for this morning's session."

And as I went out of the room, out of the corner of my eye, I saw that Father James was aglow with a bright and yet soft golden light. Oh, my God, this priest was an ARCHANGEL!

Chapter Five

THIS TIME I DID NOT GO TO MY ROOM. I WENT OUT THE DOOR towards the lake, and the geese immediately greeted me with their honking. I laughed and said, "hello" to them and continued down the grassy knoll to the lake. Oh, the air smelled so crisp and fresh, and I needed to get away from everyone. I'd never expected this whole thing to go as it had gone.

WOW! Never in a million years had I ever thought I'd get into all this heavy stuff, especially not right away. I thought that I'd first start out by telling these old nuns and priests why it was that I'd first fallen in Love*Amor* with the Holy Roman Catholic Church at St. Patrick's in Carlsbad, with the smells and happy sounds of the altar boys pretending to sing back to the old half-deaf priest in Latin, but they were actually singing back in Spanish about the best way to cook wild turkey in Mexican green sauce.

And then I figured that after saying this to the old nuns and priests and getting them laughing, I'd tell them why I'd quit being a Catholic with a capital 'C,' simply meaning 'universal' as all Catholics are taught, and I was now a catholic with a small 'c' using the full definition of the word which according to the Webster New World Dictionary was 'universal; all-inclusive; of general interest in value; hence having broad sympathies or understanding; liberal,' and now I felt so much closer to God.

So I was walking along thinking all this and feeling happy and enjoying the sight of all the honkers and deer and the beautiful clear blue water, when that youngish priest came running up to me. He was all out of breath.

"Oh, I'm so glad to catch you alone," he said. "I'm Mark," he added.

"You're a priest, aren't you?" I said, because priests normally didn't give you their first name when they introduced themselves.

"Well, yes, but not for much longer," he said. "You see, I'm leaving the priesthood and getting married."

"Married?" I said.

"Yes, I, too, proposed to a nun," he said.

"Oh," I said, laughing, "then this explains why I've seen you smiling all the time. You're in love."

"Yes, I'm definitely in love," he said. "And I've never been in love like this before."

"And it feels wonderful, eh?"

"Oh, yes, of course, and best of all, I don't feel guilty about being in love and she doesn't either. But, well, it was really very difficult for both of us at first, because of all the pressure that was put on us."

"I can only imagine," I said, putting my hand on his shoulder, "that took a lot of guts. Why do you think they call it 'falling in love,' eh? It's scary."

He laughed. "You're right. It has been the scariest thing I've ever done in all my life," he said. "The feelings I've been feeling are so powerful and confusing and real!"

"Exactly, because for a person to truly allow himself to fall in love, not only takes a leap of faith as much as walking on water, but then to walk down the aisle to join hands in marriage is a commitment that takes guts way beyond all reasonable comprehension."

"Well, talking about guts," he said, "we read in *People Magazine* about you buying the rights back to *Rain of Gold* from your publisher."

"Yes," I said, "and it all got started with an article in *Publisher's Weekly* where Joe Baro – something wrote about my old mother mortgaging her home so we could buy the rights of *Rain of Gold* back from Putnam, my New York publisher, for $75,000, and how I then got blackballed all over New York."

"And you ended up going with a small press at the University of Houston," he said.

"Exactly," I said, "for $1,500, and this is when I became a Born Again Texan and reporters came at me from all across the country. Everyone was astonished.

"But my *familia* and I weren't. My parents' story wasn't fiction," I added. "But now, please, no more about that. Tell me about you and this nun. What's her name?"

"Josefina," he said, pronouncing her name with a beautiful *Latino* song-like softness.

"Josefina," I repeated, but I couldn't quite say it as romantically.

We continued walking on the grass along the edge of the lake and he told me how Sister Josefina and he had met while working together in Ecuador, and they'd been very good friends for nearly a year, but then at an All Saints Day celebration, which were always such large events throughout Latin America, they'd been so happy and excited together that it had frightened them.

"I'll never forget," he said, "it was a full moon and there were fireworks and kids running all around us and something happened to us, and we just looked at each other in a way that we'd never looked at each other before. So for the next few days we both avoided each other, but then I began to dream of Josefina in a way that I'd never dreamed of her previously. And a few years before,

I would have gone to confession and asked for forgiveness for the kind of dreams I was having, but not now. Now I knew deep in my heart and soul that these dreams weren't a sin, but instead wonderful and a whole new way of viewing love and life itself, and . . . and I then realized I could no longer be a priest. And strangely enough, this was also when I began to understand that Jesus, as a man, must've loved Mary Magdalene. How could He have not? Because my love for Josefina felt so natural and good."

He stopped talking and I saw he had tears running down his face, so I took him by his shoulders and turned him around and hugged him. He was trembling and having trouble breathing. My God, these dreams that he'd had for Josefina must've frightened him to no end. He hugged me back, squeezing me with all his might.

"Good," I said, "good. We all need to hug."

"Yes, I can see that now," he said, releasing me, "but I couldn't at first. Oh, all year I'd seen Josefina be the kindest, most loving human I'd ever met, just as you spoke about your own little nun. And so finally I, too, got up the nerve to go to her and tell her of my love for her and that I was leaving the priesthood, because I would never again feel ashamed of the feelings that I had for her. She began to cry, saying that she felt the same way about me, and that she, too, would not allow anyone to make her feel ashamed of her feelings, and this was when we took each other in our arms in a whole new way and . . . and then we announced our intent of leaving and getting married and we were, well, immediately separated and I was sent here and . . . and she was sent to a convent."

"What? You mean you've lost her?" I asked.

"Oh, no," he said. "We were told that we'd have to be six months apart, so we could pray and ask for guidance before we can legally leave the Church and marry. And it's now been five months, sixteen days, and twelve hours, and thirty-six minutes," he said, glancing at his wristwatch with the biggest smile I'd ever seen on a Human Being.

"Congratulations!" I said. "Good for you!"

"By the way," he said, "it's important that you know that Father James is the only one who knows why I'm here. All the rest think I had a nervous breakdown, instead of a LOVE BURST!" he shouted with joy.

We hugged again, holding each other a long time, then we continued walking along the lake together.

"Do you know where Josefina is?" I asked.

"I think so."

"Then you haven't been in contact with her?"

"Oh, no, like I said that's part of our deal, that we won't make contact with each other for six months."

I stopped walking and turned to face him. "Okay, all that sounds good and, well, reasonable," I said. "And yet, I hate to say this, but you can't trust these decision-makers of the Church, especially the higher and higher they get up in the politics of the Church." I took in a great big deep GodBreath. "Has Josefina read *Rain of Gold*?" I asked.

He shook his head. "No, we'd never heard of you or any of your books. I only found out about you when I arrived here and I heard all these nuns talking so excitedly about *Rain of Gold*."

"Well, I really do suggest that you get a copy of *Rain* sent to her immediately. You see, I always tell young women that when they finally find a guy that they're really interested in to have him read *Rain of Gold*, and if he doesn't love the book to dump his ass immediately, because *Rain* is all about strong women, and showing the whole world what it means to be a strong woman of substance through war, through peace, through all the twists and turns of life."

"And you think it will help Josefina not to lose faith?"

"Exactly," I said, "because they did everything they could to break the little nun that I'd proposed to, and I'm sure that they are now trying to do that to Josefina. My God, in just a few weeks Sister Theresa had aged years and lost so much weight it was frightening. I strongly recommend that you find out where Josefina is and send her a copy of *Rain of Gold*. But," I added, "do not go through normal channels. Did she have any close nun friends?"

"Oh, yes, she was extremely loved."

"Well, then contact them. No, wait. Don't contact her best friend Sophia, I do believe. Contact her other best friend Maria."

"How do you know their names?" he asked.

"Look," I said, laughing, "once we get out of the prison of our limiting five sensory perception and we access our Kingdom of God with our Multi-Sensory Perception of Our Full Natural Thirteen Senses, all of us then Know Everything! Truly, Jesus Knew what He was talking about when He said that we each have the Kingdom of God within us. Just think about it. Within the Kingdom of God is Everything, Past, Present, Future, and so then—"

"We Know Everything," he said, grinning.

"Exactly, but with five senses we don't have the tools with which to access all we Know deep inside of ourselves, and with our Full Natural Thirteen Senses, we do."

"Then this is how you Know what Einstein said about not riding on a beam of light, but that he became a Beam of Light?"

"Exactly," I said. "Albert is one of the Grand Masters that I'm now in contact with ever since my dad passed over. You see, when one of our loved ones passes over, we don't lose them. What actually happens is that we gain a stronger access to the Other Side of Living, and the Church used to acknowledge this until the 4th

Century when they then decided to do away with reincarnation and all of our other Natural Knowledge that comes to us with our Multi-Sensory Perception."

"Then are you saying that you believe in reincarnation?"

"No, belief is a weak word, so I don't believe in anything anymore."

"I don't understand."

"Look, you don't believe that tomatoes taste good. You Know that tomatoes taste good. You don't believe in taking a crap. You Know you need to crap."

"Well, yes, but a tomato is something we can see and feel, and needing to crap is a function that our body tells us."

"Exactly," I said, "and once we move out of our prison of our limiting five senses, and into our Natural Multi-Sensory Perception of Thirteen Senses, then we stop believing and start Knowing with a capital K."

"Even God?"

"Most especially God," I said. "My two Grandmothers didn't believe in God. They Knew God and they lived with the Almighty with their every Breath. But I also didn't fully understand this until I met two Native American educators in Nashville, Tennessee back in 1992 at the National Library Convention. And this is when I stopped believing and began to either Know something or not Know. Like I don't believe in God anymore, I Know God, and so just like my *Mamagrandes* I, too, now live with the Almighty with my every Breathing Breath. And about reincarnation; no, I no longer believe in reincarnation. I Know reincarnation, here, deep inside of me."

"You know reincarnation?"

"Yes, I Know that I've had fifteen lifetimes on this planet and that this is only my second time as a male, and I also Know that

I've had 1,000s and 1,000s of past lives on our other Six Sister Planets."

"Really? You Know this?"

"Yes, I absolutely Know this!"

"And you think, I mean, you Know that all of us can reach this Level of Knowingness?"

"Of course, we all have the Kingdom of God within us," I said.

He nodded and nodded again and said nothing more as we continued walking alongside the lake, listening to the little waves slapping up against the shoreline.

"You know," he said after a while, "these things you've been telling us are beginning to make sense, and I can now see they were in *Rain of Gold* between the lines, but I, well, hadn't been able to see them." He stopped, turned to me, and asked, "Did you do this deliberately?"

"Oh, yes," I said, laughing. "After 265 rejections I Knew that I had to do what old Hemingway suggested and keep 7/8 of what I was saying under water or I'd never get published."

"I see, I see," he said. "You know what really resonated within me was when you said that our planet is a very emotional and sexually driven planet. I mean, ever since I admitted to myself that . . . that I was also physically in love with Josefina and not just spiritually, it's been such a complete feeling within me that, well, I now see everything differently."

"Go on," I said.

"Well, it's like I now see everything alive and full of joy," he said, laughing. "I swear that when I first arrived here, the geese came rushing up to me and they congratulated me on Being in love. I Know this sounds crazy, but it's true! That's what it felt like, and then the trees and the grass were all happy to see me, too!" He spun around, shouting with joy. "IT'S LIKE THE WHOLE

WORLD KNOWS I'M IN LOVE AND IS SO BEAUTIFUL AND HAPPY FOR ME! And this is when I just KNEW that Jesus had been in love with Magdalene, and so, of course, they'd made love and had children! How could they not have, eh?"

I was laughing with *CARCAJADAS*! "You're absolutely right, and they had kids, and we'll get into all of that too, because this is, indeed, the most emotional and sensually driven planet of our Six Sister Planets, and so it is our duty to live with all our Heart and Soul and Body and Mind, and this is how we finally have no Illusions of Separation or Mortality, and start Living on the Active Side of Eternity!"

"Then you believe—I mean, Know—that believing is, well, in fact, misleading?"

"You tell me," I said. "You have your own Kingdom of God within you, and you're the one who's now in love, and with Love*Amor*, you are Totally Connected. You see, believing insinuates not Knowing, and as soon as you get people to not trust their Inner All-Knowingness, then this is when we become easy targets for manipulation by manmade institutions, because we've lost Our Natural Direct Connection to Our Almighty!"

"I see," he said, nodding, "I see."

And once again he said nothing more and we continued walking and I could see it in his eyes, he was letting all this soak in. This was a big one. To move from believing to Knowing had taken me years.

"Will you be talking to us about this?" he asked.

"About Knowing?"

He nodded.

"You tell me," I said.

He laughed. "I think you should. No, I KNOW you should! I'm sure a lot of us are tired of all the manipulation that was done to us!"

I burst out laughing with *carcajadas* once again. I liked this guy. I really did. I was so happy that he'd chased me down.

"Okay," I said. "I'll go for it!"

And it was now time for us to head back to eat lunch. "So tell me," I said, "what is your relationship with Father James?"

"What do you mean by that?"

"Well, you two seem very close, so I was wondering if—"

"If we're gay? Yes, a lot of the others think that, but we're not," he said.

"Well, that wasn't what I was referring to," I said. "I was wondering if you Know that he's an Angel, actually a—"

"Oh, yes, I Know that," he said. "Of course, James is an Angel, if it wasn't for him I might have lost faith in my love."

"Then have you seen his glow?" I asked.

"Seen him glow? You mean, glow with Light like an actual Angel?"

"An Archangel," I said.

"Really? You're saying Father James is an Archangel?"

"Yes."

"Well, it doesn't surprise me," he said. "In fact, it actually makes sense. Without his help our good nuns would have never been able to bring you here. The priests, as I assume you've guessed, were not that keen to have you come."

It was my time to nod and nod again. "Oh, I see," I said. "I get it now."

"So how do you know that James is an Archangel? Have you seen others?" he asked.

"Yes, in Chicago I met this chubby *Latino* teacher, who looked a lot like the comic Paul Rodriguez, who was an Archangel."

"Really?"

"Yes."

"And what is the difference between an Angel and an Archangel? They're both God's Messengers of Light, correct?"

"Yes, you are right, and what I've seen," I said, "is that an Archangel's Light is almost as bright as the Golden Light I saw surrounding Jesus when He came to me in Spain."

"Really?"

"Well, maybe not that bright, but still highly illuminating."

"So, then, was your grandmother *Doña Margarita* an Archangel?"

I laughed. "Why do you ask that?"

"Well, the relationship that she had with the Virgin Mary, and the way Jesus would come to them in Church, but then she'd tell Jesus to keep still and not interrupt the conversation that she was having with His mother, made me think this."

I laughed again. "No, she wasn't an Archangel. She was an Angel like all of us, and then she, like Walt Disney, Emerson, Einstein, Cervantes, Confucius, and Moses, was a Grand Master, and so this allowed her take on leadership, which Archangels are not allowed to do."

"Really?"

"Yes, that Archangel in Chicago explained all this to me. He was a high school teacher and I asked him if he was going to become a principal or a school district superintendent and really make a big difference in the Chicago school system, and he said no. That as an Archangel he could only illuminate but not lead and/or interfere, that we, humans, had to come into our own Enlightenment, and this was why Jesus hadn't brought down 10,000 Angels and destroyed the whole Roman Empire, but instead He'd given Illumination."

"I see, I see," said Mark. "And is this what your Great Great Great Great Great Aunt, Mother Of No Specific Child, was doing when she allowed them to rape her and burn her at the stake?"

"Exactly," I said with tears coming to my eyes, "because she was Totally of Jesus, so she, too, could've brought forth all her Miraculous Healing Powers and the Heavens would've opened up with Legions of Angels but she chose not to do this just as Our Lord Jesus chose not to. And what They both did was Inspire us to Greatness! And Jose-Maria saw this, and so did many of the young soldiers."

"But the old priest couldn't see it," said Mark, "because he saw all the Native Americans as ignorant savages, and, well, I need to admit that I, too, can relate to that. When I first arrived in Ecuador I, too, couldn't see the purity of love for God that the local native people demonstrated so naturally. Then when I did, I began falling in love with Josefina. She and her fellow native nuns were just so pure in their love for God. Will you talk to us about this?" he asked.

"You tell me?" I said.

He laughed. "Well, I guess it will depend on our availability."

I laughed. "Exactly," I said. "I never Know what I'm going to do and/or say. My Spiritual Guides guide me moment by moment. And also I don't want those guys in the back to decide to burn me at that stake."

He laughed. "Well, anyway, when you said that this is a very emotional and sexually driven planet, then a lot of the feelings I've been having started falling in place and—oh, I'm just looking forward to being married so much! I'm forty years old and I'm a virgin! And I no longer want to be a virgin!"

"How old is Josefina?"

"She'll be thirty-three next week, and oh, boy, are we going to make babies!"

I put my arm around his shoulder. "Good for you! And I'd like you to Know that not just the geese and the trees and all of

Creation here on our planet are rooting for you, but also Our Star Cousins from Our Six Sister Planets are rooting for you, too. You see, Our Beloved Mother Earth is the Hawaii of our planets, and all Six Sisters are waiting for us to open up Our HeartEyes and SoulEyes with Love*Amor*, so that they can then flood us with MIRACULOUS HEALING POWERS!"

"OH, WOW! You're right! I can feel it! Because once I let myself fall totally wildly in love *con mi amor,* Josefina, then it was like the Heavens parted for me and I was so happy! And my Dreams became Adventures of Spirit like I'd been Reconnected Directly to Creation itself!"

"Yes! Yes! Yes!" I said. "And it all begins with us allowing ourselves to fall madly unconditionally in Love*Amor*!"

"Yes, I can feel it! And this is exactly why Josefina and I will not allow anyone to make us feel ashamed of these wild feelings that we're feeling for each other!"

"Absolutely! Anytime, anywhere, any way two people fall in Love*Amor,* they are doing God's Holy Work on Mother Earth! Because only through Joy and Being Happy—BIG BIG HAPPY—do we help the Almighty spread His/Her Love*Amor* throughout the WHOLE ENTIRE UNIVERSE!"

And saying this, I took Father Mark in my arms and jerked him close, kissing him on one cheek and then on the other, and he didn't resist. In fact, he kissed me back on both cheeks, too. Then arm in arm the two of us continued up the grassy knoll through the honkers and deer and we could see there was a group of nuns and two priests waiting for us at the outside patio of the huge mansion. And they looked very excited to see us coming up the knoll. I guess that they'd been watching Mark and me. When we reached the patio, Sister Mary came rushing at me.

"I want one of those hugs, too!" she yelled, grabbing me in her arms.

And she hugged me with her whole body and then gave me a big long juicy kiss on each cheek.

"Oh, that was fun!" she said. "I haven't kissed like that since I was a teenager! And it felt wonderful back then, too!"

Margarita and two other nuns were in line and they, too, hugged me and kissed me, but not quite with the fire that Sister Mary had kissed me.

"How about you guys," I said to the two priests. "Come on, just a hug. We don't need to kiss."

One of the priests stepped forward. "I guess I'll take a hug," he said.

And so we hugged, but he made sure to keep his lower body completely away from me, and then we all went inside to have lunch. And the honkers, they could feel our Love*Amor* and they came honking up to the patio with great sound and excitement. Mark had been right. The Birds, the Trees, the Grass, the Lake, All of Creation could feel the Vibrational Frequency of Our Love*Amor*!

Book Two

Chapter Six

After lunch I went to my room and took a little nap, and then when I awoke I was so happy! BIG BIG HAPPY that I'd listened to my mother and I'd come to see these old nuns and priests. I got up, washed my face, and went dancing down the hallway to the stairs.

"Thank You, God!" I sang. "Thank You! Thank You! THANK YOU, LORD GOD! And thank you, *Mama*, and thank you, *Papa*! I'm ready now! I'm all ready, so let's just go for it! FOR WE HAVE THE WHOLE WORLD IN OUR HANDS! *EN NUESTRAS MANOS*!"

And when I walked into the room where we were having our event, I saw that my dad and my brother Joseph and a whole bunch of other relatives and Grand Masters from the Spirit World were over by the windows facing the lake. I nodded to them and they all nodded back to me, and then Bossy Bill Shakespeare stepped forward.

"Oh, no, Bill," I said to him. "This isn't your show." Then I turned to Cervantes and said, "Please handle Bill for me. I don't want him trying to take over like he does."

"I could save you years of writing, if you'd just trust me," said Bossy Bill.

"BILL!" I said with authority. "WE'VE BEEN THROUGH

THIS A DOZEN TIMES! And I'm saying no to you now just like I said no to you thirty some years ago in Ocean Beach!"

"Excuse me," I heard someone say behind me, "but to whom are you speaking?"

I turned and saw that all the nuns and priests were staring at me, except Father James, who was smiling a smile full of mischief like saying, "Okay, *amigo*, now how are you going to get out of this one?"

And I Knew what he was talking about, because I was fairly sure that only he and I could see these Individuals from the Other Side of Living.

I took in a great big deep GodBreath, and decided just to go for it all the way. "I'm talking to Bossy Bill Shakespeare," I said to the nuns and priests. "You see, ever since I took my oath to become a writer as great as Homer or greater, Bossy Bill has been a pain in the ass, coming to me and insisting that he can help me to become a great writer. But I've always brushed him off, explaining to him that I prefer to get help from Cervantes, Azuela, Dostoyevsky, Faulkner, and Anne Frank."

"But why would you refuse William Shakespeare's help if he is, in fact, coming to you and making himself available to you?" asked a priest.

I took in another great big deep GodBreath and closed my eyes. "Because," I said, "when Bossy Bill Shakespeare wrote 'To be or not to be' and he said that this was the question, he was barking up the right tree, but he'd missed the whole point, because to be or not to be is the answer. Not the question. And besides I find him to be arrogant and too much in his intellectual head and so I prefer Anne Frank who's Centered in her Heart*Corazon*."

I stopped. I could see that half of the nuns and priests were staring at me as if I'd just gone off the deep end. But then Father James saved the day. He started clapping vigorously!

"WONDERFUL!" he said. "WONDERFUL! And so should we put out more chairs? How many of these guests from Heaven are here with us?" he asked.

I had to smile. He really Knew his stuff. "Right now we have about a dozen," I said, "but I can see that others are coming." And they were. "I guess Our Ancestry in the Spirit World really wants to be included."

"Well, we'll just put out a few dozen more chairs," said Father James. "Tell me, are we going to be able to see them, too, I hope."

"Yes, I'm sure you will," I said, smiling, "especially after you sleep tonight, and tomorrow awake with the understanding that *mañana es,* indeed, *otro Milagro de Dios*, that tomorrow is, indeed, another Miracle from God."

Quickly, the priests and nuns brought out the other chairs and set them up, and this was when Father James came up to me and he was GLOWING.

"You're doing fine," he said to me quietly. "You're doing fine."

"Thanks for the help," I said to him.

"That's what I'm here for," he said.

"Yes, I learned that in Chicago," I said.

"I Know, but now just continue," he said.

And he was in Full Illumination as he turned and went to sit down with the others. And this was when I Knew for sure that Mark and the other priests and nuns couldn't see Father James Glowing any more than they could see Our Guests from Our Spirit World. And yet all the nuns and priests were smiling and looking very happy. Yes, they could "feel" the Other Side of Living, but they couldn't "see" it until they'd Activated their Kingdom of God, then to the degree that they allowed themselves to open up their HeartEyes and SoulEyes to this degree they'd Awaken.

"Okay," I said, "any questions?"

Our Spiritual Guests had taken their chairs along with the nuns and priests. Eight hands shot up.

"Okay, you in the back," I said.

"I thought we had free will," said this priest, "so then how can William Shakespeare who's in the Spirit World dictate to you?"

"You're right, we do have free will," I said, "that's why I was able to say no to Bossy Bill."

"And yet he keeps insisting?"

"Absolutely, look at all these Spirit People that just came in. I don't Know them, so I'm sure they're your Ancestry."

"Mine?" he asked.

"Some, of course, you see, it's all in us like choosing up teams to play baseball, meaning like once I made my deal with God up on that tall *mesa* out in the middle of nowhere in Wyoming, that was it. There is no turning back once you chose your team, because in choosing, I put my whole Heart and Soul into Our Deal, telling God if He didn't chicken-out on me, then I'd never chicken-out on Him."

"What does that have to do with you saying that these Spirits might be my Ancestors?"

"Choose up your team, and you'll see," I said. "Look, once you stand up to the plate and choose all your past and future are with you right here, right now, forever. That's why my 265 rejections were no big deal to me. Hell, I would've gone 300, 400 rejections. Because the Spirit World was Alive for me and I see with my HeartEyes that both of my grandmothers had suffered incredible starvation and gave witness to their children being slaughtered, so choose, renew your deal with God, my friend."

He was stunned. He was speechless. Then he said, "And you were nineteen years old when you made this kind of deal with the Almighty?"

"Yes," I said, "I was nineteen when I chose to make that deal with God. But then getting back home from Wyoming, it was like I'd lost that Inner Voice I'd had out in the wilds. And this was when it came to me that I had to get away from *mi familia* and friends, who all thought I'd gone off the deep end, because they had absolutely no comprehension of what it meant to me to become a writer in partnership with God.

"Look, I'm also sure that the same thing happened to a lot of you with your friends and family who probably thought you'd lost it when you first informed them that you were going to become nuns and priests."

Many of the nuns and priests nodded.

"So what did you do to re-establish your conversation with God?" asked another priest.

I took in a Great Huge GodBreath, held, then blew out fast. "I decided to go six months without speaking. But to accomplish this, I also realized that I had to go to a place where no one knew me, and yet I wanted to stay close to the ocean, because *Nuestra Madre Pacifica* had always felt like my connection to God. So I rented a beach shack in Ocean Beach, and I was ready to go the rest of my life without speaking if need be, but then . . . then it was, I guess, somewhere in the middle of the fourth month when I was walking along the seashore late one night and the Heavens were full of Stars, that it came to me that it was, indeed, the Darkness of Our Night that allows us to see Our Stars.

"I stopped, I'll never forget, and I looked up at all the Stars, *mi familia*, as my *mamagrande* had taught me, and now, for the first time, I saw that the Darkness was Holy and so Beautiful, because it was what gave Life to Our Stars! Tears came to my eyes, and I went back to my shack that night and I was listening to Sonny Rollins and his long pauses between the notes when it also came to me with such utter clarity that it was the Silence between the notes that gave Life to Music!

"I LEAPED UP SCREAMING! I'll never forget, I screamed and screamed and went running back to the beach, stripped off all my clothes, and went racing into the surf and the waves! For I could now clearly see that God had never stopped speaking to me! That He was, indeed, speaking to All of Us through the Darkness of Our Night which allows us to see Our Stars, *nuestra familia*, and He was also speaking to us through the Great Infinite Silence that gave LIFE TO OUR MUSIC!

"I swam out past the waves and I could now understand that God in His Infinite Wisdom had such Trust in me that He was Totally, Totally, Totally leaving it up to me to start making my own Holy Notes, my own Holy Music, for God needs us as much as we needed HimHer so we can then help plant HisHer ongoing Holy Sacred Garden Here on Mother Earth just like my *mamagrande* HAD ALWAYS TOLD ME!

"And so, of course, it was that day at daybreak on the 16th of September 1960 with Our Father Sun, Our Right Eye of God, coming up with all His Glory that I started writing, and I've been writing ever since NON-STOP to this day some sixty years later!

"And it was Sonny Rollins with his Wondrous Long Pauses of Silence between his Notes that opened up the Heavens for me, and now all of *mi familia* and the Grand Masters began coming to me each morning at about 2 a.m. when I began to write. And everything was going fine and wonderful until . . . until Bossy Bill tried to take over, promising me all these great successful riches. And I'm sure he was right, but not for me. Still Shakespeare was so insistent, that I finally quit arguing with him and just started putting up signs at the door of my writing room and in the kitchen that simply said, 'Keep Out, Bill!'"

"You really did that?" asked a nun, giggling with laughter.

"Did what?" I asked.

"Put up signs that said 'Keep Out, Bill!'"

"Oh, yes, sure, I had to. You can't fool around with the Spirit World."

By now a lot of people were laughing.

But, then, one priest became very serious looking, and said, "Are you insinuating that William Shakespeare is an evil spirit?"

"Oh, no, not at all," I said. "Bill is fine and good, but just not for me. Look, just like you guys read in *Rain of Gold* that my grandmother *Doña Margarita* finally had to tell Jesus to keep still, because she was having a woman-to-woman conversation with His Mother, I had to do the same with Bossy Bill, or he would have taken over."

"Excuse me, but I'd assumed that scene with your grandmother was symbolism," said another priest.

"Oh, no, I don't write symbolism," I said. "I write stark raw reality within the perception of Our Full Natural Thirteen Senses."

"Will you explain this?"

"Yes, of course," I said, laughing, "but first let me tell you what happened a few years back when I shared this conversation about Bossy Bill with a bunch of university professors. After my talk an older black woman ran to get in the elevator with me and she was all smiles until the doors closed. Then she started screaming and hitting me with this huge book of the collective works of Bossy Bill, calling me all kinds of names. And she was strong and that book must've weighed half a ton, and I kept pushing buttons to try to get out of the elevator before she killed me.

"You see," I said, "English, the English language, has become a religion on its own, and has all but taken over the whole world, and Shakespeare's writing encourages this to such a degree that we now brag about 'English Only' in our country, and this is not just dangerous, but self-destructive because . . . because English is the only language that I Know of that capitalizes the word 'I'. Spanish doesn't capitalize *'yo'* unless you're a California surfer and you drive a Toyota pickup and you block out the first two letters and the last two letters of the word Toyota on the back of your tailgate.

"And then add to this what I've already mentioned that only European-based languages have the word 'the' and you have a very arrogant self-serving language in English. Truly, everywhere I go I tell people that our only Hope for this nation is to start learning other languages and not just European based, because now with modern brain scans we are beginning to understand that when you learn a second language you don't just learn more words. No, you actually start accessing other parts of the brain, and a third language causes flexibility of the brain, and you then end up having a much better chance of not ending up with Alzheimer's.

"So I told this group of professors that Shakespeare was out-of-date and it was time for us to start learning African languages, and Asian and Native American languages, and so this woman who was African, I'd thought she'd gotten into the elevator to congratulate me. Not kill me," I said, laughing. "And what I guess really pissed her off was when I'd said Shakespearian plays were also totally out-of-date, and what we needed was for *Roots* by Alex Haley to be made into a musical and/or a Broadway play every ten or fifteen years like they do for all these other American classics.

"Truly, it's no accident that even that African professor became enraged. Everywhere I now give talks, I find out that high school kids have never even heard of *Roots* and of Kunta Kinte Being Raised up to the Stars in that fantastic scene that still sends chills up and down my spine, because this was what was done to me by *mi mamagrande!* Truly, we need to break loose from the prison of 'English Only'."

"That makes sense to me," said Mark, "because it wasn't until I'd been down in Ecuador for nearly six months and spoke Spanish pretty well and also a good deal of the local Native language that I could begin to open my eyes and see that there is a whole world out there beyond English."

"Exactly," I said, "and even Bossy Bill is now beginning to acknowledge this, because he has become good friends with Alex Haley. In fact, they're now *compadres*."

"Oh, godfathers," said Mark.

"Yes," I said. "Look, the most important thing for all of us to remember on This Side and/or on the Other Side of Living is to Trust with a capital 'T', because we can't access the Kingdom of God that we have within us until we have the Understanding and the Complete Trust that we live in a Wonderful Loving Universe, as Henry Miller so well said in his book *Tropic of Capricorn*, 'Once you give up the ghost everything follows with dead certainty, even in the midst of chaos,' then he took off in an Arthur Rimbaud kind of journey."

Then one of Our Spiritual Guests spoke up, but I didn't quite get what he'd said. And when he spoke again with his heavy Brooklyn accent, I laughed, because I now Knew that it was Henry Miller himself, whom I'd once met at his home out at the Pacific Palisades near Malibu in Los Angeles.

"Okay, Mr. Miller," I now said. "I'm listening. Please, go ahead. Yes, of course, I hear you, and I was going to get into all that tomorrow, but not now. All right, all right, *Papa*, I hear you, too."

"What's going on?" asked a priest.

"Well, Mr. Miller and *mi Papa* and now even Bossy Bill and *Azuela* are telling me to move you guys into Geniusing right now, then I can start sharing with you the Eight Indigenous Concepts that will free us from the past, so then automatically we'll SlipSlide into World Harmony and Peace and Abundance for All as has already been done on Our Other Six Sister Planets.

"And they're also telling me to inform all of you that back at one time Our Six Sister Planets were even more lost and violent than us, and so we can do this here on Mother Earth with ease, because, remember, we, Human People, are Hollow Bones, Buffalo Bones, Holy Instruments for helping Our Almighty plant His/Her Love*Amor* throughout the Universe!"

I took in a great big deep GodBreath. "Okay, fasten your seatbelts, because the first question we need to address before we can climb aboard Our Spaceship and BLAST OFF into Inner Outer Space is . . . is, are you a genius?

"Then after that, the next question is how many of you can imagine, just imagine, the possibility of World Harmony and Peace and Abundance for All for the next 50,000 years, even with all the problems that we have going on. And if you can see this, if you can imagine this, then please raise up your hand for each of these two questions."

"You're joking, right?" said a priest.

"Oh, no, not at all," I said. "In fact, these two are the normal questions I ask everywhere I go, and I can now see that I shouldn't have let you guys off the hook and asked you these two questions right from the start. You see, when I ask kindergarten kids these questions, they immediately all raise their hands to both of these questions, and one little *vato*-kid in Texas even flipped on the floor and raised up both feet and both hands, and I said to him, 'So you think you're a genius, eh?'

"'Yes,' he said, 'I'm really good!'

"'What makes you think you're so good?' I asked.

"'Look at my finger painting,' he said.

"I walked over and looked, then said, 'That's as good as any Picasso!'

"'Yes,' he said, 'because I'M A GENIUS!'

"'Okay,' I said, 'and since you're a genius, do you, as a genius, think we can have World Wide Harmony and Peace and Abundance for All for 50,000 years, even with all these *problemas* that we have going on?'

"'Sure,' he said quickly.

"'And why do you think this?'

"'Because it's MORE FUN!' he shouted."

And having shared this little story, I laughed and laughed, figuring that all the nuns and priests would laugh along with me, but they didn't. One priest immediately spoke up full of frustration.

"Yes, but that child had no idea what genius means or any comprehension of what it means to have world peace!" he said.

I closed my eyes. "And you do, eh?" I said. "Tell me, have you ever looked up the word 'genius' in the dictionary?"

"No, I haven't," he said.

I opened my eyes. "Well, then I'll tell you that kid in kindergarten Knew more about genius than you do! For nearly twenty years I've been asking people these two questions and adults are all so quick to say that children don't Know what genius means, and yet not once have I found any adult who has looked up the word and remembers what genius means.

"And this is no accident, because by first grade there are less geniuses, by second and third grade less and less, and by fourth grade there are no geniuses left, and then in the seventh grade the girls who get straight 'A's raise their hands and the boys who are bored stiff at school raise their hands sarcastically. You see, our educational system CRUSHES GENIUS and replaces it with kids who have learned how to cram for tests and regurgitate what they've been taught! And that's not genius!

"Okay, no more of this," I said, taking in a deep GodBreath, "now let's just go for it like kindergarten kids and have fun! BIG BIG FUN! Okay, ready? And so I now ask all of you here, who's a genius? Come on, go for it!"

Two nuns raised their hands.

"Okay, good, not bad," I said. "And I fully realize that all of you were educated to not brag, to not walk down the center of a hallway, but to walk along the edge of the hallway, so people wouldn't think that you are Being Arrogant, but . . . and this is a big 'but', Being a Genius, admitting to Geniusing, isn't about arrogance. No, it's about Activating the Kingdom of God that Jesus told us is within each of us. So now come on! Go for it! ARE YOU A GENIUS?"

Still it was only the same two nuns who raised their hands. Henry Miller had been right. This question had certainly taken these old nuns and priests even further out of their comfort zone.

"COME ON!" I said in a loud voice. "Once you give up the ghost, then all the illusions, all the fears and expectations and all the negative crap that's been fed to us since birth, dissolves, disappears, and then everything follows with wonderful dead certainty, even in the midst of chaos!"

Still no one else raised their hand.

"Excuse me," said the tall, elegant nun in the front row who'd said she'd been a mother superior, "but what is your definition of genius?"

I smiled. "Good question," I said. "Very good question. And I'd like you to Know that I'm using the definition from Webster's New World American Language Dictionary of pre-1990, which states for genius: 'guardian deity, or spirit of a person; spirit, natural ability, and according to ancient Roman belief, a guardian spirit assigned to a person at birth.' Thank you, Sister, thank you very much.

"And now can you see that originally genius had nothing to do with being smart and/or having a high I.Q., and had everything to do with Spirit?"

I stopped and Breathed and glanced around giving time for all this to sink in. "In fact," I now added, "this backs up what *mi mamagrande* always told me about coming into this world with a Guardian Angel, and this is why I was raised up with the understanding that I was a Genius, that we were all Geniuses, because *mi mamagrande* also told me that the corn had its own Guardian Angel, the string beans, too, and this was how the corn Knew how to grow and what to do and the string beans also Knew how to grow and what to do. So now that you can see that originally Being a Genius has nothing to do with arrogance, I.Q., and/or being smart, how many of you can now say 'I am a genius'?"

Three more nuns quickly raised their hands.

"GOOD! GOOD! EXCELLENT!" I said. "And now let me share a little story with you that I think will help all of us get over this hump of Being overly educated."

Saying this, I walked back over to the podium and stretched out both arms, gripping the top of the grand old wooden structure and leaned on it as I continued.

"This happened a few years back in Florida when I was giving a talk to about 1,500 teachers and librarians," I said. "And at first, I'll tell you, I was also having to pull teeth to get them to say that they were Geniuses, just as I'm having trouble now.

"But then I saw this young, very good-looking woman in her thirties in the sixth or seventh row to my right and she was crying. She just couldn't say it, and she really wanted to, and seeing this, it suddenly came to me what to do.

I asked the two women beside her to hug her, to give her Love*Amor*, and then once she'd calmed down, I asked this woman if she could please close her eyes and go back to a childhood memory before kindergarten when she'd been happy. She said she could and she closed her eyes. I then asked her to see herself in a park having fun with her friends, or playing with a puppy, or by the seashore, or wherever, then I asked her if she was there, and she nodded yes. 'Good,' I said to her, 'very good, and now can this happy child say that she's a genius?'

"Oh, you should have seen it! Her whole face lit up with joy and she nodded yes, yes, yes! And so I then said, 'WELL, THEN SAY IT! Say 'I am a Genius'. And she did, saying it with Power and Conviction and people applauded and some even had tears in their eyes, and I then had them all say it again and again! AND COLLECTIVELY WE THEN EXPLODED! WE TRANSFORMED!

"And so now I want all of you here to STAND UP AND STRETCH! Because, you see, as I said earlier, this is a very emotionally and sensually driven planet, and so you need to feel it! And/or as my dad would always say when he'd have a straight shot of Cutty Sark, 'You got to feel it!'

"And so now I need for all of you to give each other a big hug! A great big hug full of friendship and Love*Amor*! And yes, this also means you guys in the back. COME ON! IT WON'T HURT! Good! Good! Much better! And now I want all of you to close your eyes and go back to a happy day that you had before you started school. In the park. By the seashore. At a picnic. In the woods. Do you see this day? Just nod. Good! Good! Excellent! And now that you're into this happy day with feelings of joy, and BIG BIG HAPPINESS! Can that little child within you say, 'I am a Genius!'?"

The whole place now EXPLODED, too! And it was beautiful! Almost everyone was saying it, and I now Knew that Henry Miller had been an absolute Genius to give me this guidance, because you COULD FEEL IT! Really feel it! All these old retired nuns and priests had LEAPED back into the happiness they'd had as a child! And so now, Collectively, we could move mountains! Tears of joy came to my eyes. WE'D DONE IT! We really had! We'd just traveled those eighteen inches from the brain to the Heart*Corazón* and now we were really Hollow Bones, Buffalo Bones, Human Being Instruments of God ready to plant His/Her Love*Amor* throughout the UNIVERSE!

"GOOD! GREAT!" I shouted. "And now that you're all once more officially kindergarten kids, how many of you can imagine World Harmony and Peace and Abundance for All for 5,000 years? For 50,000 years? Even with all the destructive sick crap that's going on globally?"

All the nuns raised their hands and about half of the priests.

"Good! Good! Because, you see, the custom some Native American Tribes of Central America have when you meet someone, especially a stranger, is to say, "Finally we meet, for you are another me, and I am another you.' Then they put their hands behind their back and touch their foreheads together."

"Which tribes are these?" asked Mark.

"I don't exactly know," I said, "this was first gifted to me by Mariano, the insightful brother-in-law of my second successful marriage to his sister Juanita before we were divorced. But I assume that it's a greeting among many tribes. Juanita's mother is from Peru. Okay, now how are all of you feeling?"

"Wonderful!" said one nun, smiling with ecstasy.

"Happy!" said another, with tears of joy.

And so the comments went on and on and then came a statement that stopped all of us.

"I can see them!" said a nun. "I can see our Spirit Guests, and I can see my . . . my own parents!"

People were stunned. "Really?" asked several nuns.

"Oh, yes!" said this nun. "I'm back at that happy day as a child when we were all in the backyard of my grandmother's house and my parents are young and all of us kids have been given big white, furry Easter bunnies."

"Real ones?" asked another nun.

"Yes, real rabbits! And their little hearts are beating so fast as we kids hold them and love them."

"We were once given real rabbits for Easter, too," said another nun. "And it was one of the HAPPIEST DAYS of my life!"

"And you loved to hug those rabbits, didn't you?" I said.

"Oh, yes!" said the nun who was seeing the Spirit World.

"Yes," I said, "because, you see, to reach Spirit we also need to be anchored, and one of the most wonderful ways to feel anchored is to hug, especially when we sleep. Puppies all sleep rolled up together. Baby ducks and baby chicks cuddle up under their mother's wings."

"Just wait," said a priest to the nun who'd had her breakthrough, "are you telling us that you really see people in these empty chairs and that you just traveled back to your childhood and are with your young parents in your grandmother's backyard?"

"Yes, that's what I'm saying."

"But how can you be at all these places at once?"

"I don't know," said the nun, and we could see it in her face that she was losing sight of her Happy Vision.

I stepped in. "Sister," I said, "please don't try to explain anything to this Doubting Thomas. He's Our Problem! And he and his type have been *nuestro problema* for the last 13,000 years! And all of you nuns please now hug Our Visionary Sister, because, you see, it takes *mucho mucho* Love*Amor* for us to have enough Faith to open Our HeartEyes and Pass through the doors of the Garden of Eden that have just Opened up for her. Because, you see, we never, never, never lost the Holy Garden within, within our own Kingdom of God, and this is where we are all now going to go.

"NO JOKE! WE'RE ON OUR WAY! And in the future any of you Doubting Thomases talk to me! Not to the ones who've just made their first breakthrough. BUT ME, whose been going to the Garden through FIRE AND STORM FOR OVER FORTY YEARS AND 265 REJECTIONS!" Oh, I was pissed. I needed a break. "Okay. Let's take a ten-minute break, and then WE'RE GOING FOR IT ALL THE WAY! GOD BLESS US ALL!"

And saying this, I walked over and joined the nuns who were hugging Our Visionary Sister. Father James came over and so did Mark, and Our Love*Amor* Energy was so POWERFUL, that we KNEW to Our Collective Heart*Corazón,* that we had just moved A MOUNTAIN OF FAITH AROUND OUR WHOLE BELOVED MOTHER EARTH!

Chapter Seven

I WENT TO MY ROOM, WASHED MY FACE, THEN I DID SOMETHING I hadn't done in years. Instead of just standing up and talking to God, I knelt alongside my bed, made the sign of the cross over myself, closed my eyes, and thanked the Holy Creator for His/Her Trust and Patience and Guidance and Understanding. And this felt so good that I got lightheaded and had to lie down, and I was out like a light.

Then waking up, I felt so happy! BIG BIG HAPPY and ready to go, and looking at the clock on the bed stand, I could see that once more I'd only slept for eight minutes. I laughed. This was utterly amazing for once again it felt like I'd had a full night's sleep! I went dancing down the stairs, and entering the room, I saw that not all of the priests had returned.

"Okay," I said, "I can see that not all of us came back, and that's okay, because now that we're all Geniuses, we are going to start Geniusing, and so we don't want any negative energy holding us back. Because, you see, once you are Geniusing, then all of your *problemas* of the whole world disappear. No joke. They really, really do."

I glanced around, and took in a great big deep GodBreath. "All right, would anyone like to share what happened to them during our little break? Myself, I knelt down and gave thanks to the Almighty and got to feeling so good I became Lightheaded and had to lie down, then when I woke up eight minutes later, I felt WONDERFUL! And still feel ABSOLUTELY WONDERFUL!"

A nun raised her hand.

"Yes?" I said.

"Well," she said with a huge smile, "I heard a voice speaking to me in Gaelic. And I haven't heard Gaelic since my family and I visited our relatives in Ireland when I was a young girl."

I smiled. "And how did that feel?"

"Wonderful! Exciting! The Gaelic language is so beautiful!"

"Yes!" I said. "And there's a reason for that. Gaelic is an Indigenous Language, not an empire-based language, and so it comes from the Heart and Soul and not just the Head. And so a Genius with your Gaelic language, you are now Jesusing."

"Jesusing?"

"Yes, Geniusing is actually Jesusing."

"I don't understand."

"Please don't try to understand. Our thinking, analyzing brain will just keep you going around in circles. Feel it. Take in a great big deep GodBreath and Know how Geniusing and Jesusing give you the exact same Wonderful Feeling. Go on. Try it. Good. Good. And the rest of you please try it, too. Very good. I can see that most of you are participating now."

I watched, and it was Wondrous. Fabulous. Miraculous. Just as it had been Miraculous with those 1,500 teachers and librarians.

"All right, most of you are smiling now. Great Big Happy Smiles! So I'd like you to Know that what's happened to you is that you are no longer primarily connected to your given country, nations, or even your empire-based language. Now you have been reconnected to one of our own Original Native Indigenous Heart

Feeling Languages, and you are Free! FREE AT LAST and in HEAVEN on EARTH!

"Meaning that you are now once more Directly Guided by God. By our Inner Voice. By our Guardian Angel. And we are now able to See what we were never able to See before.

"And," I said taking even another great big deep GodBreath, "and realize that we have no such things as *problemas* here on Mother Earth. What we have are challenges. Situations that need to be addressed with all of OUR HEARTS AND SOULS! For the reality of WHOLE NEW UNIVERSE OF POSSIBILITIES HAS OPENED UP FOR US!"

I stopped.

I Breathed.

I held.

I glanced around, and said, "Now you Can See, Can Feel, that manmade *problemas* were deliberately created to siphon off Our Direct Spiritual Energies, so that we are, then, incapable of ever realizing who we, Human Beings, really are. You see, problems are actually an agreement of opposing opinions. One group is for abortion, and another is against abortion. One group is saying that there is global warming and another group says there isn't global warming. And each opposing group uses all the facts they can assemble to back up their side of the argument, and the key words they use in European Languages are 'the', 'or', and 'but', and these words, they don't even exist when we start Jesusing Geniusing.

"All right," I now said, opening my *Ojo*Eyes, "let's all stand up and stretch. Yeah, really stretch raising up our arms. Reaching for the sky and spreading our fingers apart. Really forcing them apart and now Breathe and Breathe as we bend our backs and move our torsos and move our legs. Delicious, eh? Oh, cats and dogs really Know how to stretch, don't they?

“Okay, ready to go on?” Most people nodded. “All right then, any questions, or comments?”

A priest raised his hand.

Yes, and please from now on give me your name.”

“It used to be Father Anthony, but now here in our retirement home, I’m called just simply Tony.”

“And may I call you Tony?”

“By all means, and what I want to say is if, well, genius is geniusing, and Jesus is Jesusing, well then what happens to God? Is God Goding?”

“OH, WOW! What a brilliant question! Please let us all give a round of applause! Because you are ABSOLUTELY correct! With Genius Geniusing and Jesus Jesusing, then of course, God is Goding.”

Hands shot up all over the place.

“No, no more right now please. Just fasten your seatbelts, BECAUSE HERE WE GO! You see, right after *Rain of Gold* came out with Arte Publico from the University of Houston, I was invited to speak at the National Librarian Conference in Nashville, Tennessee. I was pretty nervous. This was my first big talk in years and I didn’t want to blow it like I’d almost done with the English Teachers Conference back at Long Beach when my first book *Macho!* had come out. So I just gave a short little fifteen-minute talk about *Rain of Gold,* explaining that this book was so important to me that I’d asked my old mother to please mortgage her home so we could buy the rights back from Putnam in New York, because—I couldn’t believe it—they’d wanted to call it fiction!”

I stopped. I had to take in a great big, deep GodBreath before I could go on. “Then I explained to these librarians and teachers that books were Holy, that good books could take People out of their isolated existence and bring them together with Heart and Soul, and this was why Every People, Every Culture needed to have their own Holy Voice, and that *Rain of Gold* was the Holy Voice of my Human People, the Native Indigenous People of Our New World, just like the Bible was the Holy Voice of the Jews, and Homer was the Holy Voice of the Greeks, and Confucius was the Holy Voice of the Chinese.

"Tears were running down my face by the time I finished my talk, so I went to the bathroom, figuring that I'd blown it and I'd just made a fool of myself. But then coming out of the bathroom, I saw that most authors had three or four people waiting for them, but one author in the back had everyone in a huge long line waiting for him or her.

"I asked the tall, well-dressed guy, who'd come out of the bathroom with me, who that author was who had the long line, and he said that it was me. I was shocked. I had no idea what I'd said to cause this. The place was supposed to close down at 11 p.m., but they had to keep it open until 1 a.m. in the morning, because the librarians and teachers kept demanding to see me. And all this time, as I was signing books and then pamphlets, because we'd run out of books, I'd noticed that there were two Native Americans squatted down over by a corner waiting for me. And after the last person was gone, they both got to their feet and came to me with great big huge smiles. One guy was real tall and the other was much shorter.

"'You did it, Brother,' said the shorter one. 'YOU KNOCKED THEM DEAD!'

"'Yeah,' agreed the taller one with the huge wide shoulders, 'you really cleaned house!'

"'Yep,' said the shorter one, 'you really got to the Whiteman's ear, and that's not an easy task to do.'

"'But I didn't understand what they were saying, because I'd just given a little talk about my parents coming to the U.S. with their indigenous mothers from *México*. And I knew it was a good story, but so were the stories of these other writers. This was when the shorter one introduced himself, saying that he was Harry Walters from Arizona, and he was Navajo. Then the big one said he was Jack Big Shoulders from Montana and he was Lakota, then he teased how all the white women just couldn't stop kissing me and hugging me. And it was true. I must've gotten 500 kisses that night, but I still couldn't understand why my talk had touched these people so deeply.

"'You gave them Hope!' said the Navajo.

"'You gave them Spirit!' said the Lakota.

"'Yes,' I'd said, 'but some of these other speakers were really good and had great stories filled with hope and spirit, too, and yet they hardly got anyone to come to their booths. So, why me?'

"'I remember that the Navajo and the Lakota now looked at each other, and Harry said, 'Then you really don't understand what it is you did tonight?'

"'I nodded, and this was when Jack Big Shoulders said, 'Brother, you just turned all of history on its ear, and you opened up doors the Whiteman has never seen open before, or at least not for the last 7,000 years!'

"'Exactly,' said Harry, 'you brought our Native Way of thinking and viewing the world right up in their faces and touched their hearts as they've never been touched.'

"'Look,' said the tall Lakota, 'the westward movement is over. They have no more continents to conquer, no more people to annihilate or enslave, and you just gave them a Whole New World of Possibilities!'

"'You see,' said the Navajo. 'when you said that every day

is another Miracle gifted to us by God, and that your Native American grandmothers taught you to give greetings every morning to Father Sun, the Right Eye of God, and to watch Our Sister Corn smile her happy face and Our Sister Flowers open up with joy and Our Brother Birds begin to sing with Love*Amor*, you were giving people an understanding of Hope and Spirit and Love that touched their Hearts.

"'Then, when you added that Our Mother Moon was the Left Eye of God and that the Stars were our Holy Family, because we were all Walking Stars, you tied everything together.' He smiled. 'Then when you added that we, Human People, also had Our Holy Sacred Work to do here on Mother Earth, just like Our Sister Corn and Brother String Beans, you gave meaning and purpose to every person's life in that room.'

"'In other words, you were giving the Whiteman back his Original Instructions,' the big Lakota told me, and he then explained to me that Whiteman had been lost for a very long time, and that they now didn't Know where else to go or what to do, and I'd just opened a doorway for them to maybe return to their Own Indigenous Roots.

"'You showed them,' he said, 'in a way that they could understand, that their ancestors weren't ignorant savages, but, in fact, were highly intelligent, well-thought-out, good people who'd lived in a sustainable way with nature.'

"'I did all that?' I'd said to them. 'But I just talked for fifteen minutes about my family.'

"Hearing this, they both burst out laughing, and then they began to speak in Navajo or maybe in the Lakota language. I couldn't understand a single word they said, yet I kind of remembered, like in a dream, some of these throaty sounds and the use of tongue clicks that, I guess, I'd heard as a child from my Yaqui *mamagrande* and my uncle Archie, who had relatives out at the California Pala Indian Reservation. Then the two of them stopped talking to each other and turned back to me.

"'You tell him,' said the Navajo to the Lakota.

"'No, you tell it to him, Brother,' the Lakota said to the Navajo.

"'Okay,' replied Harry Walters, looking at me. 'We both believe maybe you don't really understand what it is you said tonight. And it's important you do, because obviously you will be speaking again, because you have reached the Whiteman's ear.'

"'You know,' I said, 'over and over my parents would tell me that I really didn't understand what it was they were telling me. My dad, in fact, finally said that I was *tapado,* meaning constipated in my head.'

"They both busted out laughing.

"'Your dad told it true,' said Jack Big Shoulders.

"'Thanks,' I replied.

"'Let me try to explain to you what I think it was that your parents were trying to tell you,' said Harry.

"'Go ahead,' I said, glancing at the tall, muscular Lakota. He was all smiles.

"'In the Navajo Languaging,' continued Harry Walters, 'and in every Native Languaging that I know of, there is no concept of nouns. All there are is verbs.'

"'So,' I said, 'what's that got to do with anything?'

"Hearing this, the Lakota burst out laughing again.

"Everything," said the Navajo.

"'But how can that be?' I asked. 'A tree—that's a noun. It can't be a verb.'

"'Sure it can, because a Tree is Alive and always growing and changing through the seasons and through the years. It's *Tree-ing,* a verb.'

"I gripped my forehead. 'Okay, but what about rocks? They don't change.'

"'Yes, they do. If we lived to be ten million years old, we'd see that they are constantly changing, too.'

"'Oh, my God, this is really confusing,' I said. 'But, well, didn't Einstein say that all there is, is change?'

"'Yes, he did, so he was doing it the Navajo Way, just like you did it the Navajo Way tonight.'

"'No, the Lakota Way!' said the big man from Montana, still laughing.

"'All right,' I said, trying to figure out what they were saying, 'if everything is a verb, then do you believe in God?'

"'No, of course not,' said the Navajo, without batting an eye. 'That would be silly. We *do* God.'

"'You *do* God?' I said, gripping my forehead with both hands. Having been raised a Catholic, this was just so inconceivable that it hurt my head. 'But how in the world can you *do* God?' I asked. 'Hell—I mean, Heaven—we can't even agree on the concept of who or what God is.'

"'That's the whole point,' said the Lakota.

"'What's the point?' I said.

"'Why Native People have kept the Creator as a verb.'

"'Dammit,' I said, 'talk plain! You guys are killing me in my head!'

"'Years of constipation will have that effect on a man when he's finally trying to take a good mental shit,' said the Lakota, roaring with *carcajadas*.

"But I didn't laugh. I was in terrible pain!

"'When we walk in Beauty, we are *doing* God,' continued Harry. 'When we are in Harmony with our surroundings, we *are* part of God. And when we *find* Peace within us, we *are* God.'

"'YOU ARE GOD!?!' I SHOUTED. 'No wonder the *padres* tried to slaughter all you savages! I mean, all of us savages! How in the hell—I mean, in Heaven—can we, human beings, *be* God?'

"'Easy. We *are* God as a verb, not as a noun. We *are* Goding once we *find* Peace inside of us,' said the Navajo.

"'GODING!' I shouted with my whole head EXPLODING! I had to sit down. And the damn Lakota wouldn't stop laughing.

"'Dammit,' I finally said, 'I still don't get it! Goding? Goding? Are you then saying that it doesn't really matter what you think, and it only matters what you *do*?'

"'Now you're *beginning* to get it,' said the Lakota.

"'Well, if this *is* True, then it really doesn't matter if you *are* a Catholic, a . . . a Protestant, a Jew, a Muslim, a Buddhist, a born-again Christian, or even an atheist, because all that really matters is what you *do*, right? Not what you *think* or *believe*.'

"'Exactly!' said the Lakota.

"'Then we would have never, ever had any religious wars,' I said.

"'NOW YOU HAVE IT, BROTHER!' shouted the Lakota.

"'Then we've had all of our religious wars, not because of religion, but because of the language we use to do our talking and thinking about our religions.'

"'Now you really got it, Brother!' said the Navajo.

"'This is mind-boggling! IT CHANGES ALL OF HISTORY!' I shouted.

"'And this is exactly what you did tonight,' explained Harry. 'You changed the course of history!'

"'You did it tonight,' continued Harry, 'when you said that your two Native American grandmothers didn't believe in God; they *lived* with God. You did it tonight when you said that your grandmothers didn't pray to God; they *spoke* to God. You did it tonight when you said God *was* their way of life. And you did it when you said that we're all Walking Stars and we came to Mother Earth with a Guardian Angel to plant Our Stardust Seeds that we brought with us from Our Heavens, and that God needed us as much as we needed God in order to plant His Ongoing Sacred Holy Garden. You totally changed the course of Human History, because God was no longer distant and unreachable, but instead close and very reachable.'

"I was stunned! They were right! I had said all this!

"'Yes, Brother, you had them eating out of your hand,' added the Lakota, 'and they were all ready to follow you anywhere, because in making God both male and female, you rolled back Human History 13,000 years to the last big ice age.'

"And I can tell you that those two guys kept talking to me, explaining my own book *Rain of Gold* to me, but I'd quit listening. I'd had it. They walked me to the elevator. They were staying across the way, where the rooms were more reasonable. The only reason I was staying at the hotel of the convention center was because my room had been paid for by the library association. And the big man from Montana was still talking, and I guess telling me something really important, but I just couldn't take it in. I was dead on my feet and I almost collapsed once I got into the elevator.

"And that night I had a DreamVoyage and I was with my dad shooting across the Heavens and this was when I realized that our Mother Earth really was no larger than a grain of sand on the Seashore of Creation and we, Human Beings, WERE SO HUGE that Our WingArms and WingLegs reached out to the furthest reaches of Our Universe! God was a Verb and we were Verbs, too. Supreme Being was God and Human Beings were we. Both Being. Both Verbs."

I stopped and took in several big deep GodBreaths, and glanced around, and saw that almost everyone was now Breathing in Harmony with me. Oh, this was WONDERFUL! We were on Our Way. We really were.

A nun raised her hand.

"Yes," I said.

"Sister Mary," she said.

"Hi, Sister Mary, please go on."

"This happened in Nashville, Tennessee, correct?"

I nodded.

"Did you see Harry Walters and Big Shoulders again the next day? The reason I'm asking this is that that was a lot of information to take in, and so unless you spoke with them again I don't see how you can remember everything so clearly."

"Good question," I said. "Very good question. And no, I never saw them again and when I called Harry several times — because he'd given me his card — I was always told that he was elsewhere, at some other part of the Navajo Nation in Arizona, Colorado, or New Mexico.

"And you're absolutely right about that being a whole lot of New information for me to take in, and most of it really didn't register until about a month later when I was at the wrong hotel about eighty miles outside of Phoenix, Arizona, and the next morning I was scheduled to do a TV interview at 7 a.m.

"You see," I said, pulling up a chair, "there really, really are no accidents. Because Being at THIS wrong hotel, with the Heavens jam-packed-full of Stars, was when it hit me with SUCH POWER what that Navajo and Lakota had been telling me as I'd gotten into the elevator that I went TWO YEARS WITHOUT SLEEPING! No joke! Just like Albert Einstein, I, too, became a Beam of Light!"

Hands shot up all over the place.

"No, no, please," I said, closing my *Ojo*Eyes, "no questions now!

For I'm Being told by Our Spirit World that the BIG QUESTION for All of You Genius-Jesusing People is are YOU READY TO BURST INTO YOUR OWN BEING BEAMS OF LIGHT?"

I opened my eyes. "Quit the questions. Quit your thinking with superficial manmade words, and close your *Ojo*Eyes and Breathe. Breathe deeply, and you will see that the answer to this question is within your Own Kingdom of Goding just laying Here so Peacefully. Good. Good. And keep your eyes closed, and when you see your answer within your Own Goding Self, raise up your hand, but please don't give the answer aloud.

"We need for over 50% of you to get this answer on your own, before we say it aloud. Because, like I said, when I realized the answer to this question I'm going to ask you, an Energy came BURSTING into me with such POWER that I really, really went two years without sleeping. And I then understood how my Great Great Great Great Great Aunt, Mother Of No Specific Child, had gotten to the age of 165 and how she could've gone on to the age 900 years, like Moses or Methuselah, in perfect health, because we, Human People, are, in fact, Living, Breathing Beams of Light! Okay, ready? Here is the question, but please just raise your hand," I said, wetting my lips that had gone dry. "When did Creation happen if . . . if everything is a Verb?"

No one raised their hand.

"Come on," I said, "Trees are Tree-ing, Rocks are Rock-ing, and Albert Einstein proved that all there is, is change."

One hand shot up. Then another and another. All three were nuns.

"Good," I said. "We have three people who see it, and now I want you three to put your hands down and send your Love*Amor* to all the rest of Our People, and you others to keep your eyes closed and keep Breathing in the Love*Amor* that is Being sent to you, because we're All, All, All INTERPLANETARY CONNECTED TO THE FURTHEST REACHES OF THE UNIVERSE!"

And this was when the priests, who hadn't returned to our session, now came quickly walking in and took their seats. One was a big bulldog-looking guy. I guess that they'd all been in the next room listening.

I laughed. "All right, and you guys who just came in, you, too, close your eyes, and Breathe in deeply, and I ask all of you once again, when did Creation happen if everything is a Verb? Trees are Tree-ing, Rocks are Rock-ing, and Einstein proved that all there is, is change. NOW GO FOR IT within your own Kingdom of God, and raise your hands when you see it!"

Two more hands came up, but not with as much confidence as the first three nuns.

"All right," I said, "now everyone open your eyes, and get up and stretch. We have about 25%, and what we need to happen is for all of us together to Circulate the Love*Amor* Energy that's shooting around us, so STRETCH! STRETCH! And Breathe in deeply, then blow out fast! Yes! Yes! And do it a few more times! Good! Good! And now please take your seats again."

They did so.

"Great!" I said. "And so now tell me, when did Creation happen if everything is a Verb?"

Six more hands shot up, and these came up with Energy and Confidence.

'WONDERFUL!" I shouted. "WE DID IT! We got well over 50%! So tell it! Verbalize it! When did Creation happen if EVERYTHING IS A VERB?"

"RIGHT NOW!" shouted one of the nuns who'd first raised her hand.

"ALWAYS!" shouted another nun.

"It's still happening!" said a priest.

"It has never ceased happening!" said another priest.

"It's Ongoing Forever!" said several people at once.

"YES! YES!" I shouted. "You're all right! So you see, we didn't get left out of the Super Bowl! And that guy in the wheelchair doesn't get it, because he's stuck in nouns and in five senses, because there are no beginnings and ends! IT'S STILL BANGING! Right Here! Right Now! Forever! And Ever! So how does this feel?"

"I think it's mind boggling," said a priest.

"Well, then, stop thinking. Because as I keep saying, all thinking is done with superficial manmade words for manmade words are limiting within their own definition, and so we need to get into Our Feelings, Our Knowingness, which is INFINITE! So I ask again, how does this FEEL?"

"Look," said the same priest, "this is still too new for me to think about it."

I laughed. "So stop thinking! You see, what happened is that nouns are one of the things that we ate from the Tree of Knowledge, and with nouns we solidified Creation, and then we imposed our manmade concept on Creation. We said, this empire started here and ended there. This king started ruling here and his ruling ended here. And we then took our idea of beginnings and endings and imposed them on nature. So can you now begin to See, to Feel, to Glimpse that Our Holy Doors of the Garden of Eden are re-opening? Eh, can you Glimpse this?"

All the nuns nodded and several of the priests nodded, too.

"Good, good," I said, "and now that you can clearly begin to See that Creation is Ongoing, tell me what happened to the old concept of death? Go ahead. Talk it, speak it, put it in words RIGHT NOW!"

"It . . . it disappears," said a nun, with her eyes getting huge.

"It never existed," said another nun in astonishment.

"Then we're always dying and living," said a priest.

"I read somewhere that every seven years all the cells of our bodies renew, so that infers that the old ones died," said a priest.

"Oh, my Lord God," said another nun, "then this is what you were referring to when you said that once we Activate the Kingdom of God within us, we begin Living on the Active Side of Eternity!"

I nodded. "Yes, exactly," I said, with tears of joy streaming down my face. "And now . . . that we have slipped out of the two old concepts of nouns and death that have been holding us back, and we see that Genius-Jesusing and Creation Creating have always been Ongoing, I'd like to ask you who . . . who are we in Full Partnership with?"

"WITH GODING!" shouted a nun.

"With Creation Creating!" said another nun.

"And so we now no longer believe in God, but live with God," said another nun, "just as your grandmothers were living with Our Holy Creator."

"Exactly," I said. "And so how does this feel?"

"FANTASTIC!" yelled a nun, leaping to her feet.

"WONDERFUL!" shouted another nun, standing up, too.

"For the first time in my life I can love God without fear," said another nun with tears pouring down her face.

"Can't talk," said Margret. "Too beautiful! Too beautiful!" And she also had tears of joy running down her beautiful, elegant face.

"WE NEED TO TELL THE POPE!" shouted a priest from the back. "This can REVOLUTIONIZE OUR WHOLE CHURCH!"

"DIDN'T YOU HEAR HIM?" yelled Mary. "The Pope is a man! And over and over he's told us that it's now women who are going to lead! And men need to listen and 'Follow Infront'!"

"Well, yes, but maybe it can help," said the priest, sounding defensive.

"How can it help?" said Mary. "What we need is a woman Pope!"

"A woman Pope?" said several priests at the same time.

I raised my hand, closing my eyes.

"Yes," I said, "Mary is right. We are going to have a Woman Pope." I opened my eyes and Breathing deeply. "And Our First Woman Pope will happen when . . . when the Vatican moves to Ireland."

"Then you think the Vatican is really moving to Ireland?" asked several people.

"I don't think," I said, closing my *Ojo*Eyes and raising up my right hand, palm open towards the nuns and priests. "I Know. You Know. We all Know deep inside Our Heart*Corazónes* and *Alma*Souls. And you, who said we need to tell the Pope, are also correct. But our next Pope is the one that we need to tell, because our next Pope will be from Our New World and he'll set the stage for Our First Woman Pope and our move to Ireland."

I opened my eyes, smiling. "You see, these last 2,000 years of Our Catholic Church has just been a little wrinkle compared to what She's going to do for the next 50,000 years with Women Popes leading Us in Our Global Godvolution for all religions to start moving into Being Of the People, By the People, For the People in a Direct Spiritual Relationship with God Worldwide."

I closed my eyes. "Can you see it? Can you see it? Please just close your HeadEyes and allow your HeartEyes to open up."

"I SEE IT! I SEE IT!" shouted Sister Mary. "Our next Pope is from the New World!"

"Yes," said Margret, "and he's a Jesuit. The first Jesuit to ever be a Pope he's all dressed in white and a flock of large white birds fly overhead at his inauguration. Oh, it's so beautiful! Full of Beauty as Harry Walters would say."

Tears of joy were streaming down my face. "And the flock of large white birds fly in a V-formation, correct?"

"Yes," says Margret.

"Well, those are Snow Geese, Angels of Ourselves, and this Snow Goose Pope will show the whole entire world how to Follow Infront as big strong male geese have been doing for over 20 million years, for this is, indeed, an essential part of Our Human Being Ongoing COLLECTIVE GODVOLUTION!

I stopped.

I Breathed.

I held, and I just couldn't stop crying I was so very, very happy. Sister Mary and two other nuns came up and handed me handkerchiefs and hugged me and held me.

"Thank you, thank you," I said, drying my eyes, "and now tonight I'd like all of you to please close your eyes, placing both hands over your Heart*Corazon* area, and SeeFeel that you already Know all this in a Cellular Level deep within yourselves, and this very night you will start accessing all this in your sleep. Remember," I added, "whatever we can imagine, and then put Our Heart*Corazón* and *Alma*Soul Energy into, becomes our Reality."

"YES!" shouted Mary. "Then that's why this beautiful voice sang to me in Gaelic last night! Oh, it's True!" she said, turning to everyone. "The whole sky was full of Angels singing in Gaelic! Have you ever heard Gaelic? It really can't be spoken. It needs to be sung, because it sounds like Heaven, just like Enya."

"You dreamed all this last night?" asked someone.

"It was more than just a dream," she said. "It was more like, well, a—"

"A DreamVoyage," I said. "A real actual happening, and all of you will now start experiencing DreamVoyages as you go SlipSliding into Our Collective Multi-Sensory Perception. For truly, you are now in Full Partnership with God Goding Creation Creating! In other words, like my Yaqui Indian *Mamagrande* always used to tell me, God needs us as much as we need God for Creating Heaven Here on Mother Earth as we have been Creating Heaven on other Mother Earths throughout OUR ENTIRE UNIVERSE SINCE EVER!"

"THAT'S IT!" shouted Mary. "I truly felt like I was, well, in Partnership with God, and so this wasn't just a dream at all! But something that has—how can I say it—has already happened. Can that be right?" she asked.

"Of course," I said. "Just close your eyes again, and Breathe, Breathe deeply, letting go of everything you think you know, and go into Your Feelings, Your Intuition here within Your Own Kingdom of Goding."

Mary closed her eyes, Breathing deeply.

"Good, good," I said. "You see, only when we are totally relaxed can the Spirit World come to us. You are doing very well, Mary, and . . . and don't worry about contradictions or sounding ridiculous. Remember, manmade words are shallow, one-dimensional, and have only been around for 20,000 years at best, and singing, chanting, drumming, dancing around the fire has been with us for 100s of 1,000s of years, if not millions, and this is exactly why the Vatican is moving to Ireland for 100 years and going to make the Native Language of Gaelic Her Official Language, instead of the dead, non-changing empire language of Latin.

"And then after Ireland, the Vatican will move to *Oaxaca, México* for 100 years and once more take on another non-empire based Native Language, then move to the Philippines for a 100 years and take on another Native Languaging, and then come back to Europe at that rich agricultural valley between France and Germany for 100 years and take on a pre-Roman Native Languaging, then shoot down to Africa, zigzagging from Africa and the Americas and Asia and all around the world every 100 years for the next 50,000 years, becoming Truly Catholic and setting up a Global Design of Harmony and Love*Amor*!"

"AND CATHOLIC MEANS UNIVERSAL!" shouted the big burly bulldog-looking priest.

"Yes," I said, "that's what we Catholics are always told. But have you ever looked up the word 'catholic' in the dictionary?"

He shook his head.

"Well, Father—"

"Joe," he said, "just call me Joe."

"Well, Joe, I suggest you look up the word 'catholic' and you'll find that the definition doesn't end with 'universal.' The full definition, according to the pre-1990 Webster New World American Language Dictionary, is 'universal, all inclusive, of general interest and value, having broad sympathies and understanding; hence, liberal'."

They were stunned.

"Yes, I, too, was shocked," I said, "when I looked up the word 'catholic', and . . . and now I'd like for you to consider what Bishop Malachy from Ireland said in the 12th Century."

"He said that we'd have 112 more Popes," said Joe.

"And our next Pope will be number 112, and like Sister Mary said this will be our first Pope from the Americas and a Jesuit just like Sister Margarita said, and he'll set us up for Our First Official Woman Pope just as Jesus let me Know when he gifted me His Holy Sacred Heart*Corazón* in Madrid, Spain back in 1992. And all of you . . . all of you already Know All This Deep Within OUR OWN COLLECTIVE CELLULAR MEMORY!"

I stopped again and took in a deep Breath and blew out fast.

"But," said Joe. "Bishop Malachy wasn't correct about everything, and so how can we know if what comes to us is really true or just wishful thinking?"

"Easy," said Mary, "since everything is a Verb and we are then all in Full Partnership with God, how can we then not Know what's true within Our Own Kingdom of Goding?"

WOW! This was a brilliant answer, but I could also see it wasn't quite satisfying Joe and some of the other priests.

"Joe, I suggest you just go back to that place within yourself," said Margret, "when he asked us to consider how would we all be today if Peter would have not looked down, and he would have instead walked on water alongside Our Lord Jesus. And I, then, do believe that you, too, will move past Our Doubting Thomas mentality."

"She's right!" said another nun. "And you priests didn't help raise the money to have Mr. Villaseñor come to see us, so I say, SHUT UP! Or please leave so we can continue this Enlightening Event! A WOMAN POPE!" she added, with a shout and tears of joy streaming down her face. "It makes Total Sense, especially since we are finishing up 26,000 years of out-of-balance Male Energy and going into 26,000 years of Balanced Compassionate Feminine Energy!"

Two priests got to their feet, looking all upset. I guess for being told to shut up by a nun.

"OH, SIT DOWN!" shouted Mary. "You guys are too old to revolt! And besides, it's us, the nuns, who fix your food and do your laundry, so just get off your high and mighty crap, and SIT BACK DOWN!"

The two old priests sat back down, and all the nuns BURST OUT LAUGHING with so much *gusto* that I couldn't help it, and I, too, started laughing *CON CARCAJADAS*!

Chapter Eight

We broke for dinner and I went into the large bathroom just off the main dining room where we were scheduled to dine in the evening. It was a huge, ornate beautiful bathroom and I'd just unzipped and was starting to take a pee, when the door suddenly opened behind me with a bang and there stood Joe, the big, burly priest and his face was all red with rage.

"MY GOD!" he shouted. "YOU JUST DON'T STOP!"

"Excuse me," I said, "but I'm trying to pee!"

"SO PISS! NO ONE'S HOLDING YOU BACK!"

And saying this, he turned and closed the bathroom door, locking it, and then came walking towards me. I suddenly didn't need to pee anymore. This huge man outweighed me by a good eighty pounds and it didn't look like he carried much fat, so even with all my knowledge of having been a wrestler and having been trained in advanced boot camp in the Army, I figured that I still had very little chance of defending myself against this huge guy and especially in such close quarters.

"I need to speak with you!" he said, gasping for air.

"Well, okay, good," I said, "but could we do it outside on the grass by the lake after I pee?"

"NO!" he shouted. "This needs to be private! Pee! I'll wait!"

"In here with me?"

"YES!"

"Well, okay, but I don't think I can pee with you watching," I said.

"All right, then you can pee afterward, and I'll just tell you what I need to tell you right now!"

"Okay," I said, glancing around to see if there was any chance of escaping.

"I'm a cross-dresser!" he barked.

"You're a what?" I said.

"You heard me, A CROSS-DRESSER, DAMNIT!"

"Okay," I said, "but, well, you see, I need a little help. I don't exactly know what that means. Are you telling me that you're gay?"

"NO, I'M NOT GAY!" he barked. "I'm straight! This has nothing to do with being gay! You see, I was raised by my mother, a big woman, and I'd see her put on her make up and get all dolled up to go to bars to find a man for the night, and well, it angered me that I wasn't enough for my mom, but then once, when she was gone, I sat down before her mirror and I began putting on makeup like I'd been watching her do for years, and it calmed me down, especially when I looked at myself in the mirror and saw an attractive young woman.

"So, well, after that, I then began doing it every time she went out, and I became a big kid, so by fourteen I was able to fill out her dresses, and this was when she once brought home this man who was abusive to her, and I . . . I, well, literally BEAT THE LIVING SHIT OUT OF HIM! And threw him out, and I guess she thought I was one of her girlfriends, so she thanked me and then in the morning she thought it had all been a dream."

"So then, you were dressed like a woman when you beat the crap out of that man and threw him out?" I asked.

"YES! OF COURSE! THAT'S THE WHOLE POINT!

As a man I've never beat the hell out of anyone, but dressed like a woman, I've . . . I've, well, brought many situations to justice, and then when I became a chaplain attached to the U.S. Marines and some of our G.I.s would confess to me the horrible things they'd do, not just in war, but at home with their own families, I'd go to my place afterwards and put on makeup and get all dolled up and, forgive me God, dressed as a woman I would go find these Marines and I'd beat the living crap out of them. THEN I COULD FORGIVE THEM!" he yelled and took in a huge deep Breath and blew out fast. "Do you now see what I'm talking about? As a woman I can Forgive, BUT NOT AS A MAN!"

It was me who now took in several great big deep GodBreaths. I had absolutely no idea how to respond to this, and here I'd figured that this great big tough-looking guy had probably abused altar boys and maybe even other priests. Never had it crossed my mind that he'd dressed up like a woman and defended women. Then I laughed. I mean, he'd had to have looked pretty attractive to have lured those Marines in so close.

"You're pretty big," I said, laughing. "So it must've been pretty difficult to find attractive dresses large enough to fit you!"

He started laughing, too. "It was," he said, "so I had to learn how to make alterations."

"And only as a woman have you beat the crap out of men?"

"Yes, that's true," he said. "Only as a woman, and this is why I had to see you privately."

"But not to beat me, right?" I said. "Because you're dressed like a man."

"Oh, no," he said, "I came to tell you how wonderful it is to hear all the things that you're telling us, because then, maybe, I'm . . . I'm not going to go to hell and burn for eternity when I die," he said with tears suddenly coming to his eyes. "Because revenge and not forgiveness I can now see is what I did for most of my life as, well, supposedly, a man of God."

I took in another few great big deep GodBreaths and blew out fast. My God, my God, my God, then this big tough-looking man had truly been paying attention to all I'd said.

"You know," I said, "I can now see that you've really been taking in all that I've been talking about, and here I'd thought you were really just being judgmental when you asked your question."

"Oh, no, not at all," he said. "It's quite the opposite. I believe in what you've been sharing with us, because . . . well, because I saw you levitate."

"Leva-what?"

"Levitate, rise up off the floor."

"You saw me do that?" I said, swallowing. This frightened me. Only once before had anyone ever said that they'd seen me do this.

"Yes, when you repeated the words 'I am a genius' over and over again, then you made the connection that Geniusing was, in fact, Jesusing, at that point you levitated and Prince saw it, too."

"Prince?"

"Yes, that's what we call Father James, because he was the chaplain in Washington, D.C. and all those high and mighty came to confess to him. He and Margret both saw you levitate. You're not alone, Mr. Villaseñor," he added. "Some of us have had experiences that aren't too much different than your own."

Once more I took in a deep GodBreath, flashing on the Archangel I'd met in Chicago, then I flashed on the L.A. rush hour traffic parting for me like the Red Sea, then I flashed on the realization that I really wasn't alone and so none of these Miracles, including the Levitating, were really me. No, they were simply proof that we were All, All, All Interconnected with Creation Creating, and that there were others all over our planet who were also already stepping up to the plate in preparation for Our Shift that would happen between December 21, 2012 and November 10, 2026 when Collectively we would plant all Our Stardust Seeds of Heaven on Mother Earth, and Miracles would once again become Our Norm.

"Okay," I said to him, "I think I can piss now."

"Do you want me to leave?" he asked.

"No, you might as well stay," I said. "My God, a cross-dresser and a Chaplain attached to the Marines. WOW! What a life you've lived!"

"That's not all of it," he said.

I turned my back on him, unzipped again, and began to pee.

"You should talk to Prince," he said. "He's the one who's really had the life, hearing the confessions of all those movers and shakers in Washington, D.C. Those confessions make the atrocities that I heard from our fighting boys sound like child's play.

"Your dad was right, our whole damn world really is upside down and stupid, and don't you think for a minute that the Church isn't still asking us to sprinkle holy water on the atrocities that She allows our good Christian soldiers to commit, and then has us say the equivalent to these service men that they only killed their earthly bodies, but they saved their immortal souls for the love of God and the honor of the United States.

"And these young men believe us, because we're priests, and I used to believe too, until now that I've been retired, and for these past years I've had a chance to reflect. Truly, I now believe that more of us of the Cloth are going to go to hell when we die than regular people, because we out-Nixoned Nixon. Watergate was nothing compared to what we've been doing for centuries."

"And yet you were still able to see me levitate," I said. "And I've only had one other person ever tell me that she saw me levitate.

It was a woman healer from Carlsbad who self-published a book about healing yourself."

"Carlsbad, New *México*?"

"No, Carlsbad, California, and as I'm sure you know, only a very Spiritually Elevated Human Soul can see levitation, so I'm sure that you're not going to hell," I added.

"How can I not be? Judgment Day is just around the corner and that's the Day when Jesus is returning to—"

"No," I said, "it's not coming."

"Judgment Day isn't coming?" he asked.

"No, it's already here. And Judgment Day is the day when we all stop passing judgment on each other, and especially on ourselves."

He looked all confused.

"Didn't Jesus say to Forgive them for they did not Know?" I said.

"Well, yes, He did, but—"

"There are no 'buts' in life," I said, "because you're also part of the package that doesn't Know. Stop being so full of self-importance that you think you're superior to those who drove the nails into Our Lord Jesus' flesh. You are every bit as ignorant as they were. In fact, if Jesus were to come to us right now, today, who do you think would be the first ones to want to do Him in?"

"I don't know," he said.

"Come on," I said, still pissing. "You Know. Tell me who's all full of judgment."

"Well, I guess you're pointing at my fellow Christians," he said.

"Exactly," I said. "It is us, you and me and all our most conservative and self-righteous Christians, who'd drive the first nails into Our Lord Jesus if He was to come to us once again."

"Unless He came dressed in fire and damnation!" he added, laughing. "Yeah, I guess you're right. Then you really do think that

I'm part of those who didn't know, and so I can be Forgiven?"

"Absolutely," I said, "because once we truly open our eyes to the full Glory of God, then we can only do the Sacred Holy Good, and your eyes are just beginning to open now that you're retired and have had time to reflect."

"Then I really am Forgivable," he said, with tears coming to his eyes.

"Yes, of course," I said, taking in another deep GodBreath. "You are a good man, Joe. A very good man, and I bet you make a pretty good-looking big girl, too," I added, laughing.

He burst out laughing, too. "It's true," he said. "I watched my mother put on her makeup for all those years and get all dolled up and I'd see this large, homely-looking woman totally transform. So you're right, I must say, I did look pretty snazzy when I was young and I'd get myself all dolled up."

I walked across the room and washed my hands after I'd finished pissing. "Has anyone ever seen you?"

"You mean dressed as a woman?"

"Yes," he said, becoming as embarrassed as a little girl. "Prince. He saw me once. But no one else."

"What is it about Prince?" I asked, drying my hands. "It seems like a lot of people entrust him with their darkest—no, not darkest, but their most exciting secrets!"

He yelped. "That's it! That's it! It's because he, too, manages to do what you just did. We tell him our darkest secret, and he gives our secret back to us in Light and Joy, and we then feel totally better about ourselves, and this was what he did with those big-shot movers and shakers in Washington. They all adored him!"

"Yes, and Father James is able to do this, because he's an Archangel," I said.

"Prince is an Archangel?"

"Yes."

"You know, that makes sense," said Joe. "Because he's the one who convinced us priests that it was okay for the Sisters to invite you to come and see us."

I nodded and said, "Okay, and I now need to Know how you'd like for us to go out of this bathroom. Do I go out first and you stay here for a couple of minutes, or do we just say to hell with it and go out together arm in arm?"

He looked at me. "You're right," he said, "this is a delicate situation, so, well, maybe we shouldn't go out together," he added. "But I also saw that you didn't have any trouble hugging and kissing Margret."

"Hey, do I detect a little jealousy?" I said, smiling.

"You're damn right!" he said. "I've been in love with that woman for over sixty years, and I've never so much as held her hand, and here you were hugging her and kissing her. And Sister Mary, too!"

"You've been in love with Margret for over sixty years?"

"Yes, of course! I'm a priest, but I'm also a man!" he said. "And she's the most beautiful and wonderful woman I've ever met!"

"Well, then why haven't you hugged and kissed her?" I asked.

He broke down crying.

"Is it because you're a priest?" I said. "You know, there are priests who have fallen in love and left the priesthood."

"Yes, of course, I know," he said. "And I've considered that, but then I have to admit to myself that being a priest isn't really what has held me back. What has held me back is that I don't even know how to talk to a woman, and especially not about such feelings like love. And yet I've tried, but then I get all nervous. I'm eighty-five years old, and—"

"You're eighty-five!" I said. "Hell, I'd thought you were in your late sixties or early seventies!"

"No, I'm eighty-five, and I've never been with a . . . a woman or a man. Sometimes I think these gay priests have it made. They get to have an intimacy I've never experienced."

On this one, I had to take in several great big deep GodBreaths. WOW! Never in 100 million years had I ever EXPECTED ANY OF THIS!

"May I hug you?" I said.

"I thought you'd never ask," he said, opening up his arms and coming to me, and it was a good thing that I'm strong and in great shape, because the bear-like hug he got me in could've broken ribs. And we held each other for a long time, and then I finally pulled away.

"Hey, but you kissed her!" he said. "We all saw you kissing Margret!"

"Okay, okay," I said. "I'll kiss you, too."

And so I kissed him on the right cheek and then the left cheek.

"My dad never even kissed me," he said, wiping tears out of his eyes. "Thank you. I'm in my eighties and this is my first real hug and kiss, except for my mother."

"WOW!" I said.

And so we looked at each other, smiled, then we turned and just went out of the bathroom together arm in arm, laughing with *carcajadas!*

"You know, Joe," I said to him once we were walking down the hallway, "when I was hugging *Margarita*, she told me that she hadn't been hugged by a man since her dad last hugged her when she'd been eighteen years old, and she's now ninety-one."

It was he who now took in a big deep GodBreath. "Then you think," he said, "that she might be open for me to take her hand and ask her for a hug?"

"Absolutely!" I said. "You're a big strong handsome-looking man."

“Really?”

“Yes, and you don’t need to get dolled up,” I added.

“Hey, that’s confidential! Please, not one word!”

People looked at us as we walked down the hallway, but it seemed like they really didn’t care or even made the connection that we’d just come out of the bathroom together. They were just happy to see us happy.

I was thirsty. I decided to get a glass of water, and then drink some wine before dinner. WOW! This encounter with Joe had just TOTALLY BLOWN ME AWAY!

Chapter Nine

"ALL RIGHT," I SAID, "WE'VE JUST HAD A WONDERFUL, relaxing dinner, and so I'd like for us to keep this good relaxing feeling before we turn in for the night." I took in a great big deep GodBreath, and as usual it caused most people to take in a deep GodBreath along with me. "And I'm very proud of us," I continued, "for having gotten as far as we have. This is all major stuff. Myself, it's taken me years and years to truly comprehend these things I've shared with you today, and many of you, well, got it so quickly."

A priest raised his hand. We were still in the dining room, sitting at our different tables and sipping coffee, but I didn't drink coffee. If I did, it would keep me up all night.

"Yes," I said.

"Did you really mean it when you said that you went two years without sleeping?"

"Yes, I really meant that."

"But that's totally impossible! You must have slept!"

"Ask your guides, ask your Guardian Angel tonight to help you with this, and then tell us all about it tomorrow. Because I agree with you, it does seem totally impossible, but walking off a cliff seemed impossible, too, and parting L.A. rush hour traffic, and yet all those are True, too."

"And not just a dream?" he asked.

I took in a deep Breath. How could I handle this, because all of Living Life, *la Vida,* was a DreamVoyage. Then it hit me.

"Look," I said, "I wasn't going to get into this tonight, and yet I now believe—I mean, I now Feel and am also Being told that I should get into this Right Now.

"You see, in *Oaxaca, México* before the European people came, it was recognized that we have three centers, not one, for processing information. One center is the Brain Computer and it has Four Senses, all located at the head: sight, hearing, smelling, and tasting. Specific information from specific location. Another center is the Heart Computer and it has Three Senses: feeling, balance, and intuition, and these three are done with our whole body. We feel twenty-six arms-length in all directions.

"For instance, have you ever walked into a room and instantly felt something was wrong? Of course you have. We all have. What you did was feel twenty-six arms-length in all directions with your whole body, and if it All Felt Balanced, then everything was okay. But if something was Out of Balance, you Instinctively, Intuitively, Knew something was wrong.

"And . . . and you Knew this with a capital 'K'. You didn't think this. You Knew this and Knowing is 100s of 1,000s of years old, whereas our thinking with manmade words is only, at best, maybe 20 to 40,000 years old. So Thinking is to Our Brain Center as Intuition and/or the Voice of Geniusing is to Our Heart Center.

"All right, got that? Good. Good. And now we can move into Our Third Center for processing information, and this is Our Soul Computer, here in our gut, and this one has Six Senses. The first of these is Music, the Eighth Sense, because when God Created the Universe, He/She Created One United Verse, One United Song, and each of us comes into manifestation with Our Own Song, and then once we move into this computer, then Time and Space, our Ninth and Tenth Senses, are relative, as Einstein said, and/or they simply disappear, and we now move into our Eleventh Sense, which is our Collective Consciousness of All the Past and of All the Future, and we now have—"

"Psychic powers like Bishop Malachy of Ireland!" said the priest who'd said all this was impossible.

"Exactly!" I said. "Because Psychic is to the Soul as Intuition is to the Heart and Thinking is to the Brain!"

"OH, WOW! Then not sleeping for two years is possible!"

"Exactly!" I said. "Because we become Beams of Light just like Albert Einstein, and Light needs no sleep, and it doesn't age, either."

"I see, I see," said the priest, "then everything you've been sharing with us all day is Our Norm once we Activate our Kingdom of God with our Thirteen Senses. But what is the Thirteenth Sense?"

"Being," I said. "Supreme Being and Human Being, and this is when we are at One with Goding."

"It's making sense now!" he said. "This is wonderful! And so when I go to sleep tonight, and I stop all of my thinking with manmade words, I'll then be, through my feelings, in Direct Communications with God!"

"Exactly," I said. "And now that most of you here are seventy-eight or older, please ask tonight for your Blessed Tools with which to become a Sacred Elder. This is one of the main things we're missing in our whole western civilization. We worship youth," I added. "And I love that I'm getting old!"

"ME, TOO!" yelled Joe.

"Any more questions?" I asked.

"Yes," said a nun. "Why did you refer to the word 'the' so many times?"

"Oh, wow!" I said, taking in another deep GodBreath. "This is a big one. You see, the word 'the' only exists in European-based languages. The Russian language doesn't have it. No Asian language has it. No Indigenous language has it. Only Europe, and it was invented by the Jews and their cousins, and then popularized by the Greeks, and then all of Europe adopted it. And I'm not bad-mouthing the Jews or the Greeks. My ex-wife is Jewish. My two sons are Jewish Mexican Americans. And I'm Jewish through digestion. All of us have many labels. One label is out of date.

"And at first the word 'the' is innocent sounding, because you use it to say 'the tree' in front of my house. And the rest of the world has 'that tree' and 'this tree' to show location. Only Europe has 'the tree', but then European people jump from 'the tree' to 'the truth' and what happens to truth? Go on, tell me what happens to truth when you place 'the' in front of it? Come on, you're all GeniusesJesusing."

No one said a word. They all just looked at each other, and then finally one nun spoke.

"It becomes singular," she said.

"Okay, good, and what else does it do?" I asked.

"It, well, in a way elevates truth," said a priest.

"Okay, excellent, and what else does it do?" I asked again.

People shook their heads.

"Come on," I said, "go for it! What does it do to all other truths?"

"It voids them," said Joe.

"Yes, it voids them, and what else happens?" I asked.

"The truth becomes absolute and there can be no other truths," said Mark.

"*Exactamente!*" I said. "And then how do the words 'or' and 'but' back up 'the truth' Eh, what does 'or' do?"

"It gives us choice," said a priest.

"Does it really?" I asked.

"It limits us into only two choices in respect to 'the'," said Mark.

"*Exactamente*!" I said. "So if I have a third or fourth opinion, I can't voice it, because I've been forced into polarity of mind. I either get it or I don't. I agree or I don't. And because you have 'the truth', then I am totally intimidated and so I fold up. And if I don't fold and do speak up, you now use the word 'but' with one 't' and what have you done?"

People glanced at one another, not offering anything.

"Come on! Come on! 'But' is the sneakiest one of all."

"It gives us more to consider?" said a priest.

"Oh, no, that's barking up the wrong tree. I've said that this is the absolute truth, then I back that up with 'or' by forcing you into polarity of thought, and yet you're a very determined individual, so you continue trying to show me your point of view, and so I listen patiently, then say yeah, brother I hear you, but —"

"'But' cancels out everything I've just said!" said Mark, excitedly.

"*Exactamente!*" I said, "and this is why 'the', 'or', and 'but' are by far the most dangerous words in all the world, and have allowed Europe to take over the globe, and it's not because European people are smarter than others!

"Oh, no, it's that the language they speak gives them an arrogance and manipulation with the one-and-only absolute truth, so that nobody else's truth matters. That's why in *México* my great-grandfather *Leonardis Camargo* slaughtered whole Yaqui Indian villages, women and children, too, and he had no regrets, because he had 'the truth' in the name of Jesus Christ. Because, you see, when you hook up 'the truth' to God and/or politics, you have a culture that respects no other religions or cultures."

Tears came to my eyes. "And my great-grandfather wasn't a bad man. He was a good man. It's just that he didn't Know any better, because language makes us who we are. We talk with language, we think with language, we process all of Our Feelings through language. So language makes us who we are and our reality what it is. For instance, I now ask you, what happens to the Bible when you take 'the' away and instead put 'a' in front of Bible?"

I stopped and Breathed. You could hear a pin drop.

"Our Bible becomes one of many," said a priest.

"Yes," I said, "and now there can be many Bibles and many truths. Just Breathe. Breathe. And please don't panic. This is good! This is wonderful! Just don't panic, and keep Breathing in and Breathing out. Good. Good. And now can you begin to see how 'the' has been keeping us in a prison in science, in politics, and not just in religion. Because we're always searching for 'the' answer, 'the' origin of man, 'the' cure for cancer, 'the' cause of this and that, and so we've locked ourselves out of ever gaining understanding, and instead are forever just coming up with new, improved shallow theories and arrogant, self-serving opinions.

"Truly, understand that when your heads hit your pillows tonight, you are going to be Goding. No joke. You will once more have Direct Contact with Our Almighty, and this is how Our Six Sister Planets finally started moving out of chaos and violence and being lost and began regaining Unity and Harmony and Peace with Creation Creating.

"Like I said, words are manmade and limiting within their own definition and they've only been around 40,000 years at best, and so right now words own us. We don't own them. And this has all been part of Our Ongoing Stages of Godvolution, so tonight ask your Guardian Angel, your GeniusJesusing, for Guidance of the Highest Vibrations and you will go on a WONDERFUL ADVENTUROUS DREAMVOYAGE!

"And also, ask to awake in the morning rested and happy. BIG BIG HAPPY! And Totally at Peace and in Harmony with all the rest of Creation! Ask this, and Truly, you will RECEIVE, RECEIVE, RECEIVE even from the furthest reaches of the Universe! For you are a HOLLOW BONE! A BUFFALO BONE! AN INSTRUMENT OF God Goding FOR SPREADING HIS/HER LOVE*AMOR* THROUGHOUT OUR UNIVERSE!"

Book Three

Chapter Ten

AND THAT NIGHT I WENT RIGHT TO SLEEP AND I HAD ONE of my old flying DreamVoyages. Once more I was on a dirt road on Mount Palomar just east of our *ranchito* in Oceanside, California. A whole bunch of Happy People were with me and we were spreading out our arms into the wind and laughing and laughing like little kids.

Then when a strong gust of wind came up, our arms turned into Wings. Magnificent wings! And we just took a little short run and leaped off the mountaintop and we were flying over the great mountainous land of Southern California, going west to the sea.

At the beach, some of us joined in with the seagulls, but like always, I joined in with the pelicans, and now I, too, was gliding along the crest of the waves. Oh, it felt so free and wonderful and easy! BIG BIG EASY! And thusly, I awoke, feeling WONDERFUL!

I started laughing, I felt so good! Then I smelled Wildflowers just as I'd smelled in Madrid, Spain when Jesus had come to me, but this time I didn't see Him. Still I said, "Good morning," and heard Jesus say, "Good Morning," back to me.

Then He said, "We're all very proud of you. You're doing very well."

"Thanks," I said, laughing, "but I'll tell you, I was a little unsure a couple of times yesterday."

"So were we," He said, laughing, too.

"You? But how can You be unsure?" Hearing this, he laughed all the more. Then I saw it. "Oh, yeah," I said, "we, Human People, have Freewill. I forgot."

And just like that, I couldn't smell Jesus' Wildflowers anymore.

I stretched and stretched, and then got up. Oh, I was feeling fabulous! I went to the bathroom, showered, dressed, and then went out on the balcony to give thanks to the Father Sun, the Right Eye of God. Then I went downstairs and I could smell freshly baked rolls and hear happy conversation before I'd even entered the room where our event was being held. It was Heaven! A group of nuns were bubbling with joy, but the few priests didn't look so good. I guessed that some of these guys hadn't had a good night.

Sister Mary came rushing up and gave me a big hug and kiss on each cheek and then so did Sister Margret and two other nuns, but only Father James and Mark came and greeted me. And big burly Joe watched Mary and Margret hug and kiss me, and he shook his head. I waved for him to come over, but he just shook his head again. Myself, I wasn't all that hungry this morning and so all I ate was fruit and cottage cheese, and then I went over to the large expanse of windows to say 'hello' to the geese and deer. What Beauty! What Abundance! Oh, what a Beautiful World and when I turned around everyone was seated.

"Good morning," I said. "Good morning! Good morning! I hope you all slept very well. Myself, I slept like a baby and had a DreamVoyage of flying from the mountains of Southern California to the sea. I awoke laughing, I felt so good. But," I added, "before we start today, I'd like us to form a circle with chairs so we can all be participants. After all, you are now all GeniusesJesusing, and so there are no more leaders. For . . . we've all accessed Our Kingdom of God that Our Lord Jesus so wisely told us about. And please bring along your coffee and these delicious wonderful rolls that were freshly baked for us this morning. Mmmmmm, good, eh?"

Everyone brought up their chair, even a couple of priests who seemed pretty reluctant.

"All right," I said, once we were all seated, "so, how did you all sleep? Like I said, I slept like a baby and had a wonderful flying dream. So I'd now like you all to share, and please give your name when you do. Okay? So who'd like to start?"

Sister Mary instantly raised her hand with a screech of joy!

"So hit it," I said, laughing. "Go for it!"

"Well, my name is Mary, and I'd like to say that usually when I wake up in the middle of the night, I try to go back to sleep, but last night I didn't try to go back to sleep, because I was so excited! So I got up and came down to the kitchen to make myself a cup of coffee and I found Margret and Eve already here and they, too, were so happy and full of energy, but I only visited with them for a little bit, because I just Knew that I had to start writing.

"And they were baking anyway, so I didn't feel bad about leaving them in the kitchen and I went into our den, started a fire in the fireplace, and I could barely contain myself, because all these great ideas and insights just kept coming to me. I felt Blessed! I felt like I'd finally really Awakened! And I bet that this is how you felt when you were writing *Rain of Gold*," she added.

"Yes, exactly," I said, laughing, "every day was Christmas with all these great insights that were being gifted to me from Heaven."

"Yes, this is exactly how I felt this morning," said Mary. "And I hadn't felt like that since I was a very young nun!"

I took in a great big deep GodBreath. "That's wonderful, Mary," I said, "and I'd like you to Know that writing, that keeping a journal, is, in fact, Bibling, and that Bibling is Our Salvation. Bill, not Shakespeare, but Bill Cartwright my longest best friend who hiked into the Rain of Gold canyon with me that first time and has been a family counselor for over thirty years, he has always told me that the opposite of depression is expression, and when you write down what you're feeling deep inside, you then instantly make room for new possibilities to come into your life. And this is what you were doing, Mary. You were giving Birth to God! Because like I said earlier *mi mamagrande* always explained to me that we come into this world, into this Dimension of Reality, pregnant with Our Holy Creator, and so this is Our Holy Job."

"Then you equate writing a journal to writing the Bible?" asked a priest.

"Sure. What is the Bible? It's a group of stories that connect a tribe to God and Creation, and this is what Mary did last night, and Anne Frank did, and we all do when we get up in the middle of the night and the Stars, Our *Familia*, are talking to us. Like Mary said, she felt Blessed. She felt like she'd finally Awakened. And hopefully you'll feel the same thing soon.

"You see, it took me four months of not talking to get to where Mary got in just one night." I turned back to Mary. "Thank you," I said. "You're on your way, Mary. You are doing your Holy Work here on Mother Earth, which is, of course, to give Birth to God, to give Life to God with All your Life within your very Own Kingdom of God that Jesus was sent here to tell us about."

"Yes!" she said. "This is exactly what I was feeling! It's like I Awoke with this great excitement to give Voice, to give Life to all the Goodness that I can feel that I'm Receiving in Abundance from the WHOLE UNIVERSE! A Hollow Bone I've become! A Buffalo Bone I've become!

"And yet I could never have allowed myself to feel any of this until I understood that Everything is a Verb and that Creation is still going on. It was like my life had reopened in a way I haven't felt since I was a young nun and the bride of Our Lord Jesus Christ! OH, I AWOKE WITH SUCH FEELING OF ECSTASY! And warmth and joy! And all these feelings and thoughts that, I guess, I'd been holding back for all these years, they now came FLOODING BACK TO ME! Oh, I can hardly wait to go back to sleep tonight, so I can Awake again and continue feeling like I'm once more Directly Receiving from God through His Son Jesus!"

"WONDERFUL!" I said. "WONDERFUL! And so how many of you also Awoke in the middle of the night feeling like this?"

Three more nuns raised their hands, but not one priest.

"I never even got to sleep," said the priest who'd asked if I equated journaling to Bibling. "And what kept me up was, well, WHY YOU?" he added with anger.

"Why me?" I said, taking in a deep Breath.

"Yes, why you!" he repeated. "I don't see you as being that special, or educated, or anything else!"

"Why me, eh?" I said, closing my eyes so I wouldn't have to keep looking at this priest's angry face, and I could stay focused. "Well, I'd like you to Know that I used to ask myself this same question. I mean, I'd meet people who were slender and all smiles and very spiritual looking and didn't swear, didn't drink *tequila,* didn't look at women and were vegetarian, and they didn't lose their temper, and I say why not them? They're certainly much nicer people than me.

"But then I remembered that I wasn't a very good wrestler, either, and yet as a freshman I tied the senior who took the California State Championship. And in chess, I beat all the smartest students at school, plus all the faculty, and then it came to me that the real question isn't why not them, but WHY NOT ME? Because by asking why not them, I was giving away all of my Powers to them over there and leaving me here, inside, with *nada, nada*, nothing.

"And yet by asking why not me with all of my Heart*Corazón* and *Alma*Soul," I said, taking in a deep Breath. "I could now see in a flash that I was bringing in All of the Powers of the Universe into me! And this is what Johann Wolfgang von Goethe wrote about when he so brilliantly said: 'Whatever you can do or dream you can do, begin it! Boldness has genius, power, and magic!'"

"Well, yes," he said, "but—"

I raised up my open hand, palm towards him, closing my eyes, and said in a loud voice, "Please, no 'but' here! Let me finish what I'm saying, because you have asked a very important question! Either we start empowering ourselves, or . . . or we just keep finger pointing at others, passing judgment, and never take in our full potential, because by you asking this question tells me that you, sir, have over and over chickened out on your OWN GREAT FABULOUS POWERS!"

I stopped, opened my eyes, staring at him eye to eye and took in several great big deep GodBreath. "For instance," I said, "take my last confession back in 1959 when I was nineteen. It's going to be well documented in my book *CrazyLoco Love*."

"You haven't been to confession for forty years?" he barked at me.

"No, I haven't, and that's not the point!" I barked back. "The point is I started taking my powers back then, and I didn't realize it until later. You see, I did my last confession at the Chapel of the Catholic University of San Diego where I was going to school, and . . . and it suddenly came to me that yes, I could confess my sins for my Love of God, but not for my Fear of God and the pains of hell. And so I told the priest, no, that I would not say that, that I would rather burn in hell for all eternity than to think for one moment that I was supposed to fear God and believe that Our Almighty would ever even create such a place as hell.

"I was pumped! I was ready to burn for All Eternity, but I would not back down, and finally the priest was so exasperated at me that he said that if I didn't say that, then I couldn't be a Catholic. This had never entered my mind, but when he said this to me, I then said, 'GOOD! GREAT! Then I'm no longer a Catholic!' And I opened up the little curtains of the confessional and stepped out. He got out, too, and started telling me that I just couldn't do that, because I'd been baptized and I'd gone to confirmation and etc. and etc. And I said to him, 'Hey, Father, I don't have to listen to you anymore, because I'm no longer a Catholic. Goodbye!'

"And I turned and went running and shouting with joy out of the Chapel, and outside I'd never ever seen the WORLD SO BEAUTIFUL! And that's the night I looked up the word catholic in my Webster Dictionary to find out what I wasn't anymore, and to my shock, I found that it didn't just say universal as we Catholics were always being told, but it also said, 'all-inclusive, of general interest and values and having broad sympathies and understanding; hence, liberal.'

"I SCREAMED WITH JOY! Because, then, I was now a real catholic! I REALLY REALLY WAS! And this old priest, who'd insisted that I had to have fear of God, wasn't a real catholic, because being a catholic meant not just universal, but all-inclusive and having broad understandings and sympathies AND SO THIS INCLUDED ME!

"So I quickly got in my car and drove over to my cousin's apartment in Ocean Beach where he lived with a bunch of ex-G.I.s, who were also students at the Catholic University, and I told them what had happened and showed them the definition of catholic in my Webster, and instead of rejoicing, they asked me to leave when I wouldn't stop talking so excitedly.

"And those big strong ex-soldiers, who were all older than me, reported me to the priests and the priests informed my parents, but I would not back down, because like I kept telling them, once you get past Our Fear of God, then you automatically only FEEL AN ABSOLUTE JOY and LOVE*AMOR* FOR GOD AND ALL OF CREATION! The Stars Sing! The Ocean Waves Dance! And the Flowers and Trees smell of Heaven, and for the first time in all my life, I felt Whole and Connected and BIG BIG HAPPY AND FREE!

"So why me? Well, I'll tell you, because I didn't ask why about anyone else and because there are no accidents! Particularly in the Spirit World, and this incident, I'm sure, was what helped prepare me for what Harry Walters and Jack Big Shoulders told me in Nashville, because I was able to grasp what it was that they meant when they told me that they didn't believe in God, that they *did* God, and they *lived* with God like my *mamagrande* had *lived* with *Papito Dios!*

"You see, to go even further, 'belief' is a weak word. You don't 'believe' in your car. You Know your car. And to Know is strong. To 'believe' is weak. It takes us out of the realm of Concrete Solid Knowledge and responsibility, and gives us something to hide behind, because you can't argue with belief, and a person can believe anything they want, and cover up their real agenda. And on the other hand, by *doing* God by first Walking in Beauty, and then by Harmonizing with All of Creation, then actually Being with Supreme Being Goding and you Breathe and find Peace with a capital 'P' within your own self. Right Here! Right Now! The buck stops with you!

"Do you see—no, I mean feel—what I'm saying? You no longer pass judgment on others. You no longer use the Bible so you can be righteous and full of contempt for others. Eh, are you with me? Like you no longer see handicapped children as even being handicapped. You now see them as Holy Gifts straight from God Goding that are giving you the opportunity to see the Light of Goding in Everything and Everyone, Equally!" Tears came to my eyes. "You no longer see Down Syndrome Kids as weird looking, but as so God Goding Beautiful with their Big Smiles and Innocent Joy, because you now start doing as the Native Tribes of Central America say when they meet someone, particularly a stranger, 'You are another me, and I am another you,' and you then put your hands behind your back and touch foreheads.

"And in homeless people I see me, and I see my dad and his poor old Indian mother coming to the Texas border, starving and desperate, and I also remember that my dad went to prison at thirteen for stealing six dollars' worth of copper ore from the Copper Queen Mining Company of Douglas, Arizona, so he could buy food to feed his starving family." Tears were pouring down my face.

"So why me? Because I asked 'why not me?' and FLOOD GATES OPENED TO ALL OUR POWERS OF OUR UNIVERSE and came pouring into me! And I was then able to make a deal with the Almighty to become a writer as great as Homer and/or greater and I didn't even know how to read!

"So why me? YOU TELL ME! You open up your HeartEyes and see me as you! And special! And wonderful! And as a Gift Straight from God Goding! BECAUSE THIS IS HOW I SEE YOU!"

I quit.

I couldn't stop crying, this answer had totally drained me. He looked stunned. He just kept staring at me.

"Look," he finally said. "I'm sorry. I really am. I just thought that you were all about wanting to be an author and famous."

I started to laugh, but felt so drained that I had to sit down. Tears had come to my eyes.

"Tell me," I said, "did you even read *Rain of Gold*?"

He suddenly looked like a little mouse that'd just been caught in a trap. "I think I better, well, just shut up," he said, glancing around and seeing how everyone was staring at him. "I'm sorry. I'm really sorry."

"No, please don't be sorry," I said, wiping the tears out of my eyes. "It was a question that probably needed to be asked. I'm sure others have been thinking the same thing, but didn't have, well, the guts to ask. Okay, who else?"

Another priest raised his hand. "Go on," I said.

"Matt," he said, "and I, too, didn't sleep the whole night, but what kept coming to me was that you said you didn't sleep for two years. So I finally got dressed and went for a walk, and, well, quite honestly, I began to wonder if you'd been on drugs when you had all of these experiences. Because, well," he said, turning red, "I dropped acid when I was a teenager and we went to visit relatives out in Santa Monica, California. And what I experienced frightened me so much that I never took any drugs again, and especially not after one of my cousins in California died from an overdose. So my question to you is this, do you do drugs?"

"Okay," I said, "I'll answer you, but I first need to put this in perspective. As a rule I drink. I don't do drugs, and yet I've taken *peyote* a couple of times in Native American ceremonies with complete supervision and ritual. And I've done mushrooms once in the same way, and I smoke grass now and then with friends."

"How often?"

"Oh, maybe four or five times a year, because what I do on a regular basis is drink. But now," I said, "getting to your real question, was I under the influence when I've had any of my

Miraculous Experiences? No, not even a little bit. I was totally clean and sober."

"Okay," he said, "before last night I wouldn't have believed you, but since what happened to me last night, I'm now inclined to believe you, because I swear that the Trees began singing to me last night just as they had when I'd dropped that acid as a kid, and then the Stars began Waltzing, too. Everything was Alive! Totally Alive with Light and Color and so Beautiful! And yet I didn't have the fear that I'd had as a teenager when I'd dropped acid.

"In fact, I felt at Peace, and then I began to hear Music. A Symphony. And I remembered that you said that when God created the Universe He created One Verse, One Song, and that we all came into manifestation with Our Own Song, and so I understood for the first time in my life, that I do have my Own Song, and this is what I was hearing and it was making me so happy! Like you say, BIG BIG HAPPY!"

Tears of joy were running down his face, and I went across the room and took Matt in my arms, hugging and kissing him, then I stepped away.

"You, my dear *amigo*," I said, "have just become a Sacred Elder!"

"Me? A Sacred Elder?"

"Yes, you and Mary have Awakened, and become Sacred Elders! Because to be a Sacred Elder is to Be in Tune with your Own Holy Song that you brought with you from the Heavens along with your Guardian Angel. And so now as Sacred Elders you and Mary need to come out of retirement, and EXPLODE INTO INSPIREMENT! For you are now in Harmony with the HOLY MUSIC OF God Goding!"

"You know, maybe you're right," said Matt, wiping the tears that were pouring down his face. "I do Feel like this is Now a Whole New Me just Beginning."

"Yes," I said, with tears of joy streaming down my face, too. "I remember what my good friend Louis L'Amour, the western writer, once said to me: 'There will come a time when you believe everything is finished, and that will be your beginning.' And Mr. L'Amour, who finally even outsold John Steinbeck with almost half a billion books, KNEW what he was talking about. You, *mi Amigo*, and you, Mary, *mi Amiga*, have AWOKEN! Shooting past all FEAR and you are now SongShifting and MiracleMaking just as *Espirito* who followed a deer and her fawn in search of water in the first sentence of *Rain of Gold*.

"And when *Espirito*, meaning Little Spirit, saw the sunlight reflecting off the waterfall in the early morning light, he said, 'It's a rain of gold!' and thusly it became, and that first sentence used to be 300 words long, but I finally had to just simplify it or I would have lost all my readers, and especially the ones who only speak English. Congratulations! For you two are now Living with one foot on This Side and another foot on the Other Side, and are now with every Breath GodBreathing just like *Espirito* in *Rain of Gold*! Can you Feel it? Is all this finally Beginning to make sense to you?"

"Yes," said Matt, "I can Feel it."

"Me, too," said Mary with a smile of pure joy.

"AND HOW ABOUT ALL THE REST OF YOU!" I shouted. "Can you also FEEL it? Eh, can you now also Begin to SeeFeel all of Our Spiritual Guests who've been helping us?"

Most of the nuns and priests nodded, and a few actually got up and walked across the room to *be* with Our Spirit Guests.

I watched.

I said nothing and just watched these Awakened Ones and Our Spirit Guests interact and it was ABSOLUTELY BEAUTIFUL!

I pulled up a chair and sat down. Time and Space had disappeared for Our Awakened Ones. A fast ball now came in so slowly to these people that they could hit HOMERS all day long! And this was exactly what had happened to me with *mi Papa* in New York, and with Jesus in Madrid, and with my brother Joseph and Jesus at the big black rock just north of Buccaneer Beach in Oceanside.

"Okay," I now said, "stretch. Stretch like a cat waking up after a good long nap. Yeah, stretch and realize that this now is just a Beginning. Our whole Spirit World is starving for us to Awaken and make contact with them, and so they'll now Be coming to you so fast and so often that at times you'll have to tell 'em, 'Eh, please back off!'"

Hands shot up all over the place.

"No, no, please, no questions yet. What I'd like to do, while you guys are Totally Open of Heart*Corazon* and *Alma*Soul, is to put into perspective what has just happened to you.

"You see, you have now entered a Holy Place, and so it's important that you guys Know . . . that before Columbus Sacred Elders and Holy Healers would come from all over South and North America to enter into this Glowing Holy Red City of Spirit Light." I took in a deep Breath. "And at this Holy Place there is no separation from This Side of Living to Our Other Side of Living, so Our Vibrational Frequencies Automatically Glow.

"Breathe. Just Breathe," I said, closing my *Ojo*Eyes, "and for ten years Sacred Elders and Holy Healers would come to this Glowing Red City and exchange Sacred Knowledge and Interplanetary Wisdom with Parrots listening. And then they'd go back north and south with their Parrots for ten years, planting *this* Sacred Knowledge of All of Us Being Interplanetary Miracle Makers."

"With Parrots? Why parrots?"

"Please, can you hold your questions?" I asked, still keeping my eyes closed in concentration.

"No, not really. I'll be thinking about parrots so much that I honestly won't be able to hear anything else you have to say."

"I agree," said another priest. "My head is already full of flying, squawking parrots."

"Mine, too," said several other nuns and priests.

I opened my *Ojo*Eyes. "Okay, okay," I said, "I really didn't want to get into this, especially not right now, but I guess this was meant to *Be*, and so here we go. You see, recently the feathers and carcasses of large parrots have been found as far north as northern Canada, and no one can figure this one out. But you see back at one time people Knew that a Parrot can retain as much information as an entire Britannica Encyclopedia, and so Parrots were revered and great assets for Our Sacred Elders and Holy Healers. Also, when a tribe, no matter how war-like, saw these people coming with a Parrot, they'd put out their red carpet.

"Why? Because for 100s of 1,000s of years if not millions, Human Being People have been going to these 13 Global Spiritually Glowing Red Cities that Light up 10,000 Times Brighter than modern day Las Vegas for this *was* and *is* what happens when there's No Separation from This Side of Living and Our Other Infinite Side Of Living." I Breathed. "And the Great Pyramids outside of Mexico City and the Birth Village of Confucius in China are just two of these 13 Holy Red Cities and they are now ready to BURST INTO ILLUMINATION ONCE AGAIN!"

I stopped.

You could hear a pin drop. They were all just staring at me.

Oh, yeah, I'd over done it once more just as I'd over done it in South Chicago a few years back. I'd been on a roll with one of my evening talks when this older Black woman had screamed.

"SLOW DOWN! You're going too fast! Half of what you're saying, my grandmother also used to tell us about a Glowing

City in the jungles of Africa, Please slow down! I can't take notes any faster!"

"Don't take notes," I'd said to her. "That's a distraction. Just close your eyes and imagine yourself Being a big beautiful Parrot, and you'll instantly retain everything I'm saying, plus all that your grandmother ever said to you will come back to you."

Remembering this, I continued Breathing deeply. They were still processing. They weren't raising their hands and asking questions. No, they, too, were Breathing deeply and allowing God Goding to help them.

Oh, I, too, had totally been blown away by this Parrot thing, until I'd actually been in a Lower Secret Chamber of the Moon Pyramid outside of Mexico City, and I'd seen a carved drawing in the stone wall of a large Parrot with her Red Tongue sticking out, and she'd instantly Gifted me Our Entire Global Story of Our Sacred Elders and Holy *Curanderos*.

"Okay, may I now please go on?" I asked.

"I don't know if you should," said a priest. "This whole parrot thing and 13 Glowing Spirit Cities around the world has really stopped me. And yet it's so outrageous that I feel it must *Be* True. How could anyone make up such a story? And if this is True, then everything that you've shared with us is just the tip of Our Iceberg."

"I agree," said another priest, "and I haven't read Rain of Gold, but you can bet your boots that I'm going to read it now, and — WOW! I'm excited to get to KNOW ALL YOUR WRITING."

"Thank you," I said. "thank you, but remember I didn't write any of my books. I'm a Hollow Bone. A Buffalo Bone. A Receiver and a Giver and *nada, nada* more. You see, back then Healing People was done by Our Healers by Receiving and Chanting and bringing a person's Holy Song back into Harmony with the Symphony of God Goding's Universe. Disease means not-at-ease, and so when a Human Being is Totally-at-Ease, Totally-in-Tune with Supreme Being, then BINGO! Diseases disappear. And so this is now your calling, your Holy Work as Sacred Elders to help Heal Human People and Our Mother Earth and Father Sky."

"Will we need parrots?" asked Matt.

"You tell me," I said. "You, too, are now a Receiver."

"You're right," said Matt. "You're absolutely right! Because I can now see that I too, was there at this Red City last night, and I heard Our Symphony of Creation. But still, I'm sure I'll not go two years without sleeping like you did. But I will go at least a week—I'M SO EXCITED!"

"Myself," said Mary, "I didn't go to the Red City, but I'm so happy and excited that I'm going to go the rest of my life with just little cat naps. Oh, this is WONDERFUL! And I can now see that your Great Great Great Great Great Aunt, Mother Of No Specific Child could have easily lived to the age of 165. How could she not when she was Goding!"

Margaret stood up and began cheering Matt and Mary. All the nuns immediately stood up, too, and joined in with the ex-Mother Superior's exuberance. And then they were hugging and kissing Mary and Matt.

And big burly Joe was just watching. So I finally walked over and got hold of him, and came pulling him across the room and threw him into the mass of hugging, kissing people.

And there was Margret-*Margarita* in the middle of the whole thing, and when she turned and saw big Joe, she opened up her arms to him, but he was so shocked that at first he didn't know what to do. But then this face burst into a huge smile, and he went for it, hugging this woman that he'd been IN LOVE WITH FOR OVER SIXTY YEARS!

Chapter Eleven

WE TOOK A BREAK. I WENT TO MY ROOM, PUT ON MY RUNNING shoes, and took off running around the lake. I'd been running for nearly forty years, ever since I'd taken up wrestling in high school and I usually ran about twenty to twenty-five miles a week. Four runs of about three to four miles, then one day a week I'd go a ten-mile distance, and on these runs, I'd do the first mile at about an eight minute pace, then I'd drop down to a seven-minute pace, and at this speed I'd no longer be jogging but racing! And it would be much easier on my knees, because I'd be using the front part of my feet more, and pushing off with my toes and I'd be sailing!

Oh, I loved RUNNING! It was a natural high! And also I'd get to be alone, so I could let things kind of catch up with me. Oh, boy, had we just covered a lot of ground. Never in a million years did I ever dream that these old nuns and priests would be so Alive and Open and Available!

Then up ahead, who did I see, it was Mark and he was running, too, and really kicking ass. And normally I would've pushed myself dropping to an under six-minute pace to catch the person and/or people ahead of me, but I didn't. I stayed well behind and just followed Mark as he went on trails through the woods and alongside creeks and it was wonderful. Once we jumped a herd of deer. We came back laughing, and yet never having said a word until we'd returned.

"So how did it go for you last night, Mark?" I asked.

He took in a deep Breath. "Very productive," he said, "and yet very strange, but I'd like to save my comments for the group," he added.

"Okay," I said, and we parted and I went up to my room, took a quick shower, then went back downstairs.

Instantly, I could feel the difference. The whole room felt in Harmony and Alive and Full of Love*Amor*! Even the priests as a group now seemed happy and relaxed. People were talking excitedly and laughing and having a very good time!

I got myself a cup of hot water and brought out my lavender Yogi Licorice tea bag. I sat down in our circle of chairs and began dunking my tea bag up and down in the hot water until it was a golden color. I never drank coffee or caffeinated tea. I was always already so naturally high that if I felt any better I'd probably get arrested. Seeing me sit down, the others began taking their seats, too.

"Okay," I said, once everyone was seated, "as you can all see we've become a pretty relaxed happy group."

A priest raised his hand. "Okay," I said. "Go on."

"Have you ever read the book *The Outsider* by Colin Wilson?" he asked.

I shook my head.

"I think you should," he said. "Because what Wilson does, is that he gives us understanding of the human mind and shows us how the human mind can only handle so much before it, well, cracks, or goes insane. And he uses the examples of Van Gogh, Vaslav Nijinsky, Lawrence, Rimbaud, T.S. Eliot, all these gifted heavyweights of the arts, and so not only did I have trouble sleeping last night, but I ended up throwing up my dinner." Tears were streaming down his face "And what kept coming to me was, well, if we do, in fact, take 'the' away from the Bible, then does this mean that you're suggesting that we take 'the' away from what Jesus Christ told us about Him being 'the' only way?"

It was me who now took in a big deep Breath and closed my eyes, asking for guidance. This was a big one. Maybe even the biggest one, because this one hit the nail right on the head of our entire Western Civilization. I took in more great big deep Breaths and suddenly I smelled Wildflowers, and I once more Knew that Our Lord Jesus was here with us.

I opened my eyes, and no, I couldn't see Jesus, but I could sure feel His Full Powers of Love*Amor* and nothing but Love*Amor* and His Sacred Energy was going up and down my spine with a Tingling Sensation that got so hot I began sweating.

"Well," I said, turning to this priest. "I can well understand why this would be a pretty disturbing thought, because I, too, got pretty upset when this notion first came to me. But then I prayed and asked for guidance, turning it all over to God."

"BUT," he yelled, "how can I now turn it all over to God through His Only Son Jesus, if we take 'the' away?"

I closed my eyes again and took in another few deep Breaths, smelling His Wildflowers, and I now opened my eyes, feeling Totally Connected.

"Excuse me," I said, "but with whom am I speaking?"

"Oh, Adam," he said. "Sorry. I forgot. I haven't been thinking very clearly."

"Well, Adam," I said, getting out of my chair and moving back by the large expanse of windows so I wouldn't be affected by his energy, "you know, I'm being told right now . . . that what you need to do is to find this answer on your own. Because, for me to tell you my answer wouldn't be a good fit, and this is a big one. Maybe even 'the' biggest for most Christians."

"All right, but how do I do this?" he asked once again. "Last night, I swear, I felt so confused and upset that it was even difficult for me to pray. I kept losing focus, because so much of what you've shared with us seems True, and even feels True, and also, I read your whole book more than once, so . . . well, I just don't know what to do, because I'm afraid that if I lose my Church and the whole structure that I've been brought up with, I might lose God and end up cutting off not just one ear, BUT BOTH EARS!"

He stopped and took in several deep GodBreaths, and blew out fast each time. "I now realize why there was a very large part of me that was against having you come to see us. We're old! We're retired! And so we just want to make peace within us, so we can—"

He was trembling, and tears were pouring down his face, but he wasn't bothering to wipe them off. I walked over to him and took the white handkerchief out of my back pocket that I always carried that my mother had given me years ago and had little red flowers and green leaves that she'd embroidered on it.

"Here," I said, "from my mother to you."

"Thank you," he said, taking the white handkerchief and wiping his eyes.

"No, thank you," I said. "For Totally Opening your Whole Heart and Soul."

He laughed. "Trust me, I didn't mean to," he said. "It just all came out."

"Yes, and that's the way it normally is in giving and in receiving. For this is who we, Human Beings, really are, Hollow Bones, Buffalo Bones, Holy Instruments of God."

"There!" he shouted. "YOU'VE DONE IT AGAIN! And this is awful, because I really did love *Rain of Gold* and I really do love most of what you've told us, but it also, well, destroys the Church! MY CHURCH! THE WHOLE WORLD'S CHURCH! Just look what all this profound thinking has done to you! You're not even a Catholic anymore!"

The whole room was silent. Adam had certainly brought everything back to square one. Then *Margarita* spoke with such a gentle tone that it helped us all to regain composure.

"Does it really destroy the Church?" she asked. "Or does it help Our Beloved Church to become what it originally professed to be, universal and all-inclusive?"

"BUT THAT'S NOT WHAT JESUS OR THE BIBLE SAY!" shouted Adam.

"Excuse me," I said, "but you do know that most scholars now agree that Jesus spoke Aramaic when he was with us here on earth."

"Yes, I understand that," said Adam.

"Well," I said, "there is no word for 'the' in the Aramaic Language."

"What? What are you saying?"

"I'm saying," I said, "that Jesus never said that He was 'the' only way. The Greek's translation added 'the' and 'only' was added by the English. So Our Lord Jesus said that He was 'a way', and/or He simply said He was 'way', and so His message was Totally about Inclusion and He was inviting All of Us to Be Sons and Daughters of God, Equally. Even the Romans and not just the Jews. And this only makes sense, because the Roman Empire controlled the whole known world and Jesus, Son of God, wanted to bring Peace to Our Whole World just as He wants to do today."

Adam bent over, gripping his stomach. "Then you're really serious about all this you've shared with us, even about the Vatican mo...mo...!" He began gagging, but nothing was coming up.

Mark and Joe rushed to help Adam over to a couch to lie down, and his body continued trembling and jerking.

"Okay," I said, "is anyone else feeling kind of sick?"

Half a dozen hands went up.

"You know," said another priest, "if we'd been told all this as young seminarians I'm quite sure we wouldn't have had any trouble accepting all this, because it does make sense. Why would the Son of God not invite us all to become sons and daughters of Our Holy Creator equally? And I can also see how this could revolutionize the whole Church and help unite all the different religions of the world. So, yes, I can see all this in my mind. I really can. But here, in my gut, I'm too old to accept any of this. I agree with Adam. You've come to us fifty to sixty years too late and what we now want is peace and tranquility."

"And who are you?"

"Oh, excuse me. Michael," he said.

"And how old are you, Michael?" I asked.

"I'm eighty," he said.

"Look," I said, "you're only eighty. You've only been into the most perfect age of seventy-eight for two little years, so come on, stop bullshitting yourself and realize that you're just getting started and you have a RESPONSIBILITY OF BECOMING A SACRED ELDER!" I shouted, startling him.

"But look what just happened to Adam," he said sheepishly, "and to Van Gogh. There's only so much that the human mind can take."

"You're right," I said. "There is only so much that the human mind can take with five senses, but now you Know that we have three centers for processing information, and with Our Full Natural Thirteen Senses, then there are no limitations. Van Gogh, Nijinsky, Rimbaud, all of these guys would have had no *problemas* if their Full Natural Thirteen Senses had been firing."

"Really, you think so?"

"I Know so!" I said. "And you Know it was a capital 'K', too. Look, Western Civilization is like a big twelve-cylinder engine that's only using four of its cylinders, so, of course, it's easy to go berserk. And also note, all those who broke down were men, not women, and Anne Frank and my two *mamagrandes* endured 10,000 times more horror and confusion and still they didn't go insane. Instead these women rose up with their full powers as ANGELS STRAIGHT FROM GOD!

"So, no! You will not check out! You are eighty years and Totally. Available. So stand up. Come on, get up out of your chair, and LEAP into your Balanced Female and Male Energies and take on your responsibility of becoming a Sacred ELDER!

"Look, *Amigo,* there's really no turning back for you guys. You took an oath to Be Of Service for God Goding, and so you now keep your word, because, you see, the aging process from a Spiritual Point of View starts reversing when you reach the age of sixty-five and you have Balanced your Male and Female Energies, because Spiritual Aging can actually override physical aging to the degree that you accept your Full God-Given Spirituality. Ask Mary. Ask Matt."

And so Mary told Michael that she was eighty-six and she, too, had thought she was over the hill and her days of service were over, but then last night all these great feelings of Love*Amor* had come BURSTING into her Heart and Soul, and she now felt as Full of Energy and Purposeful as when she'd been a young nun.

"And I can now see," she said to him, "that I'd lost faith, well, not in God, but in my ability to make a difference, because of all the undermining politics of clerical life and all the terrible news that we see on T.V."

"Exactly," said Matt, "but now with the Vatican moving to Ireland for 100 years, and then to *México* where my grandparents were from for another 100 years, has sent my whole world into such a spin of wonderment and possibilities, that if I just keep calm and don't let myself go into fear or doubt, then I'm flying in ECSTASY WITH ENERGY. And also remember that the Vatican was moved to France for nearly a century," he added. "So there has been a precedent."

"No, that's not entirely true," said Michael. "What happened was that the King of France appointed his own Pope. And what Mr. Villaseñor is suggesting is that the Vatican itself will move to Ireland. Is this correct?" he said, turning to me.

I nodded. "Yes, this was part of the information that was Transmitted into me in Madrid."

"When Jesus came to you?" said Michael with a little smile.

"Yes," I said, refusing to be taken in by his tone of sarcasm.

"And it makes so much sense!" shouted Matt excitedly. "Because back then our whole known world was centered around the Mediterranean Sea, and so Italy, Rome, seemed the logical location to place the head of the Catholic Church, but now that we Know about the entire globe, it only makes sense to move the Vatican, and keep moving it every 100 years around the globe! OH, THIS IS SO EXCITING! And it makes so much sense that I can actually see it already done!"

"Yes!" I said. "Because it's already written in the Stars! You see, the Future doesn't necessarily come after the Present. Time is circular. This movement is, in fact, already completed, finished, done, and a long forgotten memory in the furthest reaches of Our Universe!"

"He's right!" said Matt. "And Our Lord Jesus is with us Right Here! Right Now! He's never left us. Oh, I can now see it all so clearly! This is WONDERFUL! And Gaelic makes perfect sense! And then in *México* an Indian dialect of the Yucatan! Yes, the language of your Great Great Great Great Great Aunt, Mother

Of No Specific Child! And in doing all this, Our Holy Catholic Church becomes of Goding. Not of men. But of men and of women with us having Women Popes and Women Cardinals and Women Bishops and Women Priests. Can't you all see it? Our Church becomes not stagnant, but SACRED AND FOREVER CHANGING and will then continue for 50,000 years. Could this be right?" he asked.

"It's perfectly right," I said, "because Our Mother Earth works in 26,000 year cycles. One cycle Being of Male Energy like we're just completing, and the other Being of Feminine Energy that we are just starting. So 52,000 years is One Complete Cycle of Male and Feminine Energy, which includes the last 2,000 years."

I stopped and glanced around. They were listening. Not necessarily agreeing, but listening. I took in a large deep GodBreath.

"You see, back at one time, before organized nations and religion, we were all Natural Indigenous People, as I've said again and again. And we weren't ignorant savages, but highly Spiritual Beings and so by us Collectively going Back To Our Future Our Holy Church will then Be in the Sacred Flow of Creation Creating, and hence, Eternal!

"And this is exactly what Jesus Transmitted into me in Madrid, Spain back in November of 1992 when *mi familia* and I and a group of Native Americans went to Spain to Forgive the king and queen for all of the atrocities that Spain committed around the globe, and as a United Group, we Planted Our Snow Goose Global Thanksgiving Flag for World-Wide Harmony and Peace and . . . and Abundance for All."

"Did the king and queen attend your ceremony?" asked a priest.

"No, they didn't, but they did send their nephew."

"So you're telling us that all that really did happen and it's not just a wild figment of your imagination?"

I closed my eyes, and took in a big deep Breath, blowing out fast. "Yeah, looking back I, too, almost feel that it really didn't happen, and I'm just full of crap. But, then, I go back to that time and I remember how I'd been so confident that the king and queen would understand and come to our ritual, but then once we got to Madrid, I began to lose all focus. My thinking, doubting brain took over, and I became so full of fear and . . . and feeling ridiculous. Who was I to have ever thought that I could come with a group of people to forgive a king and queen? So feeling exhausted and full of confusion, I lied down in my little hotel room bed and reminding Our Almighty that We had a deal, and I really needed help.

"Well, I must've fallen asleep, because when I awoke, I could see that there was a man at the far end of my little room and he was surrounded by a Bright Golden Light that lit up the whole room, and yet was soft and didn't hurt my eyes.

"I rubbed my eyes and looked again, and suddenly I Knew with a capital 'K' that this was Jesus Christ. I got up on my elbows to see Him better and I could see that He was hovering about two feet off the floor. I got up and went to Him and this was when He reached into His chest and brought out His Most Holy Sacred Heart.

"A real pulsating heart with arteries and everything and He reached out handing me His Heart*Corazón*, and . . . and in the act of doing this, I understood He was endorsing our trip to Spain and everything we were prepared to do, and then Miraculously He, who'd been of brown skin and looking part American Indian like me, now changed into all the different Human People of the world. In features! In skin color! In robes! In eyes! In everything! And this was when I Knew that Jesus is in Everyone of Us. You, Me, We, all of Us! And I was no longer lost or confused. No, I once more KNEW EXACTLY why we'd come to Spain, and what we were to do!"

"But the king and queen didn't come to your ceremony so you could forgive them and Spain?"

"No, they didn't, but like I said they did send their nephew because we'd contacted their Spanish embassy, and so they Knew about us and our intent. WOW! Let's just call it a day, and we'll get more into this *mañana*. Remember, tomorrow is *otro milagro de Dios*!"

Mark raised his hand. "Excuse me," he said, "but when we got back from running you asked me how it went for me last night. And I told you very productive, and yet very strange, and that I didn't want to say anything to you about it, because I wanted to share it with our group."

I nodded. "Okay, so please do share."

He stood up. "You see," he said, turning to everyone, "I'm not here because I had a nervous breakdown as some of you might believe. I'm here, because, well, I, too, proposed to a nun and she accepted." He stopped, taking in a deep Breath. "So we are now both leaving the Church so we can marry. And I'll tell you," he said, "I'm so much in Love with Josefina, whom I met in Ecuador, that my whole world has literally changed upside down, and I've come to the realization that Our Lord God can Be Nothing but Love*Amor*, and that all there is, IS LOVE*AMOR* THROUGHOUT OUR UNIVERSE!"

He stopped again, Breathing deeply. "You see," he added, "I'd never heard of Mr. Villaseñor or of his writings, but then I was sent here for six months so I can, well, reconsider what Josefina and I are proposing to do, and I found that our nuns were talking about nothing else but *Rain of Gold*, so I read the book not once, but five times so far, and I now see that what I saw in our Native American Sisters of Ecuador is what *Rain of Gold* is really all about. Just like his two beloved grandmothers, *Doña Guadalupe* and *Doña*

Margarita, didn't 'believe' in God, but 'Lived' with God and were so full of Wisdom and Pure *Amor* and Indestructible Faith in One Almighty, so are our Sisters in Ecuador.

"And it troubled me, because Our American and European Sisters are good-hearted wonderful people, too, and yet I could feel that something was missing, but I had no idea what that something was until now that Mr. Villaseñor, himself, told us that even he, who wrote *Rain of Gold*, didn't understand his own book until that Navajo and big Lakota explained his own book to him. Then I understood that Language Truly does Own Us, as Mr. Villaseñor has stated.

"Also, it now makes sense to me that we have more than five senses. For instance, when I was about ten years old, my younger brother Luke suddenly awoke in the middle of the night and started telling us that our dad had had a car accident and that he was dying, so we had to pray or he'd die. So my mother and I and my sisters and little brother all started praying, and we received a call about an hour later that our dad had been in a terrible wreck, and yet miraculously he was going to live.

"And so, what I'm saying with all this is . . . that with our Natural Multi-Sensory Perception of Our Full Thirteen Senses and Our Understanding that Creation is still going on at this very moment, then that experience my younger brother had becomes available to all of us. And this is Our Future! Our Destiny! For the Miraculous to become part of Our Norm. Tell me, how else can we expect to keep going if we don't move into a Reality of Miracles!"

He glanced around.

"There is no other way," he continued. "Because it's going to take Miracles to get us out of our present situation, and now that we know that we have Three Centers for processing experience and information we can do it. We really can, especially now that we Know our Thinking Brain Center is our smallest computer, and that Our Intuitive Heart Center and Our Psychic Soul Center are LIMITLESS! Just imagine if all of our Catholic schools began teaching that we have a Multi-Sensory Perception of Thirteen Senses! Our youth would automatically start GeniusJesusing!"

He couldn't stop smiling. "What a concept JesusGeniusing! What Possibilities! What Energy! What Purity! What—oh, my God Goding! This is all so wonderful! It's like all, all, all of ME HAS BECOME ALIVE and I'm now no longer *'WITH'* JESUS. I am 'of' Jesus, meaning that I, too, am now a Son of God."

Smiling, he glanced around once more. "And now I can see that this is the something that was missing with Our American and European Sisters and Priests—the understanding that we have Thirteen Natural Senses, that Creation is ongoing, and so we are in an Active Partnership with God. Then like Mr. Villaseñor's grandmothers, I am now FULL OF HOPE AND INDESTRUCTIBLE FAITH, because I no longer 'believe' in Miracles! Oh, no, I 'KNOW' Miracles, and so I can now 'DO' Miracles just as my younger brother Luke did at such a tender age!"

He stopped and took in a great big deep GodBreath.

"Oh, for the first time in my life I feel Complete and Whole," he added, "and I'm so happy! BIG BIG HAPPY! Being not 'WITH' Jesus, but Being 'OF' Jesus and remembering that Jesus told us that what He did, we would do more, and we can! We really can do more!"

Father James stood up and began applauding. Instantly everyone joined him, standing up and applauding, too.

I was crying.

I was crying with tears of ecstasy streaming down my face, and the scent of Wildflowers came to me. I smiled, and said, "Thank You, Jesus."

"Thank you," I heard Him say right back to me.

I wiped the tears out of my eyes and glanced around. I could see that many people were Aglow with Golden Light.

"We're Glowing," I said. "Glance around and you'll see."

"Yes, we are," said Mark, "and I can also see that—as we Catholics come out of hiding behind archaic dogma and take on what it means to Be A Complete And Real Catholic with the whole definition of all-inclusive, of general interest and value, having broad sympathies and understanding, hence liberal, that we will all start Glowing as we move into the Holy Light of God Goding. Albert Einstein was right, all there is, is change, and Creation never stopped and never began and is ongoing right here. Right now. Forever Within Creation Creating.

"And this isn't a wild dream, but Our responsibility—not just as Catholics but as Human Beings—and true followers of Jesus Christ to do as Our Lord did on the cross and show Compassion, Forgiveness, Kindness, and drop all of our archaic dogma of judgment and righteousness and exclusion.

"And we do this—as I learned in Ecuador and Mr. Villaseñor shared with us—by doing as some tribes *do* in Central America. When walking through the rainforest and two strangers meet, they automatically drop their weapons, place both of their hands behind their back, touch foreheads, and say, 'You are another me, and I am another you," and they then look into each other's eyes and smile. And this morning I did this with myself in the mirror, and I saw—"

"AND YOU SAW AN ANGEL!" shouted Mary.

"That's right," said Mark. "I saw an Angel and realized for the first time in my life that that's who we all really are. Angels, Messengers of Light, as Albert Einstein said he was when he received his Theory of Relativity."

"The same thing happened to me!" said Mary. "And I wasn't going to share this, because I was so embarrassed, but now I'm not, because I can now see that this is who we True Followers of Jesus are, Angels!"

With great excitement people began now talking among themselves. Father James winked at me and I nodded to him, then big, burly Joe came forward.

"Well, I didn't see an Angel in my mirror this morning," said Joe, "but I did see a very happy face!"

Everyone laughed.

And it was *Margarita* who now also spoke up. "I also didn't see an Angel in my mirror," she said. "But I, too, saw a very happy face."

And saying this, she began walking across the room to Joe with such regal confidence. Joe was all eyes, taking in her Beauty, and maybe they didn't see it yet, but I'm sure that most of us did see it. *Margarita* and Joe were, indeed, Aglow with Angelic Love*Amor* Energy as they drew closer and closer to each other.

Then *Margarita* placed both of her hands behind herself and bent forward. Joe placed his two hands behind himself, bending forward, and they touched foreheads, oh, so gently. Then they straightened up, and looked into each other's eyes. No happier smiles had ever been seen on this side of Heaven. Before our very eyes, Joe and *Margarita* had TRANSFORMED! Not only becoming Angels of Illuminating Light, but actually getting younger and younger and younger!

Then it was *Margarita* who reached out to take the large man in her arms. And Joe wasn't shocked this time and took her in his arms, too. There wasn't a dry eye in the whole room. *Margarita* ninety-one. Joe eighty-six. And they'd known each other for over sixty years and now, at last, they were in each other's arms, and . . . and kissing.

"Well, well," said Mark, "I almost wasn't going to share any of this, but look at the results it has caused. So are you two," he continued, "going to join Josefina and me and also get married? Remember, this is a very emotionally-driven planet, so any time we bring Love*Amor* to Our Mother Earth we are helping to heal her."

"Well, then, if that's the case," said Joe, turning to *Margarita*, "then I say—"

"YES!" shouted the ex-mother superior. "We certainly want to do our share of helping to Heal Our Beloved Mother Earth!"

"Sounds good to me," said Joe, never letting go of her.

"Oh, I remember the first time I saw you, Joe," she said. "You were clearing land of rock and brush in preparation for a garden behind our convent. It was a hot summer day and you took off your shirt and, well, you looked like a Greek god. I couldn't stop staring at you, so I ran and would never let myself ever look at you again, even when you were fully clothed."

His eyes got huge. "And all these years I thought that I'd done something or said something that had offended you."

"Oh, no!" she said. "All these years I've been afraid of these feelings I've had for you, Joe!"

"And I've been afraid of these feelings I've had for you," he said.

You could hear a pin drop. Two Hearts, two Souls, finally coming together after all these years.

I took in a deep Breath, instantly smelling Wildflowers again. I glanced around, and here was Our Lord Jesus by the windows at the far end of the room. He was smiling. I smiled, too, and then in a quick flash, Jesus came SoulSpinning all through us with a Wildflower Scent of Holy Love*Amor*!

"Well," said Mark, Glowing with Jesus's Light, "I can now see that it was no accident I was sent to Ecuador and fell in love. And it's no accident I was sent here for the six months and introduced to *Rain of Gold*. And . . . it's no accident that you, brilliant good Sisters, had Mr. Villaseñor come to us. For it's True, everything he has shared with us, we, all of us, already Knew deep within Our Kingdom of God, which we have finally Activated.

"And to move Our Holy Church to Ireland makes total sense. And not because I'm part Irish, but because, remember, Ireland saved Western Civilization by keeping all the records and books through the Dark Ages, and then what did the English do? Starve us! Enslave us through indentured servitude. So, yes, Ireland, then *México*, who's suffered even more, then the Philippines, of course, and the Purity of Love*Amor* for God Goding, a Verb, will be re-established, and these last 2,000 years will then be nothing compared to our Grand Fabulous All-Inclusive Future of Our Holy Church. And then Josefina and I can be married, and we don't have to leave the Church, and Joe, you and *Margarita* can do the same.

"OH, I, too, AWOKE LAUGHING THIS MORNING, I felt so happy with all that Mr. Villaseñor has been sharing with us!" said Mark. "And then I looked in the mirror and saw that I'd given Birth to God by becoming my very own Guardian Angel, and so yes, of course, it's True that I, that We all come across the Universe gathering Stardust to help God Goding plant His Ongoing Garden of Heaven on Earth. And so I say, 'THANK YOU, God Goding! Thank You for orchestrating this Whole Living, Breathing Symphony of Creating Creation! WE ARE BLESSED!"

And having said all this, Mark just stood before us, SMILING AND GLOWING WITH ECSTASY! And his VIBRATIONAL FREQUENCIES were of such Intensity that they didn't just affect us, who were in the room with him, but they affected all of

Creation Creating around Our Whole Mother Earth, and to the furthest REACHES OF OUR UNIVERSE!

Outside the Canadian Geese began HONKING with *gusto,* and coming up to the windows, flapping their GREAT GIGANTIC WINGS!

And the Trees began dancing their limbs.

And the Grass and Flowers took on Jesus's Holy Scent Of Heaven On Earth!

Oh, yes, Our Beloved Mother Earth certainly was Our most Emotionally LOVE*AMOR* DRIVEN PLANET of Our Six Sister Planets! And so by healing her, we also helped heal HER BELOVED TWIN SISTER!

Chapter Twelve

TIME STOOD STILL.

Holy Timeless Time stood still. We were now all like in a Trance within Our Own Delicious-Smelling Kingdom of God, feeling smooth relaxing Big Big Happy. Finally it was Father James who spoke.

"Well," he said, "to help all the rest of us become Our Own Guardian Angel, I suggest that this is a good time for us to bring out that special bottle of *tequila* that we purchased in your name, Victor. Eh, what do you all say? Should we go over what we've learned before we break for dinner, or should we have a shot of *tequila*?"

"*TEQUILA*!" shouted everyone.

"Good, then *tequila* it is!" said Father James. "And we had difficulty finding it, Victor," he added, turning to me, "but we were finally able to locate a few bottles of your favorite."

"*Herradura*?" I said, licking my lips.

"Yes!"

"Oh, wonderful!" I said. "So then, by all means, let's have a shot right now!"

We all went into the big main dining room with the large stone fireplace and Mary brought out a tray of those tiny beautiful wine glasses that people normally use after dinner for sherry or port. We were each served a generous shot of *tequila,* then we gathered in front of the fireplace, which had a good-size fire going.

"TO OUR SISTERS, who had the courage to invite our author of *Rain of Gold* to come to see us!" said Father James.

"And to Victor, who also had the courage to accept our invitation!" added Mary.

We all lifted our beautiful little crystal glasses and took a sip of our *Herradura*, which originally had been made by Villaseñors.

"And now I'd like to make a toast to Our First Woman Pope!" I added.

"TO OUR FIRST WOMAN POPE!" people shouted, and most of us shot down our remaining *tequila.*

"Oh, that feels SO GOOD!" shouted Sister Mary. "The burn of *tequila* and the image of Our First Woman Pope Being Guided by Our Blessed Mother and Jesus and Legions of Angels to Ireland!"

And saying this, Mary now gave a SHOUT OF JOY, then suddenly threw her glass into the fire where it shattered against the stone.

We were all SHOCKED!

But no one more than Sister Mary herself.

But then she started giggling and laughing with such wild abandonment that two other nuns followed her example, finishing off their *tequilas* and throwing their own glasses into the fire, too, and now all three nuns were beside themselves, laughing with *carcajadas*!

The priests, I could see, were stunned. But not the nuns. Oh, no, now it became a major event of more nuns finishing off their *tequilas* and throwing their glasses into the fire, then laughing with WILD CRAZY*LOCO GUSTO*!

"Well, well," said Father James, serving Mark and me and himself another *tequila*, "I can now see why Native Americans call liquor fire water. Our good nuns are, indeed, ON FIRE!"

"Amen!" said Mark.

"Awomen! Achildren! Amen!" I added as we now sipped our second shots. "My dad, a bootlegger, always told us that in the first half of a liquor bottle you find God, but in the second half you find the Devil if . . . if you're not careful."

They both laughed and Matt now came over to join us along with two other priests. Father James was serving them their second shot when we saw that our good nuns were not going to let us, the men, out-do them. Oh, no, a couple of giggling full-of-mischief sisters had brought out another tray of crystal glasses and Mary now opened up another bottle of *Herradura* and began serving.

"FANTASTIC!" said Mark. "Just look at them and hear their laughter! It was also Josefina's great joyful laugh that opened my Soul and gave WINGS TO MY *CORAZÓN*!!"

"There's no turning back for them now!" said Matt.

"Yes, and it's about time!" I added.

"I agree," said Father James, "and in support, I'm joining them!"

And saying this, this most dignified looking of all priests, who was, in fact, an Archangel, now walked across the room, drank off his *tequila*, then with a shout of *gusto* he, too, threw his antique French crystal glass into the fire where it also shattered against the stone.

"TO OUR FIRST WOMAN POPE!" he shouted.

"YES!" screeched the nuns. "TO OUR FIRST WOMAN POPE!"

"May she be full of LOVE AND COMPASSION!" yelled one nun.

"MAY SHE BE AS STRONG AND CUNNING AS VICTOR'S FANTASTIC GRANDMOTHERS!" shouted Mary.

"AMEN! AWOMEN! ACHILDREN!" shouted several nuns.

"AWOMEN! ACHILDREN! AMEN!" shouted Matt and Mark.

"EXACTLY!" I said. "Snow Geese flying in V-formations across the Father Sky with mother and children leading and men Following Infront!"

And so we continued celebrating, but, I can tell you, not all the priests were happy with what was going on. Finally one priest stepped forward.

"This is PRECISELY why so many of us priests were against bringing this author of *Rain of Gold* to see us! Look what has happened to us! These glasses are genuine antique French crystal, and you're behaving as disrespectful as when the author's grandmother would pray her rosary in the outhouse!"

I was impressed. This tall elegant-looking priest had never uttered a single word until now that he was livid with rage. And I was just about to go over to him and offer him a double *tequila* when our feisty little Sister Mary came forward, getting right into his face.

"OH, STOP IT, JOHN!" she barked. "We're the ones who wash and care for these glasses! NOT YOU! So don't pretend as if these French crystal glasses are important to you! What's really bothering you? Eh, John, could it be our exuberance, and that maybe we won't do your laundry anymore!?"

And saying this, Mary burst out laughing like there was no tomorrow! And all the nuns followed her, laughing their heads off! The tall priest looked mortified.

"OH, JOHN, JUST LOOK AT YOU!" shouted Mary. "You, who's always so full of yourself and can never stop lecturing us, now doesn't Know what to say! THIS IS WONDERFUL! Here, let me hug you and give you a kiss, my frightened little boy!"

But John bolted, not letting Mary get near him.

"Excuse me," said *Margarita*. People quickly quieted down. "Because, you see, even though I haven't thrown my glass into the fire and am going to keep this little glass to remind me of this day for the rest of my life—I *do* accept Sister Mary's behavior."

She stopped and coughed, clearing her throat and she now took on the full power of her well-practiced air of a Mother Superior before continuing.

"You see, we must begin to understand what it means to relocate our Vatican from Rome to Ireland. This is going to be nothing less than as large a Global Statement as when our Thirteen Little Colonies broke away from the eminent powers of Great Britain. It was the fall of royalty and the rise of everyday people. For the people, of the people, and by the people, and this time we women, along with the help of priests like Father James and Mark and Matt and Joe, will be an equal part of The People, by The People, for The People, as we move to Ireland and not just have Our First Woman Pope, but also move away from the extravagance of French crystal to goblets in Ireland, then *jarritos de barro* in Mexico!"

"*Jarritos* of what?" said Father John.

"BRILLIANT!" shouted Mark, putting two fingers to his mouth and whistling an ear-piercing whistle. "You are ABSOLUTELY right, *Hermana Margarita!* Cups made of clay that are affordable by everyone! Instead of French crystal that's only affordable by the very rich!

"Oh, yes, I can see it now, our move to Ireland will include bringing a halt to these last 2,000 years of excess and corruption and bring us back to the reality that Our Lord Jesus was born in a manger, and so the Foundation of Our Church has always been about Humility, Kindness, and Forgiveness. In other words, not just supporting the poor like Mother Teresa so well did, but for us to walk Our Talk, embracing the purity that less is more, and Create a World of Inclusion where it's easier to *Be* Good-Hearted People!

"Truly, after working with the poverty of Ecuador, it was an embarrassment for me to see all the wealth that Our Church has accumulated over the centuries, and how so many of my fellow priests would brag about how much money they'd brought to their diocese as if they were working on Wall Street. Is this what God had in mind when He sent His Son to us? COME ON! LET'S GET REAL!"

"Are you then suggesting that we abandon, or worse, destroy the Vatican in Rome?" asked John.

"Of course not," said *Margarita*, stepping in. "That great ostentatious place will be made into a museum of some sort and opened to the public!"

"I agree," said Mark. "The walls of exclusion will come down, and it will become a great museum and concert hall for all to see."

"And as we were prepared to tell Our Queen and King of Spain," I said, "that all the gold that was taken from Our New World by Our Church, through mostly Spain and Portugal, will be given back through the education of the poor over a 1,000 year plan. And this is how the Queen of Spain will redeem herself by once more leading Our Way, just as she did 500 years ago with Columbus. You see," I said, closing my *Ojo*Eyes, "it's always really been about Music, Our Eighth Sense, that Activates Our Third Center, Our Soul Computer for the Greater Glory of God!

"So, yes, the Vatican in Rome will continue to lead by 'following infront', but no longer with dogma and . . . and instead through Our Sacred Symphony of Creation Creating, which is Our Holy Voice of God Goding, and as our locations of the Vatican move around the globe for the next 50,000 years so will the Music of Our Beloved Church keep Changing and Growing and Glowing with Compassion, meaning passion in common, realizing that Our Church's Holy Locations are, in fact, a LOVE*AMOR* Global Rosary Design that can be seen GLOWING from Outer Space."

I stopped, took in a deep GodBreath and blew out fast. "Oh, I'll never forget the first time I heard Enya. I just Knew that through this Incredible Instrument of Pure Heartfelt Music, God was calling, calling, and informing us all about Our First Woman Pope and Our Godvolution Movement of Our Church to Ireland.

"Truly, next time you listen to Enya close your eyes, place both hands over your Heart and your Soul will come Alive, HARMONIZING OUR SPIRITUAL VIBRATIONAL FREQUENCIES WITH THE SYMPHONY OF OUR UNIVERSE!"

"ONE UNITED VERSE! ONE UNITED SONG!" shouted Mary, finishing off her second *tequila* with *gusto!*

"Yes, thank you, Mary," I said. "And this is exactly why Jesus came to me in Madrid, Spain, because it's never been about great cathedrals and accumulating gold—which automatically lead to corruption. No, it's always been about each of us reaching into our own chest and giving each other Our Most Precious Treasure, OUR PULSATING HEART*CORAZÓN*, and in doing this we will *be* Activating OUR DORMANT ILLUMINATION of Our Global Rosary Design OF OUR CHURCHES!"

"Are you saying that Our Catholic Churches make a Rosary Design around the globe?" asked a priest.

"Yes," I said, "almost."

I took in a deep GodBreath. "You see, Our Catholic Churches are a Wondrous Heart*Corazon* Miracle. It's only our all-male based control that's out of whack. Check it out and you'll see. And now by us Collectively dropping all Our Doubts and Fears and putting Our Hands behind Our Backs and Touching Foreheads, we will then Activate this Design. For you are —"

"For you are another me, and I am another you," several nuns and priests quickly added.

"Exactly," said *Margarita*, "and for me to come to this Illumination was when I finally had the courage to not *be* afraid or ashamed of these feelings I've had inside of me for all these years for this wonderful gorgeous man!"

"Me, gorgeous?" said Joe.

She nodded. "Yes, Joe," she said with tears coming to her *Ojo*Eyes, "all these years you have been my Greek god!"

"That's how I see you, *Margarita*," he said with tears of joy also pouring down his face. "For over twenty years I was attached to our Marines and I saw action. I was beside our boys when they were dying. And yet I can tell you it takes more courage to admit and accept these feelings that I've been carrying within me for years for you, my dear Angel, than to go to war.

"WAR IS EASY COMPARED TO THESE TENDER FEELINGS WE CARRY INSIDE OF US! Since kids we play war games! We see war movies! Football included! Which leads us to *be* more and more frightened to open Our Hearts, until there with Our Last Dying Breath, we can't run away from Our True Feelings anymore. So yes, I love you, my fabulous fine lady with ALL MY HEART AND SOUL!"

"And I love you, my dear man, with all my Heart and Soul."

And they put their hands behind their backs and bent forward touching foreheads, and they began to Glow, and we, too, then began Glowing. Like smiles, like laughter, so did Spiritual Glowing cause others to start Glowing.

And once more the Honkers could Feel Our Wonderfulness, and they came rushing up to the windows FLAPPING THEIR GREAT WINGS AND HONKING WITH *GUSTO*!

Chapter Thirteen

We broke for dinner.

We were a very different group now.

None of us even needed to take our rest time before we had dinner.

The nuns, not the priests, led us in prayer at the table. It was a delicious meal of wild turkey cooked in Mexican green sauce, just as the altar boys used to chant in Church back in *CarlosMalo*. Then we went into the lounge area to wrap up. Father James took center stage.

"Is there anything more you'd like to share with us?" he asked me. "If not, then we'd like to open a session of us asking you questions."

I took in a great big deep Breath. "Yes," I said, "now I do Feel is a good time for me to share the story of my mother Lupe's Miracle Mango Tree." I glanced around. "You see, this story will put into a very real perspective everything that we've been going over in a nutshell. Ready?"

They all nodded their heads, even the priests who'd had *problemas* participating.

"Good, so fasten your seat belts, because we're BLASTING OFF," I said, suddenly Feeling Full of Wonderful Energy! "It all got started back in 1948 when I was eight years old and my little sister Linda, who's four years younger than me, went racing out of the house, shouting, "Papa and Mama are home! Papa and Mama and Tencha are home!

"Tencha was our older sister, who was eighteen, and she and our parents had left for Mexico right after our older brother Joseph's funeral, who'd died at sixteen.

"I'd come running down from the corrals when I'd heard my sister Linda shouting and my dad honking his car horn. I'd been feeding livestock and helping milk our cows, then with my fingers sticking up out of the warm sweet-smelling sticky milk, our calves would suck the milk off my fingers, emptying the bucket in no time.

"That evening, I'll never forget, our mother took my little sister Linda and me aside and told us that she'd brought something special from Mexico that was full of magic. My sister and I were all eyes as my mother took a little flat box out of her purse and began to unwrap it.

"This is a *mango* seed," she said to us full of enthusiasm.

"The seed was oval shape and dry and white and flat and about the size of my hand. My sister Linda and I turned and we looked at each other. I guess we'd expected something like Indian jewelry or a stuffed frog with great big eyes.

"This seed comes from the sweetest, most beautiful *mango* I ever ate!" said our mother with a big smile.

"And it has magic?" asked my sister.

"Yes, you'll see," said our mother.

"Is it from deep in *México*?" I asked.

"Yes, from right outside of *Mazatlan, Sinaloa* in a beautiful rich valley where I'm sure my mother's Yaqui People once lived. You see," she said, handing us the big long seed, "I am going to nurture it and plant it with Love*Amor* and it's going to give us the most beautiful sweet *mangos* you have ever tasted!"

"The seed had long little thin lines running its length and a rough-feeling texture and tiny white whiskers along its edge. My sister and I took turns inspecting it and then we handed it back to our mother. We were really disappointed.

"But then I'll never forget, the next day when I came home from school my mother was in the kitchen banging a small nail into the middle of the *mango* seed. Then in each hole she'd made with the nail, she inserted a wooden toothpick, and all this time she'd be smiling and humming and singing and Being So Happy which was really good, because ever since my brother died our mother had mostly been crying.

"Then after she'd inserted toothpicks all the way around the middle of the *mango* seed, she filled a small glass with water and put the *mango* seed lengthways into the glass and the toothpicks only allowed the seed to submerge halfway into the water, because the long toothpicks stuck out beyond the rim of the glass. Then I'll never forget, my mother dropped a Bayer aspirin into the glass and I watched it go to the bottom and start to dissolve with little white smoke-like lines going upward.

"There," said my mother, "the poor little seed got a headache with me poking holes in her, but now with her crown of toothpicks and my Love*Amor*, she will heal and flourish!"

"Saying this, *mi mama* began making dinner and I changed clothes and hurried out to the corrals to help my dad and our workers feed livestock and milk cows and feed our calves.

"Well, what can I say, for the rest of that school year I'd come home all excited to see my mother Being So Happy with her *mango* seed that she kept it on the windowsill above the kitchen sink. The seed began to grow long white whiskers that in no time filled up the little jar. My mother explained to us that these were roots, and then one day she told me to get her some old dried out horse manure.

"Not cow manure," she said, "because it's too strong and these young roots are still too tender."

"So that day I watched my mother plant her *mango* seed in a little pot with top soil and horse manure and talk and sing to it, explaining to the *mango* seed that yes, she was far from home, but with *amor* and nourishment this could *be* her new home.

"Then with summer coming and school ending, I was out with the horses with my dad and little sister almost all the time, so I all but forgot about the *mango* seed until one night at the dinner table our mother said, "I have a very important announcement to make, and so I want you all to pay close attention."

"There was just my dad and mother and sister Linda and me at the dinner table. Our older sister Tencha was living in San Diego.

"I want all of you to Know that I've been taking my little *mango* plant and putting her in sunlight for a couple of hours every day, and she now feels strong enough for me to plant her. And so," said our mother, taking a deep Breath, "I want you all to Know that I'm going to start walking around our ranch and asking my little *mango* tree where she would like to live."

"My little sister and I almost burst out laughing, thinking it was pretty funny for our mother to be asking a plant where it wanted to live. But our dad coughed that special cough of his, and we Knew better than to laugh.

"And I will not permit anyone to laugh or make fun of me and my little *mango* tree, because just as my mother taught me that all of God's Creation is Alive, you too will get to see this *mango* far from home grow big and strong and flourish, because of all the Love*Amor* that I have shown her.

"So not one snicker or joke, because this is a Sacred Holy Quest that I'm doing, just as *mi Madre* did up in the Rain of Gold canyon, where so many others couldn't get their corn and string beans and squash to grow, and yet your *mamagrande's* garden flourished. Do you understand? And also I want you to know that once I plant this little tree, every day at three in the afternoon I will sing and give her all my Love*Amor*."

"Yes, of course, we understand," said our father. "My Beloved *Madre* did the same thing up in the high lands *de Los Altos de Jalisco* and that's why we, too, had such delicious corn."

"My sister and I both nodded, but in truth we didn't understand. All we Knew was that for well over a week we saw our mother walking around our ranch talking to her little potted *mango* tree, asking the eight-inch tall plant if she felt at home at this place, or if she felt more at home at this other place.

"Then one day at dinner, our mother informed us that she'd found the place where the little *mango* wanted to live."

"How do you know?" asked Linda.

"Because every time we get near this spot, her leaves pick up and begin to smile. Plants Know where they want to nest just like birds," she added. "The place she chose is near the swimming pool area next to the driveway so she can get plenty of sunlight, and yet be close enough to the house so she wouldn't get lonely."

"Trees can get lonely?" asked Linda.

"Of course," said our mother, "all of Creation needs Attentive Love*Amor*. My mother always told me that this is what we were sent to do here on Mother Earth, to help *Papito Dios* plant His Sacred Garden with Attentive Love*Amor* throughout all of Creation."

"So we all helped our mother plant her little tree and she now began to water her tiny *mango* tree with a mixture of cow manure and other ingredients. AND OH, WOW, DID THAT LITTLE TREE TAKE OFF LIKE NOBODY'S BUSINESS, and within three years it was taller than me with strong little branches and a profusion of large dark leaves, then it began producing *mangos*. Big ones! Little ones! And all so colorful—red and yellow and orange, and with a fragrance of heaven that you could smell all the way to my mother's rose garden in front of our home! And yes, they were the sweetest tasting *mangos* we'd ever tasted!

"The years passed and it seemed like every other year our *mango* tree gave us—not just a few *mangos*—but a bumper crop of 100s of pounds of *mangos*, and yet different than in Mexico where *mangos* got ripe in the summer, our *mangos* didn't ripen until mid-October through late-November and sometimes even into December and January, because I guess, Being this far north, they needed those extra days of sunlight in order to get ripe.

"Years later, I married Barbara and we had two sons, David and Joseph. One year we went to the huge San Diego County Fair in Del Mar to look at the livestock, see the horse shows, and ride the Ferris wheel. Then we were walking around seeing the sights when we came to a place that was selling young *mango* trees that they guaranteed would produce fruit, even this far north.

"We stopped. My wife Barbara and our sons all Knew the story of my mother's Miraculous *Mango* Tree.

"Do these really produce fruit?" I asked, fully realizing that most *mango* trees throughout Southern California didn't produce fruit and were simply used as ornamental trees because of their big dark green leaves.

"Yes," said the man, who was probably in his mid-sixties and was sitting alongside a younger man and woman. "Would you like to take one home?" he asked.

"Oh, no, thank you," I said. "We already have a *mango* tree at home that produces 100s of pounds of *mangos*, so many, in fact, that we can't eat them all."

"Impossible!" said the man, glancing at the woman and man beside him. He got to his feet. "Do you have any idea how long it takes for a tree or plant to acclimate to its environment before it can produce?"

"No, I don't," I said.

"Well, scientists say it literally took corn 100s of 1,000s of years to acclimatize from its origin in Central America and go up into Mexico and North America and down to Peru and South America."

"I could see that the man was upset.

"But my mother-in-law's *mango* tree does produce fruit," said Barbara.

"I took Barbara's hand and glanced at our boys. My heart was pounding.

"Look," I said to the man, "we might not know anything about corn taking 100s of 1,000s of years to acclimate, but we do know that the grandmother of these two boys has a *mango* tree that produces fruit every year, and a huge amount every other year." I took in a deep Breath. "I was just a little boy back in 1949 when my parents went to Mexico and my mother came back with what she said was the seed of the sweetest *mango* she'd ever tasted, and she told us that she was going to do Great Magic with that *mango* seed just as she'd seen her own Indian mother do Miracles with corn and string beans up in the mountains of Chihuahua."

"The man now really looked at me and Barbara and our two sons.

"What's your mother's name?" he asked.

"Lupe," I said. "Lupe Villaseñor."

"Lupe Villaseñor!" he shouted. "That's what this strain of *mango* trees was originally called! All the *mango* producing fruit trees in Southern California, Arizona, and parts of New Mexico and Texas came from your mother's tree. But lately a grower's association is trying to take credit, because they say that without genetic altering no one could have developed a *mango* fruit-bearing tree this far north. Does your mother live? Do you know how she did it?"

"The man was nothing, but smiles now.

"Yes, she lives," I said, "and yes, I know how she did it."

"Tell us," he said, turning to the man and woman beside him, "because, you see, Charlie, the old man who introduced us to this miracle tree, protected your mother's privacy so much that we didn't know if she even lived anymore."

"Charlie?" I said. "He was really old, right?"

"Yes, and he's passed."

"Well, I think I remember him coming to our house to see my mother, and he'd get *mango* seeds and trimmings and they'd visit for hours."

"Oh, this is wonderful!" said the woman. "You see, we have basically devoted our lives to the natural procreation of exotic plants and your mother's *mango* is one of our cornerstones in our opposition to genetic alteration, which destroys the essence and food value of everything it touches."

"And so I told them the whole story and how my mother had poured all her Love*Amor* into that *mango* seed with song and joy, then I explained how my mother had told me that her Yaqui mother had done the same thing with her vegetable garden up on the mountain of Chihuahua.

"In fact, my mother explained to us," I said, "that women, that mothers, that grandmothers have been doing this for 100s of 1,000s of years, if not millions, making a home for themselves, their family, and their plants wherever they went. And a Home is where the Heart and Soul of Our Plants and Family Flourish."

"The two men and one woman were astonished."

"Well, this then sheds a whole new light on civilization," said the woman.

"And shows that maybe everything we know about botany could be incorrect," said the young man, "and it didn't take 100s of 1,000s of years for corn to acclimate to a new area. Do you know from where in Mexico your mother brought her seed?"

"Yes, from a rich beautiful valley not far from Mazatlan, Sinaloa where her mother's tribe had lived before they were annihilated."

"Then her people were Native Americans?"

I glanced at our two sons. "Yes, of course," I said. "Yaqui Indians. Great Farmers. And so the Mexican government and the Catholic Church started the propaganda that they were cannibals and they ate Christian babies, so that the Mexican people would rise up and help slaughter them. Women and children, too, so they could take their land. And," I added, "these awful lies that the Church and the Mexican government put out became so real that even today you say Yaqui in Mexico and some people will quickly say, 'Oh, those cannibals.' And Yaqui were mostly vegetarians."

"Oh, that's awful," said the woman. "I'm part Cherokee. The same thing happened to them. You know, the Trail of Tears?"

I nodded. "Yes, I've heard," I said, taking in a great big deep Breath.

"You know," she said, "we're just beginning to realize how so much important information was lost by the annihilation of Native People all over the world. Many were excellent farmers with a sustainable relationship with nature."

She was now the one to Breathe deeply. "So, what you are saying is that your mother Lupe acclimated a *mango* well-over a 1,000 miles from its origin in just a few years?"

"Yes," I said, "that's what happened."

"This is nothing short of a miracle," continued the woman, smiling a great big smile, "because then when tribes were migrating all over our planet, women were able to have their plants acclimate to their new environment immediately. Do you see what this means? Women have, then, been doing the miracles of Our Garden of Eden since ever!"

"Yes, that's how I was raised," I said, "with the understanding that women, who carry the seed of life, are Our Miracle Makers and Our Natural Leaders, and that men, like snow geese, who fly across the sky in V-formations in their migration, 'Follow Infront' breaking the wind so that it then takes 30% less energy for the mother geese and young ones to keep up, and in this way then we, Human People, are in Tune with Creation."

"This is almost exactly what I was told by that group of Navajo women last year," said the woman.

"So we visited a little longer, traded names, phone numbers, and then Barbara and I invited them to our home in South Oceanside, and left. All the way home our two boys were talking about nothing else but Miracles — they were so happy and all excited. And I could now see that my mother had been absolutely right when she'd told my little sister Linda and me that she'd brought us something from Mexico that was Full of Magic."

I stopped. Tears of joy were streaming down my face.

"Did they ever come to your ranch to see your mother's *mango* tree?" asked Sister Mary.

I shook my head. "I don't remember," I said. "Maybe they did. Or maybe it was just the woman. Excuse me, but I can't talk anymore. I need a break. OH, MY GOD! MY GOD! That woman was right, so much Sacred Holy ANCIENT KNOWLEDGE WAS TOTALLY DESTROYED!"

"And yet," said Father James, "now with your writings, we can once more start rekindling this Sacred Ancient Knowledge within each of us. Yes, let's take a break. And thank you, Victor. That mango story really does wrap up everything that you've shared with us."

I mumbled my thanks, and quickly headed for the bathroom. I was totally drained. I'd given it my all, and my tears just wouldn't stop. How long was I in the bathroom, I don't know, but I must've washed my face with hot water and then cold water about a dozen times. Then when I went back, no one noticed that I'd returned — they were all so busy talking amongst themselves.

I LOVED IT!

I walked across the room and went out in the patio, and the crisp clean air was marvelous! And oh, they were so excitedly sharing amongst themselves! And who was leading? Well, it wasn't the priests. Oh, no! Our nuns were All ON FIRE with loud voices and *CARCAJADAS* AND GREAT BIG FLYING HAND MOVEMENTS!

"Well, for me," Sister Mary was saying, "it makes perfect sense that we never did lose the Garden of Eden, and in fact, the Garden is still here with us all over the world, and it's women like Vic's mother Lupe and his Yaqui grandmother *Doña Guadalupe*, who were and are the keepers of this Garden!"

"All I can say," said another nun, "is that this is a far better story than the one of us women being blamed for losing the Garden."

"From now on," another nun was saying, "I'm starting out my morning prayers by saying, 'Hello, to Our Father Sun, Our Right Eye of God, with the realization that everyday *es otro Milagro de Dios*!

"Me, too!" said Mark. "Thank You, God Goding! Oh, I want to SHOUT MY THANKS in every language, in every religious denomination all over the globe! For there's only One Race, Our Human Race with different cultures, and they're ALL EQUALLY BEAUTIFUL AND WONDERFUL!"

I, too, now quietly said, "Thank You, *Papito Dios. Gracias.*"

And the honkers were once more coming up towards me honking and flapping their great wings, and then I saw that they were all Angels. Glowing Angels. This was when Father James came out to see me and he, too, was AGLOW, and smiling a fantastic smile. So I, too, began smiling, and I guess that, well, I was also GLOWING. Sure, why not?

Then I suddenly remembered what my mother had sent with me to give to these nuns and priests.

"Excuse me, Father James," I said, "please just wait for me here. I need to go to my room and get what my mother sent for all of you."

"I'll wait right here," he said, Aglowing.

I went back inside and rushed to my room and brought down my overnight bag. Seeing me, Father James came inside and picked up a crystal glass tapping it with a knife. Oh, the sound was so elegant. People quickly settled down. I came forward and I put my bag on the table, opening it.

"Mangos," I said. "From my mother's Miracle Mango Tree!"

Instantly everyone gathered around, and saw that my travel bag was full of big juicy colorful mangos, and their aroma was so strong that it filled the whole room with intoxicating Miraculous Mango Fragrance just as Wildflower Fragrance filled a room with INTOXICATING LOVE*AMOR* WHEN JESUS CAME SOULSPINNING to us!

Book Four

Godvolution

THE NEXT DAY THE SAME DRIVER WHO HAD PICKED ME UP WAS taking me back to the airport, and once more here in the back seat with me was a cooler with a note attached to it. I smiled. The note was hand written once again with beautiful penmanship and had — not only little red Hearts all about its border — but little Angels, too.

I smiled, feeling warm all over.

"Thank you for coming," said the note. "We all love you and your *familia* so much, especially your aunt Carlota who's so human and full of mischief."

Once more there was no signature. But this time at the bottom there was an imprint of a red lipstick kiss. I took in a great big deep GodBreath, figuring it was Mary, but I wasn't sure until I opened the cooler and once more there were a couple of Stella beers, and not one, but two great big thick pastrami sandwiches.

I took in another deep Breath, thinking about my little nun that I'd fallen in Love*Amor* with. WOW! What if she'd said yes? Would she have waited and we'd married when I got big? I laughed. Oh, I was going Crazy*loco*!

"Hey," I said to the driver as I looked out on the beautiful lake, "why don't we pull over and have a sandwich together. These nuns have made me two big thick pastrami sandwiches with plenty of hot mustard."

"Sounds good to me," he said. "We have plenty of time. In fact, there's supposedly a storm coming in, so your flight I'm sure is going to be delayed."

"Good," I said, "so pick out a nice place where we'll be close enough to the lake to hear the little waves."

Up ahead, he took a little grassy pasture road right down to the edge of the huge body of water. It was absolutely beautiful, and the tiny waves made relaxing gentle music, nothing like the roaring crashing waves of Southern California. We got out of the big black car and walked over to a large fallen tree trunk to eat.

"So how did it go for you?" he asked, eating his pastrami.

"You mean with the nuns and priests?"

"Yes, you see, I've been their gardener for over 20 years, and this is the first time they've asked me to rent a limo."

"Really?"

"Yes, and they've had Bishops and even Cardinals come out to stay with them."

"I see," I said, opening up my second Stella. I'd offered him one, but he'd said no, he was driving. "Well, it went very well, especially this morning. You see, they'd had a chance to sleep on what we'd covered for a second night, and it's in our sleep where we can finally let go, and DreamVoyage."

"DreamVoyage?"

"Yes, Dreams are actually Voyages into Our Subconscious where we store All Our Past and Future. And so, if we'd been able to keep going for a week, I'm sure we would've reached Our Collective Level of Being where then we're able to Create Rain Storms just as my Indigenous Indian grandmothers were able to do during the Mexican Revolution, and stop battles."

"Your grandmothers were able to create a rain storm that stopped a battle?" he asked.

"Well, yes, of course," I said, "You see, back at one time people all over the world used to Know how to do Miracles like this, or else we could never have survived volcanos and 1,000 year ice ages and drought as a species for all these 100s of 1,000s of years, if not millions."

"Very interesting," he said, taking in a deep Breath.

"Sure," I said, "look, we don't have fur like a bear. We don't have claws like a lion. We don't have wings like an eagle, so we were gifted by Our Almighty God with the ability to be Miracle Makers. This is all well documented in my book *Rain of Gold* that all the nuns read and got them to invite me out."

"I'll be, sounds like something I'd like to read. But still for your grandmothers to create a rain storm strong enough to stop a battle is so, well, far beyond credibility that — I just don't know."

"Didn't Moses part the Red Sea?"

"Well, yes, of course, but the Jews are God's Chosen People."

"And you aren't? Oh, no, we're all God's Chosen Children, too. What are you, Irish?"

"Yes."

"Do you know that it was Ireland who saved civilization during the Dark Ages, when Europe was being devastated by the Eastern Europeans, and all books were being burned by these hordes of infidels. So all European scholars fled to the farthest northwest reaches of Ireland where the Irish people kept them in hiding for several centuries, so they could keep their handwritten journals."

"No, I didn't know that."

"And do you know about St. Patrick's Brigade and why the Irish do not have to be Mexican Citizens to be allowed to buy land in Mexico?"

"No, I don't know about this one either."

"St. Patrick's Brigade is a fantastic great true story. And the reason you don't Know all this is because a great important Bible-like book hasn't been written about this long range understanding of how Great and Spiritually Connected to God the Irish really are. You see, the Irish, the Welsh, the Scotch, all of Humanity is equally Spiritually Connected to God just as much as the Jews. The Jewish Bible was just a beginning. Not an end. Because God Goding is still talking to all of us."

"And you said all this to the nuns and priests?" he asked.

"Yes, of course, and I can assure you that I said a lot more. You see, what my book *Rain of Gold* and *Wild Steps of Heaven* are really all about — and it's going to end up being a trilogy or more — is about Our Original Global Native Indigenous Powers, and most particularly that Women are Our Biggest Untapped Natural Resource as my friend Professor Julian Nava has been saying for decades.

"I'll tell you, my grandmothers were these incredible, powerful women who brought their families from Mexico to the United States at the turn of the 20th century during the Mexican Revolution, and they never ever lost their Faith in God or Life, *la Vida*, no matter what terrible disasters they had to go through.

"Rape, war, starvation, and their children being tortured and killed in front of their very eyes. Horrible, just horrible destruction going on all around them, and still they'd give thanks to God at the end of every day, because they Knew that tomorrow is another Miracle gifted to us by God, and so everything was going to turn out for Our Good if we just kept Our Faith and kept going without getting bitter.

"And I'll tell you, my grandmothers weren't special or unusual. They were just your normal, average, poor Mexican Indian Women, and now today, all over Our Mother Earth we, also, have good, strong mothers busting their asses every hour of the day for their kids, just like my grandmothers, and a lot of them are single, and yet they still carry on with plenty of Heart and Love*Amor*, making life good for their kids as best they can.

"Men had their chance, and Women are Now Our Future! And our kick off is to move Our Vatican from Rome to Ireland where we will have Our First Woman Pope," I added, finishing off my second Stella.

He laughed. "Well, I can now see why so many of the priests were against the nuns raising the money to get you to come. But just like my own mom, once a woman, or a group of women make up their mind to do something, there's no power on earth that can stop them. My own mother, she could *Be* a tyrant, but if it wasn't for her we would've starved half of the time."

Saying this, he got to his feet. "You know, I do think that maybe this is a good time to bring out the other little present they sent along for you."

He went to the car and came back with a pretty little bag, handing it to me.

"It was supposed to be for your flight, but what the hell, with your flight going to be delayed and all, I think you should have it now."

I took the little bag and opened it, and it was a small bottle of *Herradura Añejo*, the golden well-aged cognac of *tequila*.

"With this one, I will join you," he said, smiling.

I laughed. "By the way, what's your name?"

"Coner, of course, and spelled our Irish way C-O-N-E-R," he added.

"Well, glad to meet you, Coner. *Victoriano* is my handle in Spanish.

"Well, glad to meet you, *Victoriano*."

So we opened the little bottle and took turns taking sips and wiping off the mouth of the bottle with the palm of our left hand before passing the bottle on with our right hand. Oh, Our Little Lake Waves were Singing Now, and so were Our Magnificent Brother Trees!

"You know, my dear mother is 95," he said with half of the bottle gone, "and she'd agree with you about a woman pope."

"Of course, she would," I said, feeling pretty tipsy, too. "Because she's a Woman of Substance, meaning that at her age if she's not bitter, she's become a Sacred Elder, and as such, she Knows deep inside of herself that Our Beloved Mother Earth is a good fine place, jam-packed full with good people just like your own mother who are doing good deeds at this very moment, this very second, twenty-four hours a day. And that these good people and their good deeds outnumber the negatives by 10,000 to one. Or, maybe, even 100,000 to one, but they just don't make the eleven o'clock news or the front page, and so we all tend to forget about these good deeds and good people. Am I making sense?" I added.

"Well, yes, of course, you are," he said. "And you're right, my mother isn't bitter. She rolls with the punches, but still I don't see what this has to do with us Being Miracle Makers and Creating Rain Storms."

"Everything!" I said. "Eskimos didn't just come into existence Knowing how to live in sub-zero weather and build igloos. They prayed. They opened their HeartEyes and looked around and saw how the seals and other animals did it, and they, then, listened to the Guidance of Guardian Angels, realizing that they, too, were part of this Glorious Natural World all about them.

"Look at how James Michener wrote about the Samoans crossing the great Pacific Ocean in little boats to the Hawaiian Islands, just a dot in an endless sea. What Columbus did is no big deal. He just sailed a little distance and hit a whole continent.

What the Natives of Samoa did was even more astonishing than us going to Our Mother Moon. But do we Know about any of this? No, of course, not, because of word 'the' — which I won't get into right now — and our western civilization's ignorance and self-centered arrogance.

"You see, we've always had a fabulous, wonderful world full of Harmony and Peace! All we have to do is stop listening to all the 'bad' news crap that reinforces all the negative thinking that we have about ourselves, and put Our Energies into remembering what's good and wonderful about all of us already.

"Truly, understand this simple fact, all of Human History has been a stacked deck, a lie, an illusion, recorded by men who chose to think that wars and battles were the Truth of Our Human Story, that chose to think Violence is Our Basis of Human Nature, and it's not true. War and violence has never been our meat and potatoes in real life. Love*Amor* has always been Our Most Basic Power. Unconditional Love*Amor* is what gave my *mamagrandes* the HeartSoul to endure all the terrible things that happened to them. And Love*Amor* is what gave my dad, a little eleven-year-old boy, the strength to run all day and night through the desert without food or water and catch the train that his mother and sisters were on."

Tears were streaming down my face.

"And so just imagine," I added, "where would we be today if Women of Substance, like your beloved mother, had written Herstory, instead of History? Eh, where would we *Be*?"

"In a very different world," he said, smiling.

"Exactly! We'd *Be* living in a Totally Different Reality. And what we'd think is Human Nature would be very different, too. Why? Because we're basically good people all over the world as Ann Frank wrote, and Our Time in Godvolution has come for us to turn off our TVs, stop listening to all the 'bad' news, and go back to basics, to visiting with Our Neighbors, Our Loved Ones, and 'rediscover' how wonderful we really are. To 'discover' what Columbus never 'discovered'—and that is you don't find lasting happiness or economic salvation by crossing oceans and abusing other people, but by staying home and recreating yourself and your own neighborhood and realizing that we have a pretty damn good, wonderful world already!"

"And you told all this to the nuns and priests?" he said, laughing. "No wonder the priests didn't want you coming!"

I stopped, and offered him the last few drops of the *Añejo.* He shook his head, still laughing, so I lifted up the bottle to my lips, tossed my head back and sucked in the last few drops of the little *tequila* bottle, then we got back in the car, and I was very quiet the rest of our drive to the airport.

IN CHICAGO WHERE I WAS CHANGING PLANES, I WAS TOLD THAT a storm had come in and we'd have about a five to six-hour layover. I decided to just relax, find a quiet corner, stretch out on the floor, and take a nap. Up ahead two little girls were running in the aisle and laughing and playing.

"Hi, girls!" I said. They stopped playing. They were about four and five. "I want you young women to Know you are Angels. You really are, and you're wonderful, and you came into this world with Total Recall, and so you're in charge. Because, you see, your parents also came in as Angels, but then they got stressed out and all confused, so they quickly forgot they are Angels, too, and so you need to re-teach them. Have a good life," I added, tipping my Stetson to them and I kept going.

Up ahead, I found a quiet corner by the huge windows facing the runway of incoming and outgoing planes. I put my backpack down, slipped off my western boots, and put my Stetson on top of them so the colorful boots now looked like a very short cowboy. Then I lay down on the floor, stretched out my arms and legs, closed my eyes, and was just relaxing and going to sleep when I felt a presence to the right of me.

I opened my eyes and turned to look and saw that here stood those two little girls with two more little girls and an older boy who was probably about eight years old, and they were just staring at me, and not moving or saying anything. Then it came to me.

"Oh, yeah," I said, "I'd like all of you to Know you are Angels. You really are, and so you came into this world Knowing everything there is to Know. And so you are wonderful and fantastic, and your Angel Voice comes to your head from Here in your Heart," I said, patting my heart area. "And this is your genius, your Voice of Geniusing, and so you young people are in charge, because your parents have forgotten they are Angels, too, and so you need to re-educate them and let them Know they are also Angels and wonderful. In fact," I added, "you guys still have cellular memory that your arms are really wings. So go ahead, spread out your Angel-Arm-Wings, and KNOW THAT YOU ARE WONDERFUL AND FULL OF MAGIC!"

And so they did, they spread out their Angel-Arms and began SoulSpinning around me, screeching with *gusto*!

"WONDERFUL! Great! And now I need to get some sleep, so please just go back to your parents, but don't forget, you're in charge and you are really, really ANGELS AND FULL OF MAGIC AND WONDER!"

They flew around me a couple of more times, then they flew off and I took in a few deep Breaths, put my Stetson over my eyes, and went right back to sleep. And I was dreaming of my horse Casanova and Buccaneer Beach and I was smelling Wildflowers when someone kicked the bottom of my left foot.

But I just ignored it and kept sleeping until they kicked me again and this kick was much harder. I opened my eyes, took the Stetson off my face, and I saw there was a tall girl just beyond my feet. She was maybe ten or eleven years old and she was staring at me and all about her were these smaller, shorter kids. About ten of them. And they, too, were just staring at me.

Well, I sat up, brought my water bottle out of my backpack, drank, then told them the same thing that I'd already said two times before, and when I finished they didn't go away. No, they stayed all around me flapping their arms like wings, and then here came some more kids, and some more, and then I noticed that their parents were coming, too, and when one father grabbed his little four-year-old girl to take her away, she jerked loose from him with power and yelled, "NO! I'M AN ANGEL!" And she came back to *Be* with the other children with her arms out like wings and her whole face Glowing with Joy!

The father rushed in at me. His face was red with rage.

"WHO ARE YOU? What have you done to our children?!" he shouted.

And I could now see that he wasn't alone. There were about a dozen other parents all staring at me, too.

I got up off the floor. I had no idea what to say or do. I closed my eyes, rubbed my face, took in several deep God Breaths, and once more I caught the scent of Wildflowers, and when I opened my eyes here was Jesus with his Sacred Holy Arms outstretched, too, and He was laughing with *CARCAJADAS* and SoulSpinning with all the JOY OF A CHILD!

I laughed. His laughter was contagious, but I could also see that this angry father in front of me didn't think this was a laughing situation.

"Look," I said, still smiling with *gusto*, "I'm a writer and . . . and, well, we're doing research at the University of Houston in conjunction with Yale on children having Total Recall of Being Angels. You see, children are nowadays coming into the world with a way more advanced understanding of how the Universe really works than us older people.

"We adults basically still live in the dark ages of the illusion the world is flat, time is linear, and there is separation. But these kids, who are now coming into manifestation, Cellularly Know that all of Creation is Interconnected, and so they're not fear-based, and instead are FREE TO BE GENIUSING ANGELS! Just look at them, they're so Happy! Big Big Happy, because they Know, just like a rose Knows how to *Be* a rose, that they are OPEN, LOVING, HAPPY HUMAN BEINGS OF LIGHT, JUST LIKE EINSTEIN," I added, thinking this explanation would calm him down. But it didn't.

"Do you have proof?" he barked angrily.

"Proof of what?" I asked.

"Proof that you're not a crackpot!"

"Oh, yeah, sure," I said, "in my backpack I have a copy of my National Best Seller *Rain of Gold,* and some great articles written about me in the *New York Times*, the *L.A. Times*, *Chicago Tribune*, *People Magazine* and a bunch of others. Here, let me get them out and show them to you."

"No! You don't have to do that! I just want my child to come back with me. You had no right!"

"You mean you're upset because I told your child that she's an Angel and a Genius and Wonderful?"

"Well, no, I'm not offended by that," he said. "I'm offended by her not obeying me and … and … I don't need to be explaining myself to you! She's my child!"

And I almost said, "Not really. She's God Goding's child and she's her own Human Angel Person," but I decided this wouldn't be the best thing to say, especially since all the other parents were looking at me with concern, too. So I turned to the kids.

"All right, you Geniusing Angels," I said. "Please, all of you go back to your parents, but remember you're in charge, because you're—"

"My little girl IS NOT IN CHARGE!" yelled the angry father.

But the mother only laughed. "Oh, come on, honey, you know she is," she said. "Thank you very much," she said, turning to me.

A couple of the kids came up and hugged me, and one little boy put his shoes into my boots, fell over, but then got up and his whole face was in ecstasy as he tried walking off wearing my boots that came up past his knees.

People started laughing.

"Can we get your books at any bookstore?" asked a mother.

"Yeah, sure, of course, *Rain of Gold* is the first of a trilogy, and my young adult book is *Walking Stars*, a bunch of short stories, and the first one is titled *The Smartest Human I Ever Met, My Brother's Dog Shep*. Pets are so important for kids. They teach love and caretaking and responsibility. Check out my children's books. That's where education really begins. Thank you. Thank you very much, and I'm really sorry if I upset you."

The tall girl stayed behind.

"Yes?" I said.

"Thank you," she said. "I just knew there was more to life."

And saying this she began to Glow with Golden Light, then she turned and took off running, and I heard Jesus say to me, "She's Our Third Woman Pope!"

"Really?"

"Yes, really."

"Oh, my God! Thank You, Jesus."

"Thank you, Victor."

And hearing this, I began to laugh and the whole entire place filled with the beautiful fragrance of Wildflowers! I lay back down, closed my eyes, put my Stetson over my face and went back to sleep.

Oh, I could hardly wait to get home so I could go across the grass and past the chicken coops to tell my mother what had happened. She'd been absolutely right. Coming to see these retired—I mean, Inspired nuns and priests had really been the most important talk of my life, and especially so when I'd shared with them the story of my mother's Miracle *Mango* Tree.

My God, they'd ALL GOTTEN IT!

Yes, with Our First Woman Pope, women all over the world were going to start remembering how for 100s of 1,000s of years they'd been the caretakers of the Sacred Seeds of Our Holy Garden as we'd migrated around Our Beloved Mother Earth.

And the nuns had instantly understood this.

Yes, in One Great Mighty Stroke, Women—Women of Vision, of Power, of Substance from all over Our Beloved Mother Earth—were going to come forward, Activating the Sacred Holy Dormant Stardust Seeds that we, Human People, have been carrying within us for 100s of 1,000s if not millions of years.

In fact, it was already Done! Finished! Completed! WRITTEN IN THE STARS, OUR TRUE HOME!

AMEN!

AWOMEN!

ACHILDREN!

Cookies and Warm Milk

GETTING HOME TO OUR LITTLE *RANCHITO* IN SOUTH OCEANSIDE, I immediately took my little *familia* to my mother's home past the chicken coops, so I could share with them all at the same time about what had happened in Wisconsin. It took nearly three hours for me to share everything.

"So yes, *Mama*," I said, summing up my trip up by the Canadian Border, "you were totally right. I do believe that this talk is probably the most important talk of my life, and . . . I can now see that when we do what we really don't want to do, and have been avoiding, can end up Being the experience that causes us to learn and grow the most in our lives. So thank you, *Mama*, for kicking my ass and getting me to go."

"Grandmama, you kicked my dad in the ass?" asked Joe. "I didn't know you could lift your leg that high."

David laughed. "No, Joe, Dad is talking in metaphors."

"No, I'm not, David. Your grandmother really did kick me in my ass, and hard!"

We all laughed.

"So they really liked my *mangos*?" asked my mother once again.

"Yes, *Mama*, and they really understood the story of how you were able to bring that *mango* seed so far north and away from her home and get her to grow and produce fruit, because of your mother's Sacred Indian Teachings."

"They really understood that?" she asked.

"Oh, yes, *Mama*."

"Well, then that makes my life complete," she said with tears coming to her *Ojo*Eyes. "Because my *Madre's* Teachings are how we all used to Live in *Tierra Firma* with God's Heaven surrounding us."

"And it was Women who held the keys to Our Garden of Eden," said Barbara, "all over the world for 1,000s and 1,000s of years."

"Exactly, *mijita*, and it is good that your two sons Know this and carry this forward into their own lives."

"We will," said David.

"Yes, because your Miracle *Mangos* are delicious!" said Joe, joyfully.

WELL, THERE ARE NO ACCIDENTS. I'D ONLY BEEN HOME A FEW weeks when one afternoon my mother came to me with the mail. She was looking full of mischief.

"You got another one," she said, smiling.

I took the envelope. It was from the convent of Our Mother of God Catholic Church in Louisville, Kentucky.

"Mother of God?" I said, laughing. "WOW! How in the world did these nuns ever manage to get a name like this past their local bishop and priests?"

"Easy," said my mother, grinning. "*CON GANAS! Y mucho corazon y el favor de Dios!*"

I burst out laughing with *carcajadas*! My mother, now a Sacred Elder, was certainly coming into her Full Powers. I gave her a big hug, holding her close, and then together we opened the letter.

These nuns were also inviting me to come speak to them. I couldn't stop grinning. Something MAGICAL was happening ever since I spoke with those nuns and priests up in Wisconsin. I was now invited to speak at World Peace Conventions across the whole country. And also at churches, libraries, grammar schools, high schools, universities, and even at the huge Global Peace Event that was being held in South Korea.

Anyway, I flew into Louisville, Kentucky and was picked up in an old Chevy station wagon by three older women who were dressed in regular street clothes, and yet it turned out that they were nuns. They'd all read *Rain of Gold* and were so excited to meet me that they couldn't stop talking and laughing.

Well, what can I say? That same day I spoke to over 30 nuns and a dozen local women teachers and only half a dozen priests. And it was a very different talk than the one I'd given to the nuns and priests in Wisconsin, and a lot had to do with the fact that I was a very different person. I was no longer holding onto all my old crap about nuns and priests. I could now see that they, too, were simply Human Beings.

And also these priests were so grossly outnumbered by the women, that they seemed to have no *problema* hearing what I had to say about women and children Being Our Natural Leaders and men Following Infront. Also, they didn't even seem to have a *problema* with Our Vatican moving to Ireland for 100 years and us having Our First Woman Pope.

It was totally amazing!

Had the nuns and priests from Wisconsin been in touch with these other nuns and priests in Kentucky? I didn't Know, but what I did Know was that I wasn't alone. Jesus and my brother Joseph and all of my ancestry on Our Other Side of Living had come with me to Kentucky just as they'd come with me to Wisconsin. There were no borders for Our Spirit World, and there were no Natural Borders on Mother Earth either as I'd learned when I'd been in that little old airplane with my friend John Folting and we'd had to turn around and not cross over into Mexico.

Oh, I'd never forgot that experience, and so somehow I just Knew that as I spoke to these nuns and priests and teachers here at Our Mother of God Convent, it was like they already Knew about everything we'd covered up in Wisconsin, and . . . they'd also had time to digest it.

And so I ended my talk by telling them what happened to me at the Chicago airport, and how once I'd explained to the first bunch of kids that they were Angels and Geniuses and Full of Wonder and that they were in charge, other kids had come running and joined right in and I hadn't hardly had to explain to the last bunch of kids what I'd explained to the first kids. It was like they already Knew Heart*Corazon* to Heart*Corazon* and *Alma*Soul to *Alma*Soul Everything that I'd shared with the other children.

Then I told them about the tall little girl who stayed behind and she said, "Thank you, I just Knew there was more to life." And she'd begun to Glow with Golden Light, and I'd smelled Wildflowers and heard Jesus say to me so clearly, "She's Our Third Woman Pope."

"And so then," I said, "this then means that the 100th Monkey Theory is really true, that when one monkey on an island learned that he could break a coconut open with a rock and all the other monkeys on that same island began doing it too, then suddenly, without ever having seen those monkeys on that first island breaking coconuts with rocks, the monkeys on all the other islands, suddenly began Knowing how to do it, too.

"So this is exactly what is happening to us right now on a Spiritual Level all over Our Sacred Mother Earth, and Our Vatican is already in movement to Ireland as we speak!"

The applause was HUGE! But then came the questions. Did I get that tall girl's name? Was she Irish?

I started laughing.

But the questions and excitement just wouldn't stop. Finally, I said that I only Knew what I Knew, and so it was up to each of us to go within Our Own Womb of Creation and seek these answers.

Then that evening a dozen of us went out to dinner at an ultra-modern bar and restaurant that overlooked the Ohio River. We had a fabulous meal, then still full of excitement we went to the huge bar and began shooting shots of *tequila* around a giant fireplace.

"You know, it's going to take two smart, cunning women to establish a foundation for that little girl, Our Third Woman Pope," said a feisty happy Irish-looking little nun. "It's going to take women from all over the world coming together to pull this off!"

"You're right," said a tall heavy-set nun. "If Ireland tries to do it alone, all these cardinals and bishops and priests will tear apart Our Global Women's Movement before we can even get started."

"And not just the cardinals and bishops, but all these ultra-conservative Catholic men's organizations that have so much power and money and still live in the dark ages of 'Father Knows Best' kind of crap," said another nun.

"Look," said the feisty happy little nun, "we can't be stopped! Those ultra-conservative men's organizations and cardinals and bishops and priests are small potatoes compared to ALL OF US WOMEN COMING TOGETHER FROM ALL OVER THE WORLD!

"I didn't just read *Rain of Gold*. I read the other book *Wild Steps of Heaven*, and for me this is the most Powerful and Spiritually Informative book. My God, what faith *Doña Margarita* still had even after they'd arrested her son, *José,* the Great, and taken him to *Guadalajara* for execution.

"She went to church feeling lost and without any hope. For all the people she Knew that might be able to help her had abandoned the area or been killed. But still she closed her eyes and spoke to Mary, Our Holy Mother of Jesus, and found Peace and went to sleep.

"And when she awoke, she was full of Our Powers of Our Holy Ghost, and so she instantly realized that she did Know someone who was still alive and powerful; the enemy of her *familia*.

"And so armed with Hope and Indestructible Faith in Our Almighty God, she went to see this man at his offices. And when he said, 'Don't you realize that I hate your family and there's nothing I would ever do to help them?'

"She simply said, 'I agree with you, half of the time I hate them too and don't want to do anything more to help them. But, as I was saying,' she continued speaking to the busy business man with such terrible calmness and confidence and heartfelt wisdom that this enemy of her *familia* finally realized that there was no stopping her, and so he ended up giving her money and a wagon with a driver to take her to the train.

"And what did she do? She purchased her train ticket, and gave the rest of the money to a poor hungry mother with a child, and she said, 'Without money we are Forced to Arm Ourselves with the Blessings and Miracles of Almighty God.'

"And this is exactly what we, women, are going to have to do," said the feisty little nun, finishing off her *tequila*. "Arm Ourselves with the Blessings and Miracles of Almighty God! For we are the Power! And we have always been the Power! And we all Know that! Men are basically spoiled, scared, lost little boys! Don't you agree?" she now said, turning to the two priests who were standing alongside of me.

The two priests glanced at each other. They were speechless. And all the nuns BURST OUT laughing, then the younger priest started laughing, too.

"One more *tequila*," he said, "and I can drink to that, Sister!"

"Amen!" said the older priest.

"Amen! Awomen! Achildren!" I said with a beer in one hand and a *tequila* in my other hand.

"Amen! Awomen! Achildren!" they all said along with me.

"I, too, read *Wild Steps of Heaven*," said the tall heavy-set nun. "And I do believe that it's my favorite."

"Mine, too," said another nun, "but on the other hand, I don't believe that I would have been ready for *Wild Steps of Heaven* if I hadn't first read *Rain of Gold*."

I couldn't stop smiling. This was beautiful! Ever since I'd arrived these nuns had been breaking coconuts open with great big rocks with *gusto*. The times weren't changing. They'd already had, and I was so big big happy!

Tears of joy were pouring down my face. And it was also no accident that Our Lord God Jesus had come to us SoulSpinning amongst all those children at the airport in Chicago, and He'd then told me that the tall little girl, who'd stayed behind, was going to be Our Third Woman Pope.

OH, THERE WAS JUST NO STOPPING ANY OF THIS! Jesus was with us! The whole Heavens were with us! All of Our Ancestry on the Other Side of Living was with us, too!

And so we were served another shot and we toasted and drank it down, and so I now turned to the feisty happy little nun, who radiated such power and confidence, and said, "Well, Sister, how would you like to be Our First Woman Pope?"

Without hesitation, she said, "SURE! WHY NOT?"

We all burst out laughing with *CARCAJADAS*!

The tall, heavy-set nun said, "And she'll make a great Woman Pope! She's brilliant, and she bakes the best chocolate chip cookies in all the world, and, I'm tell you, it's going to take a lot of cookies to put a smile on people's faces and make this a kinder, sweeter, and more compassionate world!"

I couldn't stop laughing. "Then this will be Our First Official Business after moving Our Church from Rome to Ireland?"

"Certainly!" said a very beautiful tiny nun who'd hardly spoken. "What else can help open people's hearts more quickly than the best-tasting chocolate chip cookies in all the world?"

"And warm milk," added another nun.

"You're right," I said. "You're absolutely right, and only women, women, women could've come up with this! OH, WOW! So, then, it's in the bag! Our First Woman Pope, then World Harmony and Peace and—not just Abundance for All—BUT CHOCOLATE CHIP COOKIES AND WARM MILK FOR EVERYONE!"

The laughter! The joy! The excitement and enthusiasm was so great that everyone in the bar was now looking at us, and the two quiet nuns now began to sing *Amazing Grace* with such HeartFelt Beauty that the whole place went silent.

Tears of joy once more came to my eyes, and I, too, began to sing along, but quietly. I didn't want to interrupt this Miraculous Magic Moment. Oh, we were all so BIG BIG HAPPY, and hugging and wiping tears from our eyes and feeling so Blessed!

"You know," said the tall heavy-set nun to me, "I truly feel deep inside of me that all us women around the world should start singing *Amazing Grace* every afternoon at 3:00 pm just like your mother did for her *mango* tree."

"Yes! That's it!" shouted the beautiful tiny quiet little nun. "We need to start planting Our Garden of Heaven on Mother Earth just like his mother did by singing with all Our Hearts and Souls at 3:00 pm every afternoon!"

"Yes!" said another nun. "Let's contact all our fellow nuns throughout the world and start this Holy Sacred Movement that's been so long overdue! Oh, I'm so excited I could pop! I feel just like I felt when I was 16 years old and I decided to become a nun!"

"And not just our fellow nuns," said the feisty little Irish-looking nun, "but contact our families and Women's clubs and organizations throughout the World! And there will be no way WE CAN BE STOPPED! And men will Follow Infront!"

"I'm glad you included men," said the older priest alongside of me, "because I can now actually see a few bishops that I know coming in with us, too."

"I agree," said the younger priest, "and I can also see some of my friends who studied to be priests, but abandoned the priesthood to get married and raise families, wanting to come in and join us."

And I almost said, "Join us with our 300 foot tall Spiritual Tidal Wave of Compassion Love*Amor* flooding across our whole planet!"

But I didn't say this.

It was already done.

Finished.

And written in the Stars Our True Home!

Yes, indeed, Miracle Makers were we, and World Harmony and Peace and Abundance for All was now Our Collective DreamVoyage along with chocolate chip cookies and warm milk for everyone!

DreamVoyage

FLYING HOME THE NEXT MORNING, I LOOKED OUT MY WINDOW at our vast beautiful planet and I was feeling kind of strange. It almost seemed to me like my Life, *la Vida*, had become a continuous DreamVoyage. And it really didn't matter if I was awake or asleep.

And getting home, I, of course, shared the box of the best chocolate chip cookies in all the world with *mi familia* that the nuns had sent home with me, but somehow I just couldn't explain to them what had happened in Louisville, Kentucky.

For I now felt that manmade words just weren't capable of portraying what had happened. Because, well, it now seemed to me that even Moses parting the Red Sea was small potatoes compared to what You, Me, We, All of Us United Together parting Our Global Red Sea of Fear and Doubt and Self-Loathing Corruption.

Why, we were planting Our Stardust Seeds not for 500 years. Not for 5,000 years. But for the next 26,000 years, and Our First Woman Pope was just one cornerstone of Our Whole New Consciousness.

Not of greed.

Not of fear.

Not of selfishness.

But of Balanced Compassionate Feminine Love*Amor* Energy of One Race, Our Human Race, and World Harmony and Peace and Abundance for All! And that Our Planting of Our Stardust Seeds will *Be* Done! Completed! Finished by November 10, 2026, 3:00 pm California time!

And I'd get these little FLASHES with complete Cellular Memory of how this had been done on Our Six Sister Planets. For yes, indeed, Miracle Makers were we! All of Us! Every One of Us! And Our Star Cousins were with Us, and they already KNEW How to do this, and so it was really going to get done quickly and easily!

So feeling good and confident deep inside, that night I went to bed early, wrapping myself up in a blanket like I was back in the womb. And yet I couldn't sleep because I kept hearing Mother Teresa's words ringing in my ears, "I Know God will not give me anything I can't handle. I just wish He didn't have so much Trust in me."

I giggled.

I laughed.

Oh, how perfect! How wonderful!

Then I heard Mark Twain's words. "Thousands of geniuses live and die undiscovered—either by themselves or by others." And tears came to my eyes. This was also really True.

And I flashed on that homeless woman who the other homeless people Knew as The Dumpster Poet of California, and they'd told me that for years she'd been traveling up and down the state from San Diego to San Francisco and writing on dumpsters like she'd done in Ocean Beach. "It's not who you are that holds you back, it's who you think you're not."

And they'd further told me that no one Knew her name, but they did Know that she'd originally been from Palo Alto from a wealthy family, and that growing up she'd gotten such awful stomach pains at hearing how her family spoke about homeless people that she'd finally joined the homeless, trying to make up for her family's heartless, judgmental ways.

Oh, my God, what a Hollow Bone! Buffalo Bone! Empty Vessel *de puro* Love*Amor* was this Dumpster Poet Woman.

I MUST'VE FINALLY FALLEN ASLEEP, BECAUSE THE NEXT THING I Knew, I was down at the Oceanside pier wearing bright red baggy pants like a clown and joyfully banging a rock and a trash can lid together!

I looked a lot like Johnny Depp and I was dancing and singing so loud and far off key that the Cats ran away from me with their tails straight up in the air, and the Dogs lay down and covered their ears with their paws.

Jesus loved it! And together He and I came running and singing and SoulSpinning along with Our Cats and Dogs.

Kids loved it! And came running and singing and SoulSpinning along with Jesus and me and Our Cats and Dogs.

Homeless People loved it, too! And came running and singing and SoulSpinning along with Jesus and me and Our Cats and Dogs and Kids!

Then I saw this tall elegantly-dressed in rags Homeless Woman going through a dumpster and pulling out cans and sticks and trash and making musical instruments. And she radiated such Love*Amor* and Beauty that the other Homeless People flocked to this tall old Woman and they, too, began making musical instruments from the trash in the dumpsters.

And now sure enough without anyone discussing the matter, this Woman and Kids and other Homeless People and Cats and

Dogs took the lead and Jesus and I 'Followed Infront' as we danced our way out to the end of our long, beautiful Oceanside Pier.

Oh, we were having such a grand time that when people saw us coming, they'd laugh and join right in with OUR CRAZY*LOCO* WONDERFUL DREAMVOYAGE!

By the time we came around the end of the pier, we had 100s of People and dozens of Dogs howling and jumping about, and even more Cats prancing with their tails straight up in the air.

This was when Dolphins began leaping out of the sea, making birdlike chirping high-pitched sounds, and Seagulls and Pelicans joined in, and the Surfers, who were catching waves, all began singing and dancing on their boards, too!

Oh, by the time we approached the shoreline there was a crowd of well over 10,000 People, and then suddenly we were all singing and dancing across a Luscious Green Meadow full of Wildflowers and 100s of sheep on the hillsides.

And Little Green People were sprouting out of the Wildflowers, and they instantly began laughing and singing and dancing and joined right in with us, but then we stopped.

Just like that, we all stopped laughing and dancing and singing out in the middle of this Luscious Green Meadow.

No more Singing.

No more Dancing.

No more Laughing.

All was Silent.

And this was when we heard One Single Note.

One Clear Single Note of a Woman's Beautiful Voice.

And then One More Clear Beautiful Single Note of a Woman's Voice came softly, softly down from the Heavens, and it was Enya!

ENYA! THE MUSICAL *ALMA*SOUL OF IRELAND!

And we, in the Luscious Green Meadow, stood TRANSFIXED!

And her Heartfelt Music engulfed US IN a Sea of Living LOVE*AMOR*!

And we, with starving *Alma*Souls, began coming from OUR FIVE SPIRITUAL CORNERS OF OUR whole WORLD TO IRELAND!

10s of 1,000s OF US!

100s of 1,000s OF US!

10s OF MILLIONS OF US!

100s OF MILLIONS OF US!

And Our Children and Women and Homeless were leading and we Knew no fear! For we were all OPEN OF HEART*CORAZÓN* AND ALIVE OF *ALMA*SOUL!

YOU! ME! WE! ALL OF US were now ShapeShifting, SoulShifting, Transforming into Being Snow Geese Human Angels of Ourselves, and this was when we all begin smelling cookies!

CHOCOLATE CHIP COOKIES!

THE BEST CHOCOLATE CHIP COOKIES IN ALL THE WORLD!

And here she came, Our First WOMAN Pope!

Our feisty little old nun from Our Mother of God Church in Kentucky, and she was moving in the Style and Grace of THE GIRL FROM IPANEMA!

And she's surrounded by Angels and Children and Homeless People and Cats and Dogs and all of us are Singing and Dancing and SoulSpinning, and . . . and I now Awake!

I AWAKE LAUGHING WITH *CARCAJADAS*!

And I now see Mary, Our Holy Mother God, arise from the very depths of Our Mother Earth!

And Our First Woman Pope turns and sees Mary and they smile, looking into each other's eyes. Heart*Corazon* Talking. *Alma*Soul Talking. Then with great big big happy smiles, Mary and Our First Woman Pope bow their heads and touch foreheads, saying, "You are Another Me, and I am Another You!"

And now Our Mother of God takes Our First Woman Pope's hand and together they start down the Luscious Green Meadow.

Carole King sings "A Natural Woman," as Our Two Great Ladies continue down the meadow.

Then Joan Baez sings "We Shall Overcome."

Then Louie Armstrong sings "Hello, Dolly" with his world famous great big smile!

And Wild Songbirds are singing and flying all about, and Bumble Bees are kissing the Wildflowers, and Butterflies are floating about everywhere in abundance, and Snow Geese, Canadian Honkers, African Geese are flying in V-formations, cackling and honking with great joy!

THEN WE SEE IT!

There just ahead of us, we see this cute little old Church at the far end of the meadow, and our feisty little old First Woman Pope now kisses Our Blessed Mother's hand, and she starts to dance with wild abandon that world-famous Brazilian dance of Bosa Nova Music of the last mid-century!

And seeing this, Our Mother of God, joyfully starts dancing, too, and now together both Great Ladies go dancing down the Luscious Green Meadow towards the little Church, passing fields of sheep and cattle and Shetland ponies.

And as Our First Woman Pope and Our Mother of God reach the steps of Our Holy Little Church, a cute tiny baby lamb comes rushing up to them, BLEATING HER HEAD OFF, and Our First Woman Pope bends down and picks up the little lost lamb, soothing her head and kissing her.

Then with baby lamb in hand, she turns to Mary, and she asks for Her Blessing before she takes her First Official Step into Our

New Vatican of Our Holy Catholic Church of Ireland for THE NEXT 100 YEARS!

Can you see it?

Can you feel it?

Can you SEE-FEEL IT deep within your own WOMB OF CREATION CREATING—for You, Me, We, All of Us, along with Our First Woman Pope, are now GIVING BIRTH TO God Goding!

Then here comes Pope Francis across the Heavens on a Winged White Horse-drawn GOLDEN CHARIOT!

ACHILDREN!

AWOMEN!

AMEN!

And Pope Francis gets down from a White Horse-drawn Golden Chariot and comes up to Mary, Our Mother of God, and Our First Woman Pope, pets the little lamb she holds in her arms, then with a great big smile, he turns about to All Us People and speaks!

"Welcome! Welcome! To this great day of Our Changing of the Guard that we've all been awaiting . . . ever since Our Lord God Jesus also first entrusted His Holy Church to His Blessed Mother and wife Mary Magdalene, a fine well-educated lady from a wonderful family.

"And I now state," he continues, "as the last Official Pope of Rome, that we completely and irrevocably entrust Our Beloved Catholic Church in the name of Our Lord God Jesus to Our First Woman Pope of Ireland."

A Joyful Global Applause Trembles the very FOUNDATION of Our Beloved Mother Earth!

Feeling this, Our First Woman Pope smiles, and extends her right hand to Pope Francis and he takes her hand, looks into her eyes, then bows his head and slips the Pope's ring on her finger and kisses the ring, and this photo goes viral all over the world!

And at the Vatican in Rome, Cardinals and Bishops and Priests are watching on TV. And here in Ireland 1,000s of Nuns and Priests and Bishops and Cardinals have joined in with the millions and millions of People who are giving witness to this historical event!

And now Our HEAVENS BURST OPEN with legions of Angels laughing and singing along with Enya, for Our Mother Earth Herself is Smiling, Healing, and Wildflowers sprout by the zillions in every valley and hillside across the WHOLE WORLD IN ALL the colors of the rainbow!

Pope Francis and Our First Woman Pope now bend forward and touch foreheads and say in unison, "You are Another Me, and I am Another You." And together they start to glow with Pale Golden Holy Light in Giving Birth to God Goding.

And Angels and Human People continue singing as Our First Woman Pope now turns and starts walking up the Three Holy Sacred Steps of Our New Vatican, leading—not just the whole Christian World back to Our Basics of Faith and Love and Hope, Reverence and Miracles and Compassion, but with the Total Understanding that there's only One Race, Our Human Race, and so we're all *FAMILIA! FAMILIA! FAMILIA!* AND EQUALLY CHILDREN OF God Goding!

Our First Woman Pope passes through the entrance of our little old Church with the baby lamb in her arms and the place is packed full of People. Some dressed in work clothes and others all dressed up.

Everyone gets to their feet, and most have tears of joy streaming down their faces. Some hold infants in their arms. Others hold large bundles of flowers. And still others have baskets of vegetables and fruit that they've brought from their own gardens to *Be* Blessed. And one little old couple holds a big beautiful red hen and a basket full of large brown eggs.

Suddenly our quiet little lamb lets out an ear-piercing BLEATING CALL, and leaps out of Our First Woman Pope's arms, rushing to her mother, who's at someone's side inside of the Church, and our little lamb instantly begins to nurse.

People laugh and applaud.

Smiling, Our First Woman Pope now comes down the center aisle Blessing all the Gifts that People have brought to Our Cute Little Humble New Vatican.

And as the People part, we now see the altar, and Jesus isn't hanging on a cross.

Oh, no! We now all see Him SoulSpinning with such Love*Amor* that here in Ireland and in every Catholic Church around the whole world, People—of the People, for the People, by the People—see Our Lord Jesus SOULSPINNING WITH His arms reaching up to the Heavens in Pure Ecstasy!

BEAUTIFUL!

INSPIRING!

WELCOMING!

And alongside Him is His Beautiful Wife Mary Magdalene and His Blessed Mother Mary and His Beloved Father Joseph, and as He slowly, gently ceases SoulSpinning, we now see Our Holy Family smiling together and surrounded by Angels and Adoring Children who have brought their dolls and baby ducks and rabbits and goats and sheep to *Be* Blessed, and one Child has a little baby kangaroo.

Outside, 1,000s of People are laughing with joy.

Around the world, millions of People are watching on their cell phones with tears of joy streaming down their faces.

And inside Our First Woman Pope now goes up to the altar, genuflects, makes the sign of the cross over herself, then she bows to Jesus and Our Most Holy Family and Pope Francis, then she now turns and goes up to the podium, signals for everyone to please be seated, and she starts to speak.

"Welcome," she says. "Welcome to Our Beloved Catholic Church of Our Lord Jesus Christ that is now going to be at last led also by Women from all our different cultures from all around Our Whole Globe for the next 50,000 years!

"Yes," she says, taking in a large deep Breath of God Goding, "I said 50,000 years! And we thank Enya, for keeping the fires of Ireland's Heart*Corazon* and *Alma*Soul Alive all these years! And we give thanks to Pope Francis, Our Beloved Last Pope in Rome, for coming to guide us with Our Almighty's Blessings full of Hope and Healing Love*Amor* and for all of us and for our most precious Mother Earth. We thank you, Pope Francis!"

With his typical grand smile, Pope Francis waves to everyone and Our First Woman Pope takes in several more deep Breaths, then continues.

"Also, I'd like to give thanks to all my fellow Nuns and Priests and Brothers and Bishops and Cardinals who have joined us. For ours isn't a movement of destruction, and rather a Movement of Fulfillment!"

She stops once again, taking in even a few more deep GodBreaths, then glances around before continuing.

"Also, I'd like to thank Carole King and Joan Baez, who've become close friends of mine, and the great indestructible Louie Armstrong, who spontaneously came to us from the Other Side of Living, for the sole purpose of inspiring us with his GREAT ENERGIZING 'HELLO, DOLLY!' Oh, I once more felt like a young school girl dancing up the valley with the grace and movement of the GIRL FROM IPANEMA!"

Saying this, she now bursts with laughter, doing a few quick little stepping movements with her arms up in the air.

Then she says, "Okay, now, moving onto Our First Official Business, I'd like all of you to turn on your cell phones, if you haven't already done so, and record what I am about to share with you, and . . . and then please send it out to the WHOLE WORLD! TO ALL YOUR FRIENDS AND FAMILY!

"Not just to Catholics and ex-Catholics! For this message is for all of HUMANITY! And Our First Official Statement is that I, your First Woman Pope, and all other Popes, both female and male, from this day on for the next 50,000 years, are not—do you hear me—ARE NOT INFALLIBLE!"

People are shocked.

You can hear a pin drop.

They don't know what to think, or feel, or say, or do. The infallibility of the Pope of Rome had always been the Foundation of the whole Roman Catholic Indoctrination, so that then no one could question anything that the Pope proclaimed had come to him, and only to him, straight from God.

People glanced around, looking at each other, and then slowly it begins to register what this means, and now THE PEOPLE EXPLODE WITH APPLAUSE!

And Our First Woman Pope sees the Holy Blessed Golden Light of Jesus SoulSpinning come into the People's Hearts and Souls, Activating their Kingdom of God Goding within them.

Seeing this, tears of joy stream down Our First Woman Pope's face and she reaches into the left sleeve of her loose-fitting white robe, bringing out the little white handkerchief that her Irish grandmother had given her sixty-some years ago, when she'd decided to take her vows to become the bride of Our Lord Jesus Christ.

Her grandmother Sarah had been blind, but still she'd managed to embroider tiny red and yellow flowers and even more tiny green leaves into the white Irish linen handkerchief that . . . that Our First Woman Pope had not used until this day.

This day that she'd only dreamed of.

This day that she'd kept in secret ever since Jesus had come and asked her for her hand in marriage on her sixteenth birthday.

This day she'd been gifted in little glimpses that One Holy Day she'd be Our First Woman Pope.

She can't stop crying.

Tears of joy just keep streaming down her face and she can feel the presence of Jesus and her grandmother at her side along with, of course, Our Mother of God and Mary Magdalene.

She giggles.

Oh, she can still remember how the Bishops and Cardinals had been against her fellow Nuns when they'd wished to name their Church and Convent in Kentucky the Mother of God. Oh, if only those Bishops and Cardinals were alive today and could see what was happening now!

Oh, she can't stop laughing and giggling—she's so happy! BIG BIG HAPPY! She and her fellow Nuns have certainly come a long ways in the last 100 years, and . . . and . . .

"And so I'd like all of you to know," she now says, "why my fellow Woman Bishops and Cardinals have unanimously decided, through the Holy Spirit and Guidance of Jesus, that . . . that all Popes from this day forth will no longer be considered infallible. Because, it is you . . . you, me, we, all of us, the People—of the People, by the People, for the People, who are INFALLIBLE!"

The place EXPLODES!

This, the People can HEAR!

This, the People can UNDERSTAND!

This, the People realize is Uniting them Directly to God!

In every form! In every name! In every faith! In every way throughout the WHOLE WORLD for they are, indeed, ALL! ALL! ALL PEOPLE—of the People, by the People, for the People since ever, and at long last, they are finally Being Acknowledged for who THEY REALLY ARE!

THE PLACE CONTINUES EXPLODING!

EXPLODING with applause and cheers and ear-piercing whistles!

And this message of Our First Woman Pope goes viral around the whole world, sending that 300 FOOT TIDAL WAVE OF HOPE AND EMPOWERMENT TO ALL! ALL! ALL OF HUMANITY!

"And proceeding in this same vein," Our First Woman Pope continues, "I'd like to announce that Our Second Official Statement, with Total Faith and Trust in God, is that from this day forward, we are Activating the full and real definition of what the word catholic really means in accordance to Our Webster New World Dictionary of the American Language, which states—"

She pauses.

She pauses and glances around and all is silent. In fact, even the sheep and cows and Shetland ponies are attentive.

"Which states: universal; all-inclusive, of general interest or value; hence having broad sympathies and understanding; liberal!"

She smiles and her whole Being begins to GLOW with such intensity that the People make the sign of the cross over themselves and glance downward—her Glowing Hôly Light is so Bright!

"Did you hear me? LIBERAL!" she repeats. "A word that has taken on negative meaning in the last few years. And yet, I ask you, where would we be today if we hadn't liberated slavery? Where would my family of true hillbilly Kentuckians be today if the

People, by the People, of the People, for the People hadn't liberated ourselves from the British Empire? And where would women be today, if they hadn't fought to get the right to vote!

"LIBERTY! LIBERTY! LIBERTY! Is the very foundation of progress and our guarantee that good things will continue to happen! And yet being conservative has its place. Because too much liberty, or too fast, causes us to lose Our Balance, and, remember, we have learned that Balance is, indeed, our Sixth Sense, and the Key to Our Multi-Sensory Perception of Our Natural Thirteen Senses, which my fellow nuns and I learned about from the author of *Rain of Gold,* a book, I'd like to add, that I, personally, keep on my bedstand alongside my Bible and the *Diary of Anne Frank.*"

And here she stops once again, and once more uses the little hand-embroidered white handkerchief that her grandmother had given her to dry her eyes. And the People, of the People, by the People, for the People, are in awe, in wonderment, feeling so empowered and validated and WHOLE for the first time in their lives!

And all around the globe in parks, in back alleys alongside dumpsters, under great trees, and in playgrounds, basketball courts, churches, shopping centers, and in homes, the PEOPLE, of the People, by the People, for the People are listening to Our First Woman Pope's words, and through the Grace of God, her words, spoken in English, are being heard . . . are being understood IN EVERY LANGUAGE OF THE WORLD through the Living Breathing Grace of Almighty God Goding!

"Third," she now says, "I'd like to share with you that my fellow Woman Cardinals and Bishops, with whom I've been communicating through computer Skype for months, have finally come to the understanding—guided by Jesus and Mary, of course—that this Spiritual Movement of Ours, in order to manifest, is not going to be a gradual event.

"IT MUST BE A LIGHTNING BOLT EVENT! A GLOBAL OCCURRENCE OF SUCH MAGNITUDE OF LOVE*AMOR* AND GRATITUDE AND ACCEPTANCE OF EACH OTHER'S BELIEFS AND LIFESTYLES, that it can no more be stopped than us thinking that we can stop A HURRICANE! A FLASH FLOOD! A METEORITE! For we are All Equally! Equally! Equally Children of God! No exceptions! And . . . and our beloved Anne Frank said it best in her diary—even as they exterminated her people—that she still believed that PEOPLE WERE BASICALLY GOOD OF HEART!"

Once more she uses her little white Irish linen handkerchief.

"This is our mantra," she adds. "Love*Amor*, Gratitude, and the understanding that we, the PEOPLE, of the People, by the People, for the People are basically ALL GOOD of Heart, and so we have it within us to Live Lives for the Greater Glory of God!

"For remember, Our Lord Jesus told us that what He did, we would do more, and that time in our Godvolution has come and it's RIGHT NOW! RIGHT HERE! IN OUR FOREVER ETERNAL PRESENT!

"Fourth! And this is a very important and far reaching one," she says, taking in another deep breath. "From this day forth, we will be Totally Transparent, meaning that all financial matters will be made public and kept public like any reputable nonprofit organization, and along these lines there will also no longer be any tolerance for abusive behavior from any member of Our Church financially, sexually, and/or any other way, for that matter!"

She coughs.

She swallows.

She clears her throat, then suddenly grabs the podium with both hands with such POWER that she shakes the large podium!

"And what does this mean?" she shouts. "It means that Our Beloved Mother Church will no longer be a safe haven for . . . for arrogant, self-centered spenders and child molesters!

"It means that there will be no more secrecy, no more moving a child molester from one of our churches to another, and instead, we will immediately call the authorities and fully cooperate so that the abusing person will be prosecuted to the FULLEST EXTENT OF THE LAW!"

She stops.

She stops, and then continues with tears streaming down her face. "In the past some of my fellow nuns have been intimidated, beaten, and in some cases even . . . even raped and then murdered to keep them from going to the authorities.

"And not just by the priests, but also, I'm sad to say, with the participation of some of my fellow nuns. Good nuns. Fine people. And yet out of fear, out of terror of retaliation, cooperated . . . just like in Germany, in Italy, in Spain when good decent people cooperated with the Nazis.

"You see, it's time for us to stop all our finger pointing and understand that it isn't . . . that it isn't just Our Own Beloved Church where such horrors have been committed and are still being committed as we speak, but . . . but to understand that all male-based, male-controlled institutions and governments have been guilty of some such horrendous abuses worldwide, and it's still going on today where . . . where young boys and girls—even small children—are being kidnapped, stolen, and sold as sex slaves.

"And why does this happen? Why? Because these are terrible people who do these kidnappings? OH, NO! It's because there is a market for these atrocities! Meaning that there are people of means who make it worthwhile for poor local people to do this kidnapping and stealing.

"Oh, yes! And more times than not, it's done by young men from wealthy, educated parents, who have witnessed the breakdown of their own family, and . . . and also have seen that greed and corruption are the realities of our world that, then, lead us directly into an addiction, yes, an addiction of war, violence, and, of course, rape, and so in order to fit in, they purchase, or help in the kidnapping, and then, in more recent years, photograph their abuses and tortures, and killings.

"And now before you start dismissing, accusing, and finger pointing so you can regain your composure, understand . . . please understand that these individuals come from the same mentality as drunken, abusive parties in colleges and universities, and . . . and the purchase of exotic foods like monkey brains, and laughing about it. The same people who slaughtered the vast herds of buffalo and bragged and laughed about only eating the tongues. The exotic royal meals, where last century, our fine royalty of Europe relished eating hummingbird breasts and tongues, saying that they'd never tasted anything as delicious!

"So, then, I ask you: who are these people? And I say that they are us; you, me, we, all of us, and then I also ask who are the young boys and girls and children who bring the highest prices, and are also our most vulnerable? Eh, who? Yes, of course, Poor People, Native People, the Indigenous population from all across my own country of the United States in places like Montana, California, Utah, Texas, and in Mexico across the border from Texas and Arizona, and then in New York, Chicago, Los Angeles, and Italy, Spain, and all across North Africa and Asia and . . . and the whole world!

"OH, THE HORRORS that young people have shared with us that happened to them! Places where six to eight girls out of ten are abused and raped before the age of twelve! And many of their friends murdered! And their holocaust isn't even acknowledged, except by a few of our fellow brave nuns and priests, who weren't and still aren't afraid to step forward and make a difference, even if it means going against Our Church's archaic position of so often finding it most advantageous to ignore the abuses of the rich and powerful."

She stops.

She can't go on.

She raises her right hand and closes her eyes, once more Breathing in God Goding deeply, again and again.

And there is Silence. Holy, Attentive, United, Sacred Silence across the WHOLE WORLD as the People, of the People, by the People, for the People truly now go within themselves and examine their own Heart*Corazones* and *Alma*Souls.

For they can now clearly see that yes, we, Human Begins, might, indeed, be basically good people, and yet just like the Nazis, we, too, are capable of doing and/or allowing horrendous atrocities to happen.

And now with this Monumental Historical Event of the Changing of the Guard for All of Humanity, People are Awakening to the razor-sharp sword of who we, Human Beings, really are, just as happened on our Six Sister Planets when they, too, finally had Instant Global Communications, and therefore were able to TRANSFORM!

And this Holy, Attentive, United, Sacred Silence deepens.

In every home.

In every church.

In every town center.

In every shopping center.

In every school and park and back alley alongside a dumpster around the world—for Our Beloved Mother Earth, herself, is Stirring. Awakening. Feeling Hopeful at long last that her Beloved Children are Awakening. And so with GREAT JOY, OUR

MOTHER EARTH SMILES, sending Healing Love*Amor* Energy to her Twin Sister who who instantly Feels it. Smiles. And also Begins Awakening.

And all across Our Entire Universe—One United Verse, One United Song this feeling between TWIN SISTER PLANETS REACHES OUT TO THE FURTHEST REACHES OF OUR FOREVER EXPANDING-CONTRACTING EXPLODING-IMPLODING CREATION-CREATING!

Our First Woman Pope now opens her eyes and smiles.

And her Glowing Smile of Pure Love*Amor* GOES VIRAL AROUND our whole WORLD!

YES! OH, YES!

Our First Woman Pope, herself, is ShapeShifting! SongShifting! Along with OUR BELOVED MOTHER EARTH AND HER TWIN SISTER, and the People—of the People, by the People, for the People can feel this within HER GLOWING SMILE!

"And this," she says as she glances around, "is exactly how we are going to turn around Our Whole Church's Abusive Situation that's nothing new. And has been happening for centuries, by forgiving and sending Love*Amor* to Ourselves and Everyone else. So, *si se puede!* Yes, it can be done!

"Look," she continues, "a few years back I read an article how the young male elephants had formed groups, because their fathers and other older male elephants had been slaughtered for their tusks that were shipped to the wealthy across the whole world. And not just to China, but all around the world. And so without the guidance of their fathers and uncles and other older male elephants, these young groups of male elephants ran rampant, raping young and old female elephants and even female hippos.

"It was a phenomenon. Nothing like this had ever been seen before. Elephants had always been considered civilized and well behaved. Photos were taken for study, and . . . and what happened? These photos of rape and abuse and sometimes actual killings quickly also found a lucrative black market. The article ended with explaining that they now realize just how fragile elephant nature really is, and how, without the loving, respectful guidance of strong older males, young male elephants can lose, in one generation, what had previously been thought of as 'elephant nature'.

"So, yes, I have high hopes for us that fathers, uncles, older brothers and cousins will now step forward, along with grandfathers, in the Spirit of Being Sacred Elders as is so well shown again and again in the *Rain of Gold* trilogy, and, of course, used to be True in all Native Cultures. And I have high hopes that these men will come forward, not with admiration for greed and violence, but with the profound understanding of what Leon Shenandoah of the Six Nations Iroquois Confederacy said, 'I, myself, have no power. It's the people behind me who have the power. But if you're asking about strength, not power, then I can say that my greatest strength is gentleness.'

"These words from the wonderful book, *Wisdomkeepers*, that I also keep by my nightstand, are the very words that our youth need to hear and understand, especially our boys who, with their testosterone, are so full of energy and want to quickly engage in living.

"And we've had many such male leaders of their strength being gentleness in Jesus, of course, and in Gandhi, Mandela, Martin Luther King, and Cesar Chavez, who, in the face of insurmountable odds, said, '*Si se puede*'. Yes, we can, and a whole nation rallied to his cause of helping our men and women and even children who toiled in our sun-baked fields, planting and harvesting the very foods we eat.

"And for me and my Kentucky family, the man who brought home this strength of gentleness for us in the most elegant and beautiful way needs no introduction. His immortal words speak volumes! 'Float like a butterfly! Sting like a bee!' I ask you, how much more can a man be in Tune with the Balanced Compassionate Feminine Energy that we are now entering into for the next 26,000 years!

"And so, of course, it will be men like Ali, full of fun and the strength to do what's right instead of following the given times, who will also be Popes in the future. And as I see it, I, personally do believe that in Our Future it will be, more-or-less, a ratio of five women to one man for our Popes, and also for our Cardinals and Bishops of Our Church. This is my opinion. This has not yet been run through our staff and made official."

She stops once again, Breathes deeply, and closes her eyes.

"Fifth," she says, "I'd now like for all of us to close our eyes. Yes, close our eyes and place both of our hands over our Heart*Corazon* and . . . and gently go within ourselves and realize that just like the seed of an oak has all the Knowledge within it, that it needs to Know how to sprout and grow into a GREAT MAGNIFICENT OAK TREE, so do we, each of us, with the Blessing of God, have within us all the Knowledge that we need to Know how to grow into MAGNIFICENT HUMAN BEINGS!

"And this is EXACTLY why Pope Francis is endorsing, wholeheartedly, Our Movement of the Vatican from Rome to Ireland for 100 years, then to Mexico for another 100 years, and so forth, so that this can ensure that YES! We, the TRUE FOLLOWERS OF OUR LORD JESUS, can and will, indeed, grow and BLOSSOM INTO MAGNIFICENT HUMAN BEINGS OF THE PEOPLE, BY THE PEOPLE, FOR THE PEOPLE!

"And as such, I ask you, do we the People, of the People, by the People, for the People want to keep the idea that our children are born with original sin? Or, for that matter, with any imperfection? These are the type of questions we will also be addressing.

"And I'd also like to ask us, the People, of the People, by the People, for the People do we want to keep ten commandments that tell us what not to do, or . . . or would we like to replace them with suggestions on what to do in order to live a good, healthy, loving, compassionate life?

"Also, we will no longer cause ourselves any such embarrassing situations as when the Church called Galileo a heretic and imprisoned him, and even though shortly afterwards it was well known that we and our planet were not the center of the universe, it wasn't until recently that we reversed our excommunication.

"And I ask was Father Serra, who started the missions in California and was recently canonized as a saint, really a good-hearted man? Or was he an enslaving, torturing, rapist of local natives? These and 1,000s of others must be brought forth with Total Transparency. It's more than obvious why Catholics have been leaving Our Beloved Church in droves. We have been stuck in out-of-date dogma and arrogance and self-serving indoctrination.

"And yet I'd like to also add that these are not questions or matters that we are in a hurry to answer. In fact, we have been thinking, feeling that it might be best for us to wait for a whole new generation of children, who have been educated in Our Catholic schools with Our Full Natural Multi-Sensory Perception, to address these questions. For here, among these children, lay OUR FUTURE POPES! CARDINALS! BISHOPS! PRIESTS! And, of course, NUNS and BROTHERS! And now . . . all of them are free to be celibate, married, or whatever."

She smiles.

She smiles and laughs.

"But, of course," she suddenly shouts, "our immediate GREATEST BIGGEST CHANGE IS THAT we are bringing CHOCOLATE CHIP COOKIES AND WARM MILK TO THE WHOLE WORLD!"

PEOPLE GO WILD!

APPLAUDING!

CHEERING!

WHISTLING!

Then after a few moments, she raises up her hands for silence, and she now says, "Sixth, and certainly not last, I'd now like everyone to turn to the person to the left of you, then to the person on the right of you, and hold hands, looking at each other in the eyes. Then softy, gently, welcome them with all your Heart*Corazon* and *Alma*Soul into our Shared New, Brave, Kind, Loving, Compassionate, Accepting World.

"Yes, take your time and do this. We are in no hurry. Good. Good. Excellent. And now gently, softly touch foreheads, and say to each other that 'You are, in fact, Another Me, and I am, in fact, Another You'. For We are ALL! ALL! ALL FAMILY! FAMILY! FAMILY THE WHOLE WORLD OVER!"

She stops.

She stops and waits for everyone to do this. She, too, is in no hurry.

"Okay," she finally says, "everyone now please place your right hand over your heart and raise your left hand, palm open and up to the sky, and say, using your full name, 'I, so and so, now take a solemn oath, within Our Womb of Creation Creating, to help Our Almighty God Create a World where it is easier to Be Kind, Compassionate, All-Inclusive, and GOOD OF HEART*CORAZON*!'"

This is when the Voices of 100s of millions of Women of Vision, Women of Power, Women of Substance unite singing, "WE'VE GOT THE WHOLE WORLD IN OUR HANDS! WE'VE GOT THE WHOLE WHOLE *MUNDO EN NUESTRAS MANOS!*"

REJOICE!

REJOICE!

REJOICE!

And NOW from all around Our Sacred Holy Planet Mother Earth the People—of the People, by the People, for the People—join in with Dancing and Singing and Fireworks, showing the whole world joy and celebration!

AMEN!

AWOMEN!

ACHILDREN!

ASTAR COUSINS!

100 Years into Our Future
Oaxaca, Mexico

WE HEAR CHURCH BELLS!

We hear beautiful, long, rich bong bong echoing sound of old fashioned church bells! It's a beautiful bright sunny spring day, and You, Me, We come zooming down into the valley of Oaxaca, Mexico surrounded by mountains in a spaceship-looking modern aircraft. Suddenly Our Modern Aircrafts stop and hover in mid-air before gently coming down for landing in this ancient state capital of red-tiled roofs and little twisting narrow cobblestone streets.

You, Me, We have ZOOMED in from Our Vatican in Ireland, from Our Village of where Confucius was born in China, from Our Village where Ghandi was born in India, from Our Village where Mother Teresa was born, from Our Village where Ann Frank was born, and so many other Sacred Holy Places like from Our Sacred Holy Pyramids outside of Mexico City, from all Our Holy Sacred Places around Our Beloved Mother Earth and from Our Sacred Holy Places of Our Love*Amor* Six Sister Planets, plus Our Twin Mother Earth, who is now once more thriving in Good Health, and then, of course, from Our Village of where Our Great Mohammed Ali was born; he, who was OUR FIRST TO PROCLAIM, "YOU! ME! WE!" on stage with shaking hands when he was no longer Our Super Human Being, and instead was reduced by Parkinson's to BEING a Totally Spiritual Male Human, Aglow with Our Entire Complete Balanced WombMan Energy of Our Next 26,000 years!

You, Me, We all come ZOOMING in Super Modern Aircraft which are TS FREE, meaning Free of Time and Space, just as Albert so well informed us nearly 200 years ago. And You, Me, We see Our Little Ancient twisting narrow cobblestone streets between the old tile-roofed buildings and Our Local People rushing with excitement down these streets, carrying enormous bundles of beautiful flowers and large baskets of gorgeous-looking fresh vegetables and fruit, and joyful little kids carrying puppies, rabbits, ducks, chickens, squealing little pigs, and baby goats calling with forceful little high-pitched voices.

The huge Church Bells continue BONGING and ECHOING throughout Our Entire Valley as You, Me, We are now also rushing down Our twisting cobblestone streets with such joyful excitement! For Our Third and Last Woman Pope of Ireland has ZOOMED in for Our Collective Heart*Corazon* and *Alma*Soul PASSING of Our Pope's Baton from Ireland to Mexico for Our World Wide Catholic Church, in conjunction with All Our Holy Spiritually Connected Faiths throughout Our Universe, One Verse, One Song, and so, hence, Our Spiritual Symphony of Creation Creating continues soothing You, Me, We, All of us.

And so side-by-side, Our Last Woman Pope from Ireland and Our First Woman Pope of Mexico walk step-by-step down Ancient Cobblestones to Our Smallest Church of all of Our 20 Catholic Churches throughout Oaxaca.

And from every Home, every Village, every City, every school, every community, every mall, every air and water ship, all around Our Beloved Mother Earth and her Six Sister Planets, plus now her own Twin Sister Planet WATCH! LISTEN! ENJOY! AND

CELEBRATE with all their Heart*Corazones* and *Alma*Souls.

And Our Two Women Popes now go within Our Ancient Little Church along with All of Us and many of Us dip our fingertips in Our Bowl of Holy Water and make Our Sign of Our Cross over ourselves as we continue up Our isle and take Our Seats. And we see that Jesus is no longer hanging on the cross up on Our Altar.

Now Our Lord Jesus is sitting alongside his Beloved Beautiful Wife Magdalene with His Holy Mother Mary and His Blessed Father Joseph at their side.

Our Church Bells have ceased ringing and You, Me, We now see a row of mostly Women Cardinals and Bishops and Priests come up each side to Our Altar. And now Our Most Holy Sacred Ceremony Commences and both Women Popes genuflect, giving their respect to Jesus and Magdalene and Mary and Joseph, then raise up their Mighty WingArms to Our Heavens, welcoming Our Legions of Singing Angels with GREAT BIG BIG HAPPY SMILES!

And so, of course, You, Me, We Smile, too, and Our Collective Human Being Smile Lights up OUR ALMIGHTY'S AGLOW SMILE THROUGHOUT OUR ENTIRE UNIVERSE!

"You, Me, We have arrived!" proclaims Our Last Woman Pope of Ireland, "to this Holy Sacred Place that those nuns up in Wisconsin saw so clearly when they read *Rain of Gold* and prevailed — with Father James' help — to invite Our Grandson of *Doña Margarita* and *Doña Guadalupe* to come and visit with them, and what did this Hollow Bone, Buffalo Bone of a Human Being do? He brought to them a travel bag full of Miracle *Mangos*, which are Our Foundation of Our Women Pope Leadership and Our Changing of Our Guard every 100 years!

"Heaven on Mother Earth WE DO PLANT!

"And every generation brings their Own Unique Stardust that they gathered from Our Heavens when they came across the Universe along with their Own Guardian Angel, so they can help Our Almighty plant his Holy Sacred Stardust Garden of Eternal *Amor* throughout All of Our Creation Creating — for this is who You, Me, We, All of Us Human Beings are, Instruments for Giving Birth to Our All-Loving God Almighty throughout OUR UNIVERSE!

"And in this vein Ireland Passes onto Mexico, this Rosary, which we have now seen Glowing even from Outer Space for Our last 100 Sacred Years! Do you accept this Holy Spiritual Baton for *la gente de México*?"

"*Con todo mi corozon y alma, Yo Maria de Gloria y Jesusita* accept," says Our First Woman Pope *de México*, who'd been a Sister, then left Our Church, married, had seven children, and when her beloved husband, who'd been a priest, died, she, at the age of 78, had returned to *Be* One of Our First Women Priests of Latin America, then a Bishop and a Cardinal as well.

So You, Me, We, All of Us cheer! Applaud! And Sing along with Our Legions of Angels! And Our Beloved Mother Earth and Father Sky rejoiced, purring together like happy fat cats.

"And We thank You, *Señora Maria, Madre de Dios*," continues Our First Woman Pope *de México*, "and Thank You, Saint Joseph! And thank you, Pope Francis, who heroically helped guide us into Our next 50,000 years of Our Universal, All-Inclusive Catholic Church, of general interest and values, hence having broad sympathies and understanding and acceptance for all! For You, For Me, For We, For All of Us are in Our process of Giving Birth to God, which means bringing out the very best in each of us out into the world!

"REJOICE!

"REJOICE!

"REJOICE!

"And also recognize that we have many guests from Our Philippines where Our Vatican will go for the next 100 years, then of course, to that rich valley between France and Germany, and then to Africa, where then Our Vatican of Our Beloved Church will continue Activating Our Zigzagging Sacred Design around Our Whole Globe!

"And with such a Sacred Design, wars and violence have become a forgotten memory of Our Past for we've already seen that with assistance from Our Star Cousins, wars and violence, hunger and unsanitary conditions have enormously diminished in the last 100 years, and we can all now see Glowing Light at the end of Our Dark Tunnel that has been SoulBent with greed and selfishness, destroying our planet just as Our Mother Earth's Twin Sister was destroyed by Human People eons of Timeless Time ago.

"So now I say, *salute* to Us! For We, the People, Of the People, For the People, By the People, have discovered in these last 100 years, that when You, Me, We Activate Our Womb of Creation Within Us, then We, Ordinary People, become Extra Ordinary with Our Blessings of Our Almighty and United Together with *Corazon y Alma*, You, Me, We can make this a better and kinder world!

"So now turn and face each other, and say, '*si se puede*,' as Caesar Chavez so well said. For We have done it, and We can keep doing it for we no longer live in the Dark Ages of fear and doubt, but in the Golden Light of Our Collective Godvolution of Being Miracle Makers.

"So now each of you place your hands behind your back and say, 'You are another me, and I am another you.' Yes, yes, take your time and look into each other's eyes, and say these Holy Words that originally came from one of Our Native Tribes here in Central Latin America."

She stops and sees how People treat each other with such gentle, kind, patient Love*Amor*.

"Oh, this Feels so good," she says, "and now each of you please bend forward and touch foreheads gently, realizing that this is Our New Strength, Our Power of Gentleness, which Gandhi taught us can move empires! For we are now well into Our Golden Age of 26,000 years of Balanced, Compassionate, Loving Energy for all, and hence, in Tune with Our Symphony of Our Universe!"

And You, Me, We, All of Us are smiling, nodding, Feeling thoroughly wondrous deep inside.

"Good, good," says Our First Woman Pope *de México*, "so now please before we begin Our Mass, let us open up for sharing with Heart*Corazon* as we've learned to do in the last 100 years from Ireland.

"And once more, I'd like for us to thank all those great brave women and men and children who participated with the helpful guidance of Our Great Heroic Pope Saint Francis, Our last Pope of Rome, moving Us into this New Consciousness. Remember, Pope Francis immediately refused to move into the great facilities of the Vatican. And instead moved into a small humble apartment.

"All right, now let's speak up. For remember, we are now all participants Of the People, For the People, By the People."

A dozen hands go up, and one little girl about six years old stands up on her bench so she can be seen and with a little brown puppy in her arms, she shouts.

"I have something very important to say!"

People laugh.

"Well, go on right ahead," says Our First Woman Pope *de México*.

"You touch *mi Corazon*," she says. "My little puppy and I love coming to Church *con mi familia*!"

"Well, thank you. I'm very happy to hear that. What is your name, may I ask?"

"*Margarita*," says the little girl. "And, I, too, want to be Our Pope when I grow up, but before I get real old like you."

Our Woman Pope and everyone else BURST OUT LAUGHING WITH *CARCAJADAS*.

"Well, then, my dear," says Our Woman Pope, "why don't you and your little puppy come up here now, so you get a feel for this job that you are going to *Be* doing."

Our little girl doesn't just get down from her bench. Oh, no! She LEAPS down with her little puppy in hand, RACING up the isle to the altar.

"So do you Know what you are going to say to Our People when you become Pope?" asks Our Present Pope *de México*.

"YES!" she shouts. "I'm going to tell everyone that from now on we give chocolate chip cookies and warm milk to everyone, instead of flesh and blood of Jesus, because everyone loves cookies and warm milk, even my puppy!"

You, Me, We ALL BURST OUT LAUGHING, and now Jesus up at Our Altar, leaps to His feet and start SOULSPINNING and HIS SoulSpinning Love*Amor* Energy goes viral around Our Whole World, and Out! OUT! OUT to Our furthest reaches of OUR Universe!

And our old Vatican in Rome, which is Sky-Linked, rejoices with a Wondrous Symphony as Our First Woman Pope *de México* now begins her First Official Mass. For this is what Our Old Vatican has become: a Spiritual Music City for all Our New Vaticans of Our Planet.

And through all of Our Catholic Churches of Oaxaca and You, Me, We see a Woman Priest, and in flashing quick ZOOMING pictures, You, Me, We see that throughout all of Mexico and Our Whole World Our Catholic Churches and Churches of other denominations are PACKED FULL!

Going to Church is Our New Global Frontier!

Praying several times a day is Our New Path!

Singing at 3 pm every afternoon, no matter where you are and what you are doing, is Our New Interconnected Miracle Seed Planting!

And You, Me, We rejoice and Wildflowers blossom by zillions and Our Mother Earth is BIG BIG HAPPY, for Her Twin Sister Planet is also now enjoying New Life! And Our Whole Universe smiles, taking in a great big deep GodBreath! WE HAVE FINALLY AWAKENED!

ACHILDREN!

AWOMEN!

AMEN!

ASTARCOUSINS!

Now What?

Here We Go!

OKAY, YOU'VE READ THE BOOK, AND NOW WE NEED TO MOVE into action, into getting an endorsement from Pope Francis, saying he whole-heartedly agrees that the time has come to have a Woman Pope, and move the Vatican to Ireland and then keep moving the Vatican every 100 years.

But he can't do it alone.

We, of the People, by the People, for the People need to help him with the Mighty Hand of GodGoding by sending him 100s of 1,000s of 1,000,000s of emails saying that we want a Woman Pope, Women Cardinals, Women Bishops, Women Priests — Women of Substance who've lived, married or didn't marry, had children or didn't have children, women who aren't perfect, who have maybe even gotten divorced, but Women who Live Life from their Heart*Corazon* and *Alma*Soul, and hence are Sacred Elders!

And this needs to get done with the quick sudden Power of a Flash Flood, a Meteorite! For according to the Mayan Calendar on December 21, 2012 we finished up 26,000 years of out-of-balance aggressive masculine energy and we've moved into 26,000 years of balanced compassionate feminine energy, and by November 10, 2026 3pm California time we need to have all Our Stardust Seeds planted for the next 26,000 years.

In other words, by November 10, 2026 3pm — the same hour my mother sang every afternoon to her Miracle Mango Tree — the Pope will not just have endorsed us, but this movement of Miracle Grandmothers leading will be already WRITTEN IN THE STARS AND JOYFULLY ALIVE ALL OVER OUR PLANET!

YOU! ME! WEEE! WEEE! WEEE! All of us are on OUR WAY, and there's nothing that can stop US!

Myself and my organization will be contacting convents and women's clubs and giving away FREE books! Millions at a pop! And this is just Our Start! For You, Me, We, All of Us have the WHOLE WORLD IN OUR HANDS!

See the film *The Two Popes.*

See the film *The Francis Effect.*

See the film *The Man Who Keeps His Word.*

These first three films will anchor you, then leap into *St. Vincent* and *Before I Go* and see what the woman in *Before I Go* puts into her box labeled God. WOW! I LAUGHED MY HEAD OFF!

People are so hungry for meaning, for purpose, for something good and decent and real. Also, see *The Dream Seller*, and revisit the oldies *Forest Gump, Grand Torino, August Rush, Phenomenon, The Gods Must Be Crazy, Whale Rider, A Man for All Seasons* and please send us your own list.

Watch movies that help you have a wonderful relaxing night full of good dreams, so you can Awaken Feeling that yes, You, Me, We, All of Us are already planting Heaven on Mother Earth with Our First Woman Pope and Grandmothers Leading Our Miraculous Way!

P.S. While watching the *Francis Effect* and *The Man Who Keeps His Word*, I realized that Pope Francis is using English and Spanish in a whole new way. He is using language from the Heart and Soul like our Indigenous ancestors used to do. He never uses the languaging of command or of law and order. He uses a languaging of Heartfelt Compassion and Empathy and Humor. In fact, Humor and Smiles and Belly-Shaking *CARCAJADAS* ARE OUR NEW FUN, FUN DREAMVOYAGE!

Bonus Stories

Miracle Magic

YOU SEE, AFTER MY VISIT WITH THOSE NUNS AND PRIESTS UP by the Great Lakes Miracles started happening. Suddenly I was being invited to give talks to all these religious groups. Twice I was invited by some nuns to go to Oakland to give a talk at the Holy Name Convent. Then I was asked to come and speak to 16 different Christian denominations in Ohio.

Then I was invited to the great world event in South Korea where they had the largest religious spiritual gathering the world has ever seen. I was invited to speak there, but I already had a commitment to go to Oaxaca to speak at the Benito Juarez University.

And while I was going to all these places, I met so many people who were giving birth to God. They were ShapeShifting, SongShifting, Accelerating Our Sacred Path into a Huge 300 foot Global Spiritual Tidal Wave.

So, here are a few Bonus Stories that show this, moving all of us into a GLOBAL WORLD OF PERSONAL BALANCE, HARMONY AND PEACE AND ABUNDANCE FOR ALL.

Buffalo Grass

A FEW YEARS AFTER MY TALK WITH THESE NUNS AND PRIESTS, I was in Iowa giving a talk at a university to faculty and students. I was talking about buffalo grass/prairie grass and how it used to grow naturally in Iowa and all across the plains. Then I explained how prairie grass had been able to survive ice ages and draughts for 1,000s of years, because it had so many different grasses per square yard.

And now I tried to explain how we, with our modern civilization, had messed everything up, but I was having such a difficult time explaining what I wanted to say that I finally just stopped and said, "I really don't know that much about what I'm talking about, so is there anyone here who can help me?"

I'll never forget, a tall handsome man who looked a lot like the movie star Gregory Peck immediately stood up. "I can help you," he said. "I have my doctoral on prairie grass, or as you said buffalo grass."

He then explained to us that the astonishing thing about this grass wasn't just that it had 10-15 different grasses — I don't remember exactly how many — within each square foot, but that there was a very short little grass that had a twenty-two feet deep root system into the earth, deeper than any tree, or anything else in the prairie. And a 1,000 year ice age only froze the first ten to twelve feet of the earth's surface and a 1,000 year drought only dried out the first ten to twelve feet, so then this little grass was able to stay alive and give nourishment to the tall grasses.

Then he said that when the good times came, the tall grasses, that grew up to the chest of a buffalo, didn't forget it had been the little grasses that had kept them alive during the bad times. So now all these tall vibrant grasses worked together, realizing they needed to nurture and keep the short little grasses alive, so then united as one entity they'd be able to survive in the long haul.

And now this tall handsome man explained to us what we, the Europeans, did when we came. We immediately set fire and plowed under all the natural grasslands and we put in wheat — one crop. And when a drought came, the wheat died and the earth dried out, and that was when the famous dust storms came and they blew the topsoil off the Midwest, that had taken millions of years for nature to develop the rich topsoil of the plains.

Then he added that this is what we've continued to do all over the world. Where ever we go, we put in one crop, destroying the natural diversity that's been keeping our environment and earth healthy for timeless time.

This tall handsome man totally blew me away. I was now able to explain that this was exactly what my Indigenous *mamagrandes de México* had been talking about when they'd raised my dad and mom to understand that there's only One Race, the Human Race, with many different cultures and beliefs, and so it is only when we accept each other as *familia* and cherish our differences that we have the wisdom with which to survive Our Mother Earth's dramatic ongoing changes.

In other words, what I'm saying is that simply the great world-reknown museum of Tolerance in L.A. isn't enough anymore. What we now need is a museum of accepting and cherishing our differences, because one crop, one way of thinking, one way of living is for sure the end for us, Human People.

King Ranch

THERE ARE NO ACCIDENTS. SHORTLY AFTER MY EXPERIENCE in Iowa I was invited to speak at the famous King Ranch, which proclaims to be the largest ranch in the world. It's over one thousand four hundred square miles in southeast Texas.

And at first, I didn't want to go, thinking they were just one more of these big bragging racist bad guys with the common Texas ignorance of saying, "remember the Alamo," not realizing that there had been more Tex-Mexicans who'd died at the Alamo fighting for Texas's independence than Tex-Anglos.

But still because of what my mother had told me about "forgiveness" when I also hadn't wanted to go see retired nuns and priests, I went. And what did I discover? WOW! I discovered that the King Ranch is one of the good guys, and is leading us with solutions into OUR WONDERFUL FUTURE WORLD!

Not only do they have their own town, they have their own hotel, and their own herb gardens and organic foods, and also most of their cowboys are of Mexican descent and they get benefits and have been working for the King Ranch for generations.

And of course, like everyone else, the King Ranch does enormous one crop planting. But different than others, they leave large round circles of nature's natural wild diversity so that the deer and native brush and plants can survive and live. And if we did this all over the world, we too could prosper like the King Ranch has done, and yet help keep a healthy vibrant Mother Earth.

The spokesperson for the King Ranch was a young woman and the first thing she explained to me was why she loves working for them and why they're always on the cutting edge of our times. Simply, they go to our top universities and hire the most brilliant young graduates they can find who have new and sometimes even radical ideas. And also the King Ranch has a program for encouraging and supporting the children of their workers to go to college.

And why do the owners and bosses of the King Ranch do this? They do this, the spokeswoman explained to me, because they're not afraid of change. They embrace change just like Einstein. And yet at the same time, they keep their stability of old fashioned Texas business by selling beef, lots and lots of quality free-range beef.

So, yes, solutions are possible even in our ever changing expanding world. In fact, many solutions are already in place and at work. It's just that we don't hear about them on the news, and also, like me, so many of us hold on to the past and assume that successful companies must be one of the bad guys.

OH, I TELL YOU IT WAS AN INSPIRATION FOR ME TO VISIT THE KING RANCH! I was thrilled to see that this huge successful modern day company is one of the good guys, and that their workers were happy! BIG BIG HAPPY! Smiling and laughing and telling me how their parents and grandparents and great grandparents had been *vaqueros*, and how they were treated well even back then when Texas was one of the most racist states in all of the United States!

Miracle Making Grandmothers

A FEW YEARS BACK WHEN ISRAEL AND PALESTINE WERE READY to go to war, the Grandmothers in Palestine started sending emails to the Grandmothers in Israel, saying, "We lovc you! We love your kids and grandkids. Don't pay attention to our leaders. We don't want war!"

Immediately the Grandmothers in Israel started sending emails to the Palestinian Grandmothers saying, "We love you! We love your children and your grandchildren. Don't pay attention to our leaders. We also don't want war!"

The Love Messages going back and forth between these two sets of Miracle Making Grandmothers went viral with such a profusion that the war communications of each country fell apart.

Why? Because the Vibrational Frequencies of Love*Amor* come from the Heart*Corazon* and are so powerful that they automatically dissolved the lower vibrational frequencies of hate, revenge, jealousy and greed.

And we can do this Worldwide with Miracle Making Grandmothers leading the way, then You, Me, We, All of Us also sending messages of Love and not wanting war where ever we have leaders who are proposing war as a solution.

War is out of date!

Our Spaceship Mother Earth has gotten small, and is getting smaller every day, so Our Heart-Soul-Centered Vibrational Frequencies of Love*Amor* can now quickly dissolve all the lower frequencies of anger, revenge, jealousy, and greed.

In fact, this is how Our Six Sister Planets did it eons of timeless time ago, and they were even more lost and violent than us. There is no other way. We all need to become Miracle Makers once again, and restart planting Our Holy Garden of Heaven on Earth on a Daily Basis just as Our Sacred Elder Grandmothers used to do and my own mother did with her Miracle Mango Tree.

This is Our Future!

For we're all One Family, and in the process of Collectively moving Our Whole Human Being Consciousness into a kinder, more wonderful, BEAUTIFUL WORLD!

Tsunami

Several years ago there was a tsunami in Asia where 10s of 1,000s of people were killed, and I read an article — I believe in Time magazine — where the writer said there was a tribe of sea gypsies, of native people who hadn't adopted modern language or modern lifestyle and that none of these people were killed.

Why? Because days before the tsunami happened they saw the elephants on land going up to the high ground, and at sea they saw the dolphins going way out to sea. So they, too, immediately began going up to the high ground if they were on land, and if they were at sea, they took their little boats way out into the ocean.

Then when this catastrophe happened and the ocean withdrew a long ways back and all of a sudden there were thousands of flopping fish along the shore and people were so excited to rush out to get the fish that they didn't see the gigantic sea wall rushing back to shore. And in minutes this tsunami demolished whole towns and villages, killing 10s of 1,000s of people, and yet not one of these native people were killed.

Why? Because simply the native people still saw themselves as being part of nature. In fact, this brilliant writer of Time magazine said that their language has no word for nature, because they consider themselves to be a part of our natural world, and hence they respect and recognize the wisdom of elephants knowing to go to high ground and dolphins knowing to go out to sea.

Can you see what has happened? We, with modern language and lifestyle, really did eat the Forbidden Fruit from the Tree of Knowledge. And in doing this, we divorced ourselves from nature and began to believe that we were the only intelligent life on this planet.

And back in the Garden, before we ate of the Forbidden Fruit, we'd recognized the profound instinctive, intuitive, intelligent, psychic powers of all God's Creation.

Why? Because each of us had been DIRECTLY connected to Our Creator. We hadn't been separated from Our Almighty by manmade male-based languages and organized religions and nations. We'd all been Indigenous People the world over and Miracles hadn't been seen as unusual, but as an Ordinary Part of Living Life for us, and all of Nature.

And this is where we're all now going. Back To Our Future with Our Grandmothers once more Being Our Natural Leaders and we once again speaking with HeartFelt SoulAwaken SingSong Languages just like the sea gypsies who didn't lose one person in the tsunami.

WE'RE ON OUR WAY!

THERE'S NOTHING THAT CAN STOP US.

IN FACT, IT'S ALREADY DONE, COMPLETED, AND WRITTEN IN OUR STARS AS WE DANCE OUR WAY BACK INTO OUR HEAVEN ON OUR BELOVED MOTHER EARTH!

Look Daddy! She's an Angel

More and more of our children are now coming into our world with such a highly developed frequency of HeartSoul Vision that they are re-educating their parents. Take for instance what happened a few years back when I was giving a talk in El Paso, Texas about Transformation through ShapeShifting and SongShifting.

This tall handsome Tex-Mex man raised his hand and asked if he could share a story with us. I said, sure, of course, and he told us how he loved being a father and loved to take his daughter with him when he went shopping, but then he added how last time he'd lost his three-year-old daughter at the mall.

"So my wife warned me," he said, laughing, "that I'd pay big time if I lost our little Rosita again, but I assured Sophia that I'd keep my eye on our daughter like a hawk, and I wouldn't lose her this time.

"'You better not!' shouted my wife as I went out the door.

"But well, what can I say, here I was at the mall and our little daughter was gone once again, and quite truthfully as I ran around searching for her, I was more concerned with what my wife Sophia was going to do to me than I was with having lost our little girl once more.

"I mean, she couldn't have gone far. I'd been holding her hand only seconds ago, but I had to admit that this was exactly what had happened last time. I'd been so caught up looking at these new electronic gadgets—things I knew I didn't even need—that I hadn't noticed when Rosita had let go of my hand.

"Then I saw the back of this extremely tall heavy-set Black woman and she was standing still and all bent over like she was getting sick or having a heart attack. So I immediately rushed over to see if I could help her, but to my utter shock there was my little girl standing in front of this huge woman looking up at her and the elderly Black woman was bent over sobbing in tears."

"What happened?" I asked. "Did my little girl do something to you?"

"'Yes, she did,' said the huge woman, 'she told me I'm beautiful!'

"'She is, Daddy,' said Rosita, taking my hand. 'Look at her, she's an Angel and she's so beautiful.'

"And I could see that our little girl's eyes were glowing with such love that it took my breath away. She, simply, didn't see this woman as I and the rest of the world saw her."

"'No one in all my life has ever said anything like this to me,' said the large woman, sobbing with such emotion that her whole body was jerking.

"People were gathering, wanting to know what was going on.

"'Can I hug you and kiss you?' now asked my daughter. 'Eh, can I please?'

"'Well, yes, of course, child, but I'm all wet from crying.'

"'Wet with Angel tears!' shouted Rosita, stretching out her arms and getting up on her tip toes.

"And as the large tall Black woman bent down to hug her, people began applauding, they were so moved.

"I was stunned. Here was this woman, who I had seen as a huge heavy-set unattractive Black woman, and before my eyes she was shifting, transforming as you've just told us about into a beautiful large woman. The years were literally falling away from her, and she was now looking at least twenty years younger, and extremely attractive.

"So I guess my little girl's saying what she'd said with such love and sincerity caused this woman to activate her Kingdom of God within herself, and SongShift, ShapeShift as you've explained to us is now happening all over our globe."

"Exactly," I now said to this man, "your daughter gave the woman the Holy Sacred Key to give Birth to God within herself, which used to be so natural for all of us, and it's just that we've been beaten down with so much crap that we've forgotten how to do this.

"You see, just like those kids at the airport who were Aglow as they raced around me with their Angel Arms stretched out, children are now coming to us in this Sacred State of Being all over our planet.

"Bob Dylan was right, the times are changing, but we no longer need to get stoned in order to bypass our interrupting word-busy-thinking heads and SlipSlide into Our Ever Loving Heart*Corazon* and *Alma*Soul Centers.

"Therefore, Fathers like this man are now needed all over the world who are strong and confident enough to protect their daughters' Natural Spiritual Powers. Because as we make this Global Shift from 26,000 years of out-of-date and out-of-balance aggressive masculine energy into 26,000 years of Balanced Compassionate Feminine Energy, there is a huge powerful Global Tsunami male-based attack still trying to hold onto control and push women backwards and take away their power.

"So we need lots of strong loving fathers, not just strong mothers, to protect these children who are now coming into our world with such a highly developed HeartSoul Vision, which of course, IS OUR FUTURE AND ULTIMATELY THERE'S NOTHING THAT CAN STOP OUR COLLECTIVE WONDROUS MIRACULOUS FUTURE!"

PS
Three Miracles

A Godsend

HELLO! HELLO! HELLO!
MIRACLES ARE COMING OUR WAY!

Look, just a couple of months back my sister Linda called me and said that there's a Villaseñor, David James Villaseñor, that has contacted us and wants to meet us and find out if he's part of our family.

I asked Linda if he's read *Rain of Gold*. She said yes, and that she has a good feeling about him, so I said sure, go ahead and invite him. She did and David James Villaseñor came down from northern California with his wife, Christine and their daughter, Alexandria.

And we found out that Alexandria Villaseñor is a close friend of Greta Thunberg and she's also world famous in her own right since the age of 13 when she sat on a park bench across the street in front of the United Nations building in New York City for 40 weeks every Friday, with a sign on each side of her about Climate Warming.

"My God," I said to Alexandria, who's now 17 years old, "what got into you to grab our global issue by the horns and just go for it? Are you a GODSEND? A MIRACLE MAKER?"

She shrugged. We were at the dinner table enjoying the delicious meal *que mi Amor* Carmen had prepared for us.

Her father James laughed. "Here, let me tell you what Lexi did when she was 7 years old, then you'll understand who our little girl is. You see, this is our second marriage so her brothers and sisters from our previous marriages are way older than her. And when Lexi was 7 years old, she came to us one day and said, "We've got to go on a family vacation. We never go on vacations, and we need to go on one together so we can get closer as a family."

Her mother and Alexandria laughed, and her father continued, "So I told her, 'That sounds great, honey, but you know we don't have the money to go on a vacation.'

"And she said, 'Yes, we do. I've got it all figured out. Look, this is where we're going to go. We'll drive and I've already made reservations for us at a motel that's reasonably priced and these are the places we can visit for free and we can buy our food at grocery stores and not eat out.'"

"We couldn't believe it," said her mother. "It was all laid out like a travel agency. So we went and had a wonderful time and we did get closer as a family."

"And so," continued her father, "ever since 7 years old, Lexi's been our leader. And when Christine went to get her master's in environmental studies at Columbia University in New York, she took Lexi with her, and I stayed home to take care of the rest of our family."

I was stunned. There was just nothing I could say. But then my sister, Linda started clapping, and so Carmen and I joined her.

"I guess it's like we're meeting a young female Gandhi or Mandela," said Linda.

"Yes, I agree," I said, "some people Know why they come into this world. Like Mozart, a music prodigy child, and Alexandria, my God, a PRODIGY GLOBAL LEADER."

"Hey, let's not overwhelm the poor girl," said Carmen.

"Exactly," said her mother, "and this is why she has decided to go back to high school, so she can have at least a couple of years of being an almost normal teenager."

"That is between already scheduled appointments," said her dad, laughing. "She keeps us so busy that I quit my job. I now work full time for our daughter raising money. It took us nearly $300,000 dollars just to take 22 children with her to the Global Climate Warming Conference they just had in Egypt, which was a disappointment, and yet good contacts were made so we can carry on this movement."

"Did anything come about from you sitting on that park bench across the street from the United Nations building in New York?" I asked.

"At first no one paid any attention to me," she said, "but after a few weeks people did, especially when they realized I was one of the young people who'd met Greta when she sailed across the Atlantic. Students and teachers joined me, and we got on the news, then we set a date for a march, but I insisted they first go to school and check in, because their schools can't get paid if they don't."

"She organized the whole march like she did for our vacation," said her dad, "and busloads of kids along with teachers and parents came. Well over 350,000 marched down main street to Wall Street, showing the business world that they refuse to be taken lightly, and now Lexi has a global following of millions, and not just individuals, but also business organizations."

My GodGoding, and so they were with us for 3 days and it turned out that David James' great grandfather, Everardo Villaseñor, was one of my father's older brothers who'd gone with our great grandfather Colonel Don Pio to Mexico City to celebrate President Porfirio Diaz's 70th birthday with whom Don Pio had fought side-by-side against the French.

But when they got to the capitol, they weren't allowed to join the celebration. Don Porfirio had built the main boulevard in Mexico City, *La Reforma*, to look like an exact replica of the main boulevard in Paris, so he didn't' want any dark Indian-looking people to be seen.

In fact, he, himself, Porfirio, a dark Indian just like Don Pio, painted his face white and gave presents of gold to all his European and American guests whom he'd invited to come and help him modernize Mexico and make huge profits for themselves.

"So," I told David James and his family, "my dad told me that when Don Pio was told that he could not enter the capitol to join his old friend's celebration that the well-dressed armed guards just laughed at him and said, "Go across the river where all the other colonels that fought alongside our great president are camped." Don Pio's grandsons felt so horrified the way their grandfather was disrespected that unarmed, that night, they went in with a white flag to protest and they were all shot to death.

"And my father told me that this is when the Mexican Revolution of 1910 got started. Because Don Pio and all the other old ex-colonels rose up with their people with such rage that they defeated Don Porfirio's army of well-dressed guards and then went back to their ranches all across Mexico to inform *la gente* how Porfirio had sold them out to the French, even after they'd defeated them in honest combat.

"And my dad, just a little 7-year-old boy at the time, told me that Don Pio, who'd looked so strong and handsome when he'd gone to Mexico City dressed in his finest clothes and riding his finest horse, returned looking like a worn out old man with only two of his 18 grandsons who'd gone with him, and so," I added with tears streaming down my face just as they'd streamed down my dad's face every time he'd told this story, "it was figured that Everardo and all the others had been killed.

"But now with meeting you, David James Villaseñor, I'm happy to say," I said, "that obviously my dad's older brother Everardo didn't die, and maybe even a few others didn't get killed. Your grandfather, I was told, was a big strong handsome and very capable man, so he must have gotten shot to pieces, because even being unarmed, I'm sure he'd given them one hell of a battle as we Villaseñors always do."

I stopped and reached out to take James in my arms, and he was hesitant at first like he wasn't used to being hugged by a man. But then he let go, and allowed me to hug him, and he then hugged with such stunning power that he almost broke ribs. And I noticed that all this time his wife and daughter watched with tears in their own eyes.

"So I guess," I said, finally stepping back, "that by the time your grandfather recuperated and got back to his home in *Los Altos de Jalisco*, the Revolution had been going on for a few years. All the cattle and horses were gone, and the ranches had been burnt to the ground, and all the people had been killed or left. So, I guess, that seeing all this disaster was when your grandfather Everardo decided to migrate to the United States, and like you say, ended up settling in the foothills of Bakersfield, California."

"Yes," said David James, "I can now see that he must have been a very broken man, giving up all hope of ever finding any of his family, so he raised us kids to become Americans. In fact, he forbade us to speak any Spanish and he would never talk about the past.

"So you don't speak Spanish?"

"No, I don't, and, well, the only reason we became interested in finding out about my roots is because of Alexandria. She started taking Spanish classes and said, 'Well, Dad, are we related to the Villaseñor family that we've read about in the book, *Rain of Gold*?'

I told her that I didn't know, and I wasn't going to bother you. But she said, 'Dad, call him. Who knows, maybe he'll be thrilled to find out we're family.'"

"Well, you were right," I said, laughing with *carcajadas*. "My God, 350,000 marching down the streets of New York and stopping Wall Street! THAT'S POWER! Wow, we, Villaseñors, really are real ass-kickers, aren't we!"

And so they stayed for a few days, and they had *Rain of Gold* and so I gave them a copy of *Thirteen Senses* and *Wild Steps of Heaven*, which is all about *Los Altos de Jalisco* and the Villaseñors. Then I told them about my new book *Our First Woman Pope* and how we needed to give away a million ebooks as fast as possible and get people to send emails to us and Pope Francis, so he can endorse us and help Transform the whole Catholic Church into a Modern Force of Women for the Healing of Our Beloved Mother Earth, and Our Heart*Corazones*.

They loved it, and Christine gave us valuable feedback, then we went out front by our huge German Star Pine where 25 years ago we did our First Global Acupuncture of the 100s of 1,000s we need to do so we can activate Our Collective Sacred Design of Healing Power that will GLOW so brightly that it will be seen from outer space by Our Star Cousins, who are eons of Timeless Time more GodGoding Evolved than us.

They loved Our Sacred Spiritual Ritual with Our Open Heart Hand, our left hand, face up Receiving, Receiving, Receiving from Our Farthest Reaches of Our Universe, and Our Open Giving Hand, our right hand, Giving, Giving, and flooding Our Entire Mother Earth with Love*Amor* and nothing but Love*Amor*!

They got it!

They felt their open palms tingling with such Vibrations that they began smiling and then giggling with joy!

Yes! Yes! Yes! We were on the same page! So we talked and planned and it was a Wondrous Miracle of Miracles to meet members of Our Lost Tribe and find that we were as close as if we'd been raised together.

There "*are*" no accidents. So like family, we sat together and watched some of Alexandria's videos on YOUTUBE. They were all wonderful, especially the 7-minute one that she did in San Francisco, and I told her that she could easily become a writer the way she thinks and talks and . . . and she then told me that she's already completed a 160-page manuscript.

I was totally blown away. She just went for it! She didn't waste any time thinking or procrastinating. OH, WOW! I hugged her for I, too, had just gone for it to become a writer at 19 years old, and I didn't even Know how to read.

I invited my agent Bill Gladstone, my close *amigo* and one of the three strongest literary agents in the world with sales of over one and a half billion dollars to meet Lexi and her parents. And of course, they hit it right off the bat!

OH, WE FELT SO BLESSED and on Our Way of Uniting and Helping Heal Our Beloved Mother Earth, and TAKING ALL OF HUMANITY OFF THE MOST ENDANGERED LIST!

Kiss the Ground

MIRACLE TWO CAME TO US AFTER WE'D MET LEXI Villaseñor and her dad and mom in November 2022. What happened was one evening in early February 2023, I was flipping channels on TV looking for something to watch as I prepared dinner for Carmen and me. And I came across a show called, "Kiss the Ground," that had a colorful picture of a bunch of beautiful vegetables, so I turned it on.

Woody Harrelson, whom I have always liked, was narrating. He's looking out on a large natural landscape and says, "I'd given up hope. And I'm sure you have too."

Then he goes on to say how we've all been inundated with so much bad news of climate warming and the 1,000s of years of us human beings destroying our planet, so that, of course, it makes sense that we only have a few years left before it all goes kaput.

He's preaching to the choir, so I start getting bored, but then Woody added that there's hope. He's found this organization that has a solution, and it's so simple, it's about the ground we walk on. The dirt. The soil. And now I really start listening. There was someone else, besides me, who isn't just talking about all the destructive crap that we misguided humans have been doing since ever, but they, too, have a solution.

OH, WOW! So I watch the whole film as I chop and cook and

it shows us that the ground we walk on is ALIVE with roots and worms and all these tiny busy microorganisms just like my Yaqui Indian grandmother always used to show me.

Then Woody tells us about the U.S. famous midwest Dust Bowl of the 1930s that I, also, wrote about in Woman Pope that took the topsoil off the plains and Woody informs us that it was the largest single destruction of topsoil the earth has ever seen, well over 200 million square miles of rich natural soil was permanently damaged.

Then the film shows that the solution to our global predicament is that we stop killing our natural wonderful topsoil. That we stop plowing it. That we stop turning it over as we've been doing for 1,000s of years. They have a new disc made by John Deere, called a non-till, and it simply cuts a thin line into our natural soil, and then another disc drops in the seeds.

WOW! So easy! So natural! So beautiful! No more all that back-breaking hard work of plowing, thank God! Because when you turn the natural living soil over with plowing, then waters evaporate quickly or just run off. And with this non-tilling they are able to hold the waters, and hence once more make deserts and dead lake beds into glorious gardens of AgroForest.

Oh, Miracle of Miracles this was exactly how my Yaqui Indian grandmother taught us to poke holes into our natural soil and grow our vegetables in little circles in our backyard in *Carlos Malo* in Carlsbad, California when I was just learning to walk.

And then the film introduces us to a Kansas farmer named Brown, and how, when he was plowing his land, he had one disaster after another, and he was ready to give up. But then he met Ray Archuleta, the man who has been going around our country and abroad for over 30 years talking to farmers about Our Natural Miracle of Living Topsoil, and that plowing and planting single crops kills our wonderful topsoil, and so we need to not plow and diversify what we grow.

Kiss the Ground shows how after meeting Ray, Brown stops plowing and just farming corn and soybeans as the government tells him to do so he can get his government subsidies. He starts no-tilling and growing an AgroForest of diversity that's gorgeous! And he starts making a 100 dollar per acre and his fellow farmers, who've continued plowing and getting part of the 25 billion dollars government subsidies that farmer lobbyists get for them, make 3 dollars per acre.

MY GOD, I'M NOT ALONE! Someone is finally talking about — not just climate warming — but also about all the destructive crap we'd done to Our Beloved Mother Earth for 10s of 1,000s of years, and then they also validate the Sacred Knowledge of my Native Yaqui Indian grandmother of how to grow nutritious organic crops that can help save our planet from destruction!

I smile.

I laugh.

When Carmen, *el amor de mi vida,* gets home from work, I serve us dinner in our TV room, and we watch the film together. She, too, loves it, saying that this is how her Native grandmother from Michoacan also taught her to farm. And she thinks that this is a must-see film that all the teachers and students of the school district, where she works as an interpreter, need to see.

I totally agree and the next day I see "Kiss the Ground" two more times and I call my two sisters, leave a message for Sita, our organic farmer, and when Linda picks up, I tell her about the film. She gets all excited and tells me she'll watch it immediately.

Later that day, Linda calls and tells me that she's watching it for a second time and she's taking notes, learning all these new terms like "re-generation," which is what they do when they come to a place where the topsoil has been destroyed, and when they bring it back to life, what they now grow, they call an AgroForest.

OH, I'M SO EXCITED, once more this is exactly what our old Yaqui grandmother taught our mother Lupe to do, and how our *mama* was able to climatize her famous Miracle Mango Tree, so I now call up Gary, the guy who runs Snow Goose Global Thanksgiving for us, and he tells me that he's already seen the film, and that our local farmer, who's in the film, is Jason Mraz and that I've met him.

"You mean, he's the guy with the great old worn-out hat towards the end of the film who's surrounded by a great big beautiful AgroForest here in Fallbrook?"

"Yes, and you and I met him up north in the Bay Area at the organic farm owned by the owners of the Gratitude Café."

"Oh, yeah! I remember now. He's the guy I told about the Indians up in Portland who gave us Our Vision of Snow Goose Global Thanksgiving, and he loved it. And he came back with a guy, who I guess is in his band, and he had me tell him the whole story again, then he went and got a tall girl and had me tell her the story, too. And each time, Jason's eyes were totally alive. He really got it, seeing how Snow Goose Global Thanksgiving can help bring Our Living Breathing Mother Planet back into Balance and Harmony, and hence the by-products are then Peace and Abundance for all." I took in a great big deep GodBreath. "I didn't realize that was Jason in the film. He's one hell of a Spiritually Alive guy!"

"Yes, he is, and his music shows this, so that's why after we met him, I stayed in touch with him," said Gary. "He wanted to come to Snow Goose and play for us. But each time he was out of the country touring and couldn't make it on the Sunday before Thanksgiving. And then we kind of, well, lost touch."

"Well, I'll be," I said. "Then we got to call him and let him and all his people Know that with his Music and their *Kiss Our Ground* and with Our Acupuncture of Our Mother Earth and Our Vision of Snow Goose Global Thanksgiving Celebration, we can Unite and TURN OUR WHOLE PLANET AROUND IN NO TIME AT ALL!"

"I'll get on it," said Gary, glowing with vitality. "I'll call and re-establish our relationship. Obviously, I guess, they were already working on this film when we met them. Woody was there too, but you didn't meet him, he was talking to some other people."

"Well, yeah, sure, of course," I said, "the whole place was packed with so many people full of Beautiful Energy."

"Yes," said Gary with a great big smile, which is the trademark of Gary's whole family and especially of his son Conor, who'd Passed Over last year at the age of 22, but he isn't gone. No, Conor is one of these Highly Illuminated Souls, who's early passage to the Other Side, is so he can BE OF EVEN GREATER SERVICE FOR US STILL ON THIS SIDE!

Dream Voyage

MIRACLE THREE STARTED HAPPENING WHEN WE HAD A Burro Genius meeting, and we were GodBreathing real easy, Carmen and Linda and Gary and I, and also Steve and Teri. We were Geniusing. We were letting go, so Our Spirit World could come to us and Guide us and we'd then Know, with a capital "K," how to team up with Lexi and the People of *Kiss the Ground*.

We are Hollow Bones.

We are Buffalo Bones.

We are Five Receivers Receiving, Knowing in Our *Alma*Souls that we are a Natural Fit.

Lexi and Greta with all their Young People around the world taking on countries and lawmakers, and *Kiss the Ground* bringing back farmers to the understanding that it all starts with Our Natural Topsoil, and then us with Our First Woman Pope and Snow Goose Global Thanksgiving and most important of all, the realization that Our Mother Earth is ALIVE, and so with Our Sacred Global Design of Acupuncture, she'll burp, give a little *pedito*, and start healing rapidly.

And yet, we also felt like something was missing.

We'd given copies of *Our First Woman Pope* to Lexi and her dad and mom and we'd done a Spiritual Ceremony where we'd put our 19 foot deep Acupuncture into Our Mother Earth, and they'd felt the Tingling Love*Amor* Vibes come into their open palms.

And we'd Prayed.

And we'd turned Everything over to GodGoding and yet something was missing, because instead of us feeling Energized, we felt tired. Really wiped out, so that night Carmen and I went to bed early, instantly falling asleep.

Then somewhere in the early morning hours, I began seeing all these Catholic Churches around the world with little sprouting gardens.

I smiled.

This was really nice, but no big deal until I heard these huge Church bells BONGING AND BONGING, and I now saw streams of People coming to these Churches, and not necessarily to pray, but to garden, and all these little gardens suddenly EXPLODED into HUGE AGROFORESTS, and they began to GLOW WITH LOVE*AMOR*! And now . . . millions and millions of People were rushing to each of these Churches all over the world, and not just on Sunday, but coming every day of the week!

100s of MILLIONS OF PEOPLE and the Church Bells continued BONGING! BONGING! BONGING! And echoing all around our whole planet, and now I could see that all these Happy People were working Our Sacred Soil of Beloved Holy Mother Earth with such *gusto* with their God Gifted Hands just as my mother Lupe had done as a 7-year-old child every day in Rain of Gold canyon, performing her Third Holy Miracle of each day!

I awoke!

I awoke smelling Wildflowers and here is Jesus SoulSpinning at each of these Holy Churches, and so this isn't a Dream!

NO! NO! NO! This is a DREAMVOYAGE!

And hence is REALLY HAPPENING WITHIN OUR COLLECTIVE CELLULAR MEMORY OF OUR FABULOUS FUTURE!

And all over Our Mother Earth People are now LAUGHING WITH *CARCAJADAS* AND SINGING IN ONE UNITED HOLY VOICE OF GODGODING as they garden at these LUSCIOUS AGROFORESTS!

I leap out of bed!

This is, indeed, how Our Six Sister Planets did it, bringing their own lost, violent planets BACK INTO SPIRITUAL HARMONY WITH THE GREAT SYMPHONY OF OUR ENTIRE UNIVERSE!

WE'VE DONE IT!

YOU! ME! WEEE! WEEE! ARE REALLY DOING IT!

With Love and Prayer and Song just as my mother Lupe did every afternoon at 3 pm with her Miracle Mango Tree!

YOU! ME! WEEE! WEEE! WEEE!

Laughing with *carcajadas,* I shout, "THANK YOU, GOD! THANK YOU! THANK YOU! THANK YOU!"

Carmen awakes. "Are you okay?" she asks.

"Yes, a Miracle is happening all over Our Planet! All of Our Catholic Churches are regenerating into HUGE LUSCIOUS GARDENS!"

"You mean like Gardens of Eden?"

"Exactly! All of Our Catholic Churches and Convents are becoming Gardens of Eden and they're GLOWING with Love*Amor*! And Our Star Cousins can see Our Glowing Collective Sacred Design all around Our Mother Earth and they're ZOOMING in to help celebrate OUR GLOBAL AWAKENING!

"And wait! Hold on! Jesus is telling us that this Mother's Day, May 10th Latino style, we are to take English and Spanish editions of *Our First Woman Pope* to Pope Francis at the Vatican or wherever he might be, and say, "This is Our Global Future Of the People, By the People, For the People to 'regenerate' Our lost Garden of Eden at all of Our Catholic Churches in a Global Design as was done on our Six Sister Planets eons of Timeless Time ago."

"Are we supposed to go personally to him, or do it Virtually?"

"I don't Know," I say, "all I Know is I'm being told that Pope Francis, Our Sacred 113th Pope and Our Last Pope in Rome, has one year in which to endorse Our First Woman Pope and Our GodGoding Movement of Our Vatican from Rome to Ireland.

"In fact, it's already written in the Stars that between this Mother's Day and Mother's Day on May 10, 2024, Nuns and Women Catholics and Women Leaders are going to start selecting who they want to be Our First Woman Pope, and Women Cardinals, and Women Bishops, and Women Priests.

"Oh, I see OUR WHOLE MOTHER EARTH EXPLODING with Women! Women! Women! Assembling in Ireland and Virtually and igniting GLOBAL HEART*CORAZON* FIRE, and setting in motion LOVE*AMOR* COMPASSION FOR ALL OF HUMANITY for the next 50,000 years with Women and Children once more Leading and Our Men Following InFront as Snow Geese have been doing in V-Formations for more than 20 million years!"

"Just as those Native Americans of Portland told you."

"Yes, Soul to Soul, Our First Woman Pope United with *Nuestra Señora de Guadalupe* will Guide Our EXPLODING SPIRITUAL FIRE! For once again OUR GOD GIFTED HANDS will be working Our Holy Mother Earth's Soil with Love*Amor* just as my Yaqui Indian grandmother taught my mother to do and as Women of Substance have been doing for eons of TIMELESS TIME!"

I LEAP!

I DANCE!

I ROAR WITH *GUSTO* AND I FLASH on that tall 11-year-old girl at the Chicago airport, who'd stayed behind when all the other Spiritual SoulSpinning Children with their arms stretched out like Angel Wings, returned to their parents.

And now I see that this tall girl — whom Jesus informed me will be Our Third Woman Pope — that she and all these other Glowing Angel Children of Lexi and Greta take their parents and grandparents by the hand, and with great big smiles of Love*Amor*, they lead them away from their TV sets and out of their homes to help "regenerate" OUR LOST GARDENS OF EDEN ALL OVER THE WORLD!

OH, YES! We're doing it, and in just the nick of time!

"Thank You, GodGoding! Thank You! Thank You!" I shout to the Father Sun that's just starting to come up over the horizon and shooting rays of Holy Golden Light across OUR NEWLY AWAKENED LAND!

Birds are singing!

Trees are swaying!

Flowers are turning their happy faces and smiling!

Rocks are warming and humming!

And here come huge flocks of Snow Geese flying across the Heavens in V-formations!

WE'VE ARRIVED!

WE'RE BACK HOME IN HEAVEN ON EARTH!

WEEE! WEEE! WEEE!

WEEE! WEEE! WEEE! ANGEL SNOW GEESE OF OURSELVES!

Burro Genius

Miracles continue when Carmen and I call a Virtual Burro Genius Team meeting. I'm so excited I can hardly speak. "I got it!" I'm finally able to say. "I was given a DreamVoyage before daybreak of what's missing."

I stop and take in several deep GodBreaths. "What happened was that I saw all these Catholic Churches around the whole world turning into luscious green Gardens of Eden of AgroForests." Tears of joy come to my eyes. "Then I saw rivers of People streaming to these Churches to do the gardening and . . . and everywhere kids were dragging their parents away from their TVs and out of their homes to come garden with them as One *Famila*!

"No big companies. No big conglomerates. And People are so Happy! BIG BIG HAPPY! Finally working together as One United Global Family, and Our Mother Earth rejoices and burps and even our deserts EXPLODE into luscious gardens with Jesus and all Our Kids SoulSpinning Together! CAN YOU SEE IT?! CAN YOU FEEL IT?! This is exactly what happened on all our Six Sister Planets, and remember, they were even more lost and violent than us!"

"I see it!" shouts Linda. "It's so easy to see!"

"I agree," says Teri, "it is easy to see, because the Catholic Church is the largest landowner in the world with — not just their churches — but also with convents and universities and high schools."

"And retirement homes and retreat centers," I add.

"Yes," said Carmen, "and now *Our First Woman Pope* will really take off, attracting not just Catholics, but everyone from all over the world!"

"Yes, and the Indigenous Wisdom of Our Grandmothers will now activate into everyone's own consciousness," says Steve.

"BACK TO THE FUTURE!" shouts Gary.

"We're really cooking now," adds Steve, "and we can activate Our No Talk Cafés, so the public in general can also start interacting with Our Star Cousins as we've been doing for over 30 years."

"Isn't that jumping the gun?" says Gary. "Don't we need to establish Our Snow Goose and Global Acupuncture first?"

I shrug. "I don't Know," I say, taking in a big deep GodBreath and remembering how my dad always told us that his mother Doña Margarita always said that 'not Knowing' opens the doors to Hearing the Spirit World and Learning. "Just wait. Hold on," I now say, closing my eyes. "Oh, my GodGoding, I'm being told that we need to ACTIVATE EVERYTHING we've been working on for the last 30 years all at once! Not piecemeal. Not do one and then do another one. BUT TO DO THEM ALL AT THE SAME TIME! That Our Star Cousins have just been waiting for us to AWAKEN, so they can finally jump us forward in ONE GREAT LEAP, so we can start Einsteining all over Our Planet with the leadership of all these Young Souls that are now BURSTING FORTH ALL OVER OUR WORLD!"

"Well, Victor," said Steve with a great big smile, "this sounds good to me. We've been holding back too long, and now we can really go for it! Oh, I FEEL SO ENERGIZED I COULD POP!"

"Me, too!" says Linda. "Oh, I see it so clearly. Deserts becoming luscious green jungles of AgroForests."

We're all laughing with *CARCAJADAS*!

We've found it! Nothing is missing anymore, and I feel so happy. BIG BIG HAPPY! And full of ENERGY! We hug together like a big bunch of loving newborn puppies.

"And this, Pope Francis will endorse immediately!" adds Carmen. "How can he not! GARDENS OF EDEN the world over!"

"Sure, of course he will," says Gary, "for this is Our Long-Awaited Global Call TO ACTION!"

We all take in several deep GodBreaths, and we see that Carmen and Gary are right. Our last Pope of Rome will, indeed, endorse this immediately, a WIN WIN WIN FOR ALL OF US PEOPLE, OF THE PEOPLE, BY THE PEOPLE, FOR THE PEOPLE!

Meet the Author

HELLO! HELLO! WELCOME TO MY WORLD!

I was born in 1940 on May 10th at midnight at home in the old *Carlos Malo* barrio of Carlsbad, California, so our old midwife put down May 11th as my day of birth.

Then I was raised primarily by my Yaqui Indian grandmother from México, behind my parents' pool hall. She taught me that every day is another Miracle, *otro Milagro,* gifted to us by God when the Father Sun, the Right Eye of God, comes up. And when the Mother Moon comes up at the end of each day, She's the Left Eye of God, so we're always surrounded by Our Almighty and HerHis Miracles.

In the mornings, she'd tell me to look at our Sister Flowers and see how they open up with such joy and turn their smiling faces to the Father Sun. And then she'd have me feel with gentle open hands our Brother Rocks warming up and beginning to purr with their joy of having been gifted another wonderful miraculous day.

Then she'd explain to me that everything is alive within the Holy Breath of Our Almighty, and so we are all equally part of God's Wondrous Creation that's in constant conversation with each other, and God, HerHim Self. And all we need to do is listen, cocking our head one direction and then the other.

Then later in the morning with Father Sun three fists off the horizon, *mi mamagrande* would have me watch the flies and see their big beautiful eyes and how smart they are. And the ants, how good and persistent they are to fend for themselves, never giving up. So this was my world, my universe I grew up in with my Yaqui Indian grandmother further explaining to me that Our Sacred Job as Human People is to learn from All of Nature's well-earned Sacred Wisdom.

Why? Because we, Human Beings, come from the Sky with a Guardian Angel gathering stardust from the different Stars to help *Papito Dios*, Little Daddy God, plant Heaven on Earth.

In fact, this is who we, Human Beings, are — Sacred Instruments of God, helping HerHim plant Love*Amor* throughout Our Universe. So, well, being educated like this, I grew up thinking we lived in the Garden of Eden, and life was wondrous . . . until I started school.

I spoke no English, so on my first day I got quickly slapped and told, "English only!" And all us Mexican kids didn't speak any English. Spanish was all we knew. School became a nightmare. I became a bedwetter. I started not believing my Grandmother's stories, and my father's and mother's stories about México and God and *milagros* now also seemed ridiculous.

I flunked the third grade twice. I couldn't learn to read. I was called a stupid Mexican, even by my friends. By high school, I was so lost and confused and angry that I stopped speaking English all-together, and I just wanted to stay on the ranch working with our workers from Zacatecas and Jalisco, and have nothing to do with the American world outside of our gates.

But then a relative from México came and told my parents, "Ship him to México," and my parents did. And low and behold, I immediately saw that the women in the parks gave *pecho*, gave breast to their children, and sang the gentle little songs that my grandmother and mother had sung to me.

I could now see that "English only" hadn't just taken away my language, but it had destroyed my entire wonderful pre-school world. With great joy, I began to walk the streets of México City and I'd see Indian women, like my Yaqui grandmother, in the streets selling handmade colorful baskets and simple elegant jewelry, and yet still they'd have time to laugh and play with their kids just as my own *mamagrande* had done with me. Oh, tears would come to my eyes, I'd be so happy watching them, and I'd hand them a fistful of money and turn, running away. I couldn't talk. I couldn't explain all that I was feeling inside of me.

But then I met this older Anglo woman, she was twenty-nine, had two kids and lived in México, and to her I could explain. In fact, she'd help me explain, and she'd take me to museums and concerts and I learned about the Mexican culture through her eyes, an American who loved the Mexican culture.

Then out of the blue one day she told me that she had the highest IQ ever recorded, way higher than Albert Einstein's, and so this was why she could understand me, and so no! No! No! I was not a stupid Mexican! I was brilliant! And more importantly, I was available, Spiritually and Emotionally, to the Grand Masters of the Universe!

I had no idea what she was talking about, but I did come back from México to our *ranchito* in South Oceanside, California, proud of being a Latino, proud of being a Mexican! And when I saw all the abuses and injustices here again, particularly towards Latinos and Blacks and Native Americans, I went into a rage and I WANTED TO KILL! TO MASSACRE! And I was excellent with weapons, growing up on a ranch, hunting and slaughtering pigs and steers to go to market.

But then in the wilds of Wyoming — I had a vision that God never chose the Jews. The Jews chose God when they took their oral story and put it into written form.

I was shocked!

My head exploded!

And I was then given the further understanding, that there would never be Peace on Earth until all of us did what the Jews had done. And we all took our oral stories, family stories, tribal stories, and put them into written form, so we, too, could pass them down for centuries like the Jews had done, telling the whole world that we were also God's Chosen People, because we, too, HAVE OUR OWN HOLY BIBLES that connected us directly with our Almighty.

And that's when I saw so clearly that the pen is mightier than the sword, or guns, or even atomic bombs, and I decided to become a writer. A great writer! And after teaching myself how to read (starting with 4th grade books) I began writing on September 16, 1960 at 6 am to help make this a better, kinder, more enlightened world, for there's only One Race, Our Human Race, and we are All! All! All! All! All GOD'S CHOSEN PEOPLE!

I get up at 2, 3, 4 in the morning with Our Stars speaking to my Guardian Angel and me, giving us wondrous gifts from the Other Side, from Our Parents, Our Grandparent, Our Collective Human Being Ancestry, who've completed their earthly work and passed over, and also, of course, from Our Grand Masters, and God, Our Almighty, HerHim Self.

I LOVE MY LIFE!

HAPPINESS IS OURS!

HEALTH AND ADVENTURE ARE OURS!

AND SCREWING UP AND FAILING IS OUR GREATEST HAPPIEST ADVENTURE FOR LEARNING!

And Our key to this Love and Happiness I've found is to laugh. To laugh your head off with *carcajadas* and to keep going, keep living with our every Breath Being Totally Connected and Available. For in many Native Indigenous languages the world over the word for Breath and God are the same word.

So, thusly, I now invite you to take in a deep God Goding Breath and come and share this beautiful world I live in with all your friends and loved ones. For Once we were all, all, laughing-our-heads-off Indigenous Native People the whole world over, and this is where we are presently going.

BACK TO THE FUTURE!

BACK TO A WONDERFUL WONDROUS WORLD where we can once more see with our HeartEyes that our planet is Alive and She's hurting, so we need to help heal Our Beloved Mother Earth.

Ann Frank said it best, even as they were exterminating her people, she still believed that people were basically good of heart.

THAT IS OUR BELIEF!

FOR WE'RE ALL ONE FAMILY, ONE RACE, Our Human Race aboard the same spaceship, Mother Earth!

So, this is what my writing is all about, and that Women are Our Natural Leaders. Not men. But men do have the last word. And a wise man will say, "Yes, my dear," and whole-heartedly support Our Collective Compassion, meaning Our Loving Passion in Common — Feminine Masculine Energy!

God Bless Us All!

Thank you! *Gracias!*

Victor E. Villaseñor

Made in the USA
Monee, IL
05 May 2023